PRAISE FOR
SOCCERWOMEN

"By tracing women's soccer from its earliest days to the young women breaking out onto the pitch right now through short biographies of some of the best women to play the sport, Clarke provides a comprehensive retelling of soccer through the words and experiences of the women themselves. This is a book of heroes, but also a book about athletes, who just want to play the game they love. And it is, of course, about triumph in the face of discrimination and diversity. It doesn't take long into the book to start to question why anyone wouldn't choose to support these athletes, forget actively working against them to keep them off the pitch. And not long after that, you'll find yourself cheering these women on, fist-pumping their achievements, and standing in awe of what they have done."

—Jessica Luther, award-winning journalist, cohost of the
feminist sports podcast *Burn It All Down*,
and author of *Unsportsmanlike Conduct*

"An excellent, thoughtful read about a topic that has had scandalously little coverage. Women's soccer needs its own heroes and legends. Gemma Clarke is helping to create them. She put her heart into this book, and it shows."

—Simon Kuper, *Financial Times* columnist and
coauthor of *Soccernomics*

"Where we are now with women's soccer is because of all those who've come before. And my goodness what stories they can tell. In this engrossing read, Gemma Clarke not only shares the battle it has taken to get women onto a football pitch, but then goes on to introduce us to players the world over who we must thank for putting the '2019 Soccerwomen' in a better place. These are stories that have at the very heart of them what it really means when we use such phrases as 'fighting against all odds.' If you want to see what that looks like, over and over again, in its many forms, you'll find it in these quite brilliantly written pages."

—Rebecca Lowe, NBC Sports anchor

"*Soccerwomen* charts the remarkable route of the world's most determined female footballers and coaches through fine storytelling and honest testimony. This book is rich with historical detail and personal anecdotes that bring to life the characters, their love of the game, and the way the trailblazers overcame challenges to influence the most popular sport on earth. Gemma Clarke writes with passion, precision, and context in this important work. It puts into action the sentiment of the final words: 'To anyone who has ever been told they can't do the thing they love: don't listen. Do it anyway.'"

—Amy Lawrence, football writer for the *Guardian* and *Observer*

"You could describe Gemma Clarke's *Soccerwomen* as a who's who of women's soccer. But it is so much more than that. Her charting the birth of women's soccer in the munitions factories of England to the nuances of its development in the US and the fights for equal rights and pay, better conditions, and just the right to play, is peppered with the rich stories of some of the game's most well-known names—and those less well known but deserving of a place in the spotlight. Rich storytelling brings to life players' sporting achievements and their off-field battles, including homelessness, alcohol abuse, injury, concussion, parenthood, the effects of natural disasters, and war and sexuality. An inspirational read that will tell any young or aspiring player going through a difficult time that they can make it and they are not alone."

—Suzanne Wrack, women's soccer correspondent for the *Guardian*

SOCCERWOMEN

SoccerWomen

THE ICONS, REBELS, STARS, AND TRAILBLAZERS WHO TRANSFORMED THE BEAUTIFUL GAME

GEMMA CLARKE

BOLD TYPE BOOKS

New York

Bold Type Books
116 East 16th Street, 8th Floor New York, NY 10003
www.boldtypebooks.org
@BoldTypeBooks

Printed in the United States of America
First Edition: April 2019

Published by Bold Type Books, an imprint of Perseus Books, LLC, a subsidiary of Hachette Book Group, Inc. Bold Type Books is a co-publishing venture of the Type Media Center and Perseus Books.

The Hachette Speakers Bureau provides a wide range of authors for speaking events. To find out more, go to www.hachettespeakersbureau.com or call (866) 376-6591.

The publisher is not responsible for websites (or their content) that are not owned by the publisher.

Print book interior design by Amnet Systems.

Library of Congress Cataloging-in-Publication Data
Names: Clarke, Gemma, author.
Title: Soccerwomen : the icons, rebels, stars, and trailblazers who
   transformed the beautiful game / Gemma Clarke.
Other titles: Soccer women
Description: First edition. | New York : Nation Books, [2019] | Includes
   bibliographical references.
Identifiers: LCCN 2018050633 (print) | LCCN 2018055122 (ebook) | ISBN
   9781568589206 (ebook) | ISBN 9781568589213 (trade pbk.)
Subjects: LCSH: Women soccer players—Biography. | Soccer players—Biography. |
   Soccer for women—History.
Classification: LCC GV942.7.A1 (ebook) | LCC GV942.7.A1 C53 2019 (print) |
   DDC 796.3340922 [B] —dc23
LC record available at https://lccn.loc.gov/2018050633
ISBNs: 978-1-56858-921-3 (trade paperback); 978-1-56858-920-6 (ebook)

LSC-C

10 9 8 7 6 5 4 3 2 1

To Stark, Griffin, and Devon.

My heart says, get up, get back in the game,
this isn't just about you.
   —*Theresa Rebeck*

If the lady footballer dies, she will die hard.
   —*The Sporting Man, April 4, 1895*

CONTENTS

A LEAGUE OF THEIR OWN
2000s

FIGHTING FOR EQUALITY
2010s

THE FUTURE IS FEMALE
2020s

PREFACE

I didn't think I could write this book.

Sure, it was my idea. It was the book I wanted to read, so it was certainly the book I wanted to write. But when faced with the prospect of actually writing it, my confidence faltered.

I thought about how when I started out as a sports writer, I didn't want to write about women's soccer at all. And although I'd been madly kicking a ball around in my backyard since I could walk, I didn't want to play women's soccer either. There was no setup for it in England, no professional league to aspire to join. I was the only girl out of hundreds of boys at the soccer schools I attended. So I grew up thinking there was nothing better than to be considered "one of the boys," to be allowed into the realm of male culture and sports and, later, bestowed with the privilege of writing about the men's professional game.

When the first newspaper I wrote for in England began sending me to report on women's soccer—simply by virtue of being female—I was clueless and reluctant. It meant fewer column inches, less pay, less glory. The beauty of soccer has always been in its stories, those age-old rivalries and intriguing characters, and the narratives of women's soccer were new to me. To make matters more complicated, I was entirely schooled in the automatic termin-ology of the men's game. Was it okay to say things like "having a man sent off" or "keeping a man on the line"? During a phone interview, I once asked a player if the support of the home crowd would be like having a twelfth—long, uncomfortable pause—*woman*? Nothing quite rolled off the tongue the way the language of men's sports did.

In the beginning, I made sure to compare female players to their male counterparts, as much for my own frame of reference as for the readers—who surely also needed a male lens through which to process things. I described Karen Carney as the female Wayne Rooney and Kelly Smith as the female David Beckham. It took time for me to understand the chauvinistic crap I was perpetuating as I came to love the women's game, slowly and steadily, until I didn't know how I'd lived without it.

Here's another reason I wasn't sure I could write this: I was scared because I had a shitty time as a woman reporting on men's soccer. I know, right? Who'd have thought? Turns out the men who don't like women's sports don't like women in men's sports either. The obstacles came from outside in the form of e-mails from disgruntled male readers, and they came from within: my questions belittled in team press conferences, my knowledge questioned by other reporters, and those murky, icky incidents of sexual harassment carried out by club executives in quiet boardrooms and by pushy players in deserted hallways. Just the idea of writing about soccer again made me feel a little panicky, like boarding an airplane after a very turbulent flight.

And finally, I was pregnant. How could I possibly write a book through the fog of the final trimester and the delirium of childbirth and into the first sleep-deprived months of infant care? I thought I needed at least three nonpregnant, nonmothering years to do it, in which I would have lengthy coffee dates with each player and tweak each sentence into oblivion. But even having that debate with myself is a function of privilege, of doing a job that affords me some agency, when more than half of US mothers go straight back to work without any paid maternity leave.

Once I started writing, I quickly discovered that I wasn't alone in questioning my capabilities or worthiness. When Sam Kerr, arguably the best forward in the world right now, walked onstage to accept the Young Australian of the Year Award in 2018, she grinned and said, "I'm pretty nervous. I guess the imposter thing is still . . . a thing."

Becky Sauerbrunn talks openly about her struggle to feel confident, even though she's the indefatigable captain of the USA, the world's greatest women's team. In the men's game, confidence is seen as something that occasionally dips and wanes but can always be recovered. For female players, self-doubt is perpetual. And evidence bears it out. According to a 2009 study in the *Journal of Sports Sciences*, female world-class athletes have less confidence than their male counterparts and are more likely to feel anxiety and to rely on "external information in establishing performance expectations."

Women are more harshly judged, and their achievements are belittled. Just look at the coverage of women's sports: while 40 percent of all athletes are female, women's sports receive just 2 to 4 percent of media coverage.

Next, let's consider language. "Sports" seems like a big, inclusive term, but it only really means men's sports. There is "soccer," and then there is "women's soccer." The Major League and the National *Women's* Soccer League. The World Cup and the *Women's* World Cup. The addition of "women's" makes it sound like a niche activity or a knitting circle. It's no longer the main event but a sideshow, worthy of less coverage. It is, as Abby Wambach succinctly puts it, "bullshit."

It's one of the many reasons women are paid less than men. Yet American soccer is a perfect microcosm of the pay gap: here you have a women's team who outperform the men, who are more popular and more famous, who attract more viewers, and who still don't get paid as much. It's not even as though they're asking for more, just to be paid equally. This is how women's soccer has become integral to the fight for gender equality.

But it goes further back than that. The origins of women's soccer are steeped in the suffrage movement and in the fight to be allowed to exist in public spaces without stifling clothing, and to participate in activities outside the home. Women's soccer transcends sport; from the beginning, it has been essential to the struggle for female selfhood.

Now, who says you can't write a book while pregnant and/or mothering? Oh, that's right—a hundred thousand articles and op-eds and advertisements, the messages women are bombarded with every day. You can't be a mother and a writer, you can't function with baby brain, you can't work and be a mother, you can't not work and be a mother, you can't be gay and be a mother, and you can't be female and *not* be a mother. You can't. You can't. You can't.

But then there's Joy Fawcett, who nursed her babies in the locker room at halftime. And Emma Hayes, who suffered the loss of one the twins she was carrying in utero while coaching a game and somehow held it together for the remainder of her Chelsea team's title-winning season. And many other players and coaches for whom motherhood wasn't part of their journey but who also overcame overwhelming odds to do what they loved.

When the women in this book were told they couldn't, they didn't listen. When there was no path, no professional league, no World Cup, they forged ahead and made one. Behind every kick of the ball in women's soccer is the power of all the women who made it possible.

I could have written about all of them, but I had to narrow it down. The selection process is mine, and there were some tough omissions. Even though the USA is number one and those teams of the 1990s made the global game what it is today, I tried to avoid bending too far to American exceptionalism. I wanted to paint a global picture, to share players' stories that otherwise wouldn't have been told. This, to me, was about all these players from around the world resting shoulder to shoulder in the same book, from Pahrump, Nevada, to Papua New Guinea.

Organizing it into a cohesive chronology was complicated. Plenty of players don't fit into one decade. Kristine Lilly, for example, played in four. So I asked her which was her favorite era, and I placed her there. For others, I went with the moment they made their breakthrough or the game they considered their best.

I've also tried to be evenhanded in terms of position and include a cross section of goalkeepers, defenders, midfielders, forwards, and coaches. Taken all together, they form a formidable squad.

It took some time to settle on a title. In publishing, ensuring that the word "girl" is in the title means you will likely sell more copies. But I couldn't demean these players, these women, by calling them "girls" just to fit some patriarchal fantasy. *Soccerwomen* is an attempt to flip the script. This isn't a niche sport, and these aren't just women who play soccer; they are women who define soccer, who use the game as a force for social and political change, who lay their bodies and their lives on the line.

This book is a love letter to soccer in its purest form, played with passion, sometimes at great personal risk, and often without expectation or fanfare. It is a love letter to the players who constantly show us what is possible—if we work hard and show courage, determination, and tenacity.

Writing this book brought me more joy than I felt writing about men's sports, and I hope that shows. It is imperfect, and it is all the better for that.

It is a testament to this:

If we question the narratives in which we've been indoctrinated, if we do what we love in spite of our fears, if we use our bodies the way we get the most from them, if we bring our best qualities to the things we do and the battles we fight, if we feel confident knowing we deserve our place in this world, we can help shape it for the better.

STEPPING OUT OF THE SHADOWS
1890s-1980s

It began as a means of attracting a husband.

Three hundred years ago, in deep, damp valleys beneath the jagged, snowcapped peaks of Scotland's Highlands, women took to the fields to play the first organized soccer games on record. But these weren't sporting contests so much as the basis of an unusual marriage custom. Women from local villages played exhibition matches, the singles versus the marrieds, while available men looked on, sizing up the athletic prowess and skills of the unmarried players and deciding whom to choose as a potential mate.

It wasn't the most progressive of beginnings, but beyond the partnerships that ensued, beyond the domestic drudgery and the confines of eighteenth-century marriage, a love affair began. Women discovered soccer. They went from playing it for nuptial selection to looking on while men took over, kicking balls around in streets and stadiums across the United Kingdom.

When the men's national football league was formed in 1885, there was fear that if large groups of predominantly working-class men gathered en masse, wide-scale violence would erupt. Several teams decided to increase female attendance as a means of nullifying the supposed threat and offered women free entry to home games. The scheme was so popular—women

1

showed up every week in the thousands—that ticket sales suffered, and within a few years, it was halted for good.

Soccer and Suffrage

Interest among women remained high, and in 1894, a mysterious young woman using the pseudonym Nettie Honeyball placed an advertisement in the national newspapers, searching for women to join the inaugural British Ladies Football Club (BLFC). Her aim was to show that women could do whatever men could do and also could function better without being forced to wear the strict, stifling Victorian dress of the day.

After the first exhibition matches, several newspapers ridiculed the club. Male reporters decried the women's play as lacking judgment, speed, and skill. Only an editorial published in the *Sporting Man* was supportive: "I don't think the lady footballer is to be snuffed out by a number of leading articles written by old men, out of sympathy both with football as a game and the aspirations of the young new women. If the lady footballer dies, she will die hard." A later article in the same publication praised the players for keeping a "pretty appearance": "The ladies, no doubt, knew what colour best suited them, and certain it was that they appeared to the best advantage. One or two of the players wore dainty white gloves, while in several other instances the ladies allowed their hair to hang down their backs."

The overwhelming disparagement continued as women's exhibition matches gained ground and spectators showed up in the thousands. Press coverage was predominantly negative and so mocking in tone that soon audiences began to thin out. Within a few years, the first real attempt to popularize women's soccer was over.

The Munitionettes

When World War I broke out in 1914, women were encouraged to step into traditionally male roles. They took over the workforce, from clerical work to bus conducting to manufacturing. Factories across the north of England were filled with women working the production lines, making weapons to supply the soldiers overseas. They were fit and strong, having honed their muscles over years of physically demanding domestic work, from beating rugs to manually washing and hand-wringing the laundry.

On their lunch breaks, female factory workers began playing soccer against the men, gambling on the score with cigarettes and chocolate. The women often won. As Alfred Frankland, manager of the Dick, Kerr munitions factory in Lancashire, stood at his office window and gazed down on the games, he sensed an opportunity.

In 1917, Frankland gathered the women together to form a team and organized an exhibition match to raise money for wounded soldiers. The game, between the Dick, Kerr Ladies and a team of women from a nearby munitions factory, took place at Deepdale, a men's Football Association (FA) stadium, on Christmas Day and attracted over ten thousand spectators.

In the sporting vacuum left behind by the war, during which men's professional soccer was suspended, women discovered more opportunities to gain ground. The Dick, Kerr Ladies began drawing vast crowds, showing their prowess against local teams until they were well known enough to take on a women's team representing France.

The Dick, Kerr's reputation grew with their audience. In 1921, the Ladies played sixty-seven games in front of over nine hundred thousand people in total. But not everyone was impressed. Critics bemoaned their attire, their shorts, and the fact that they kissed their opponents on the cheek before kickoff. Within the FA, the outrage was palpable. Yes, the women were raising vast sums for the war effort, but they were including trade unions as their beneficiaries. They were becoming too powerful, too political, and, worst of all, too popular.

The FA began a concerted campaign to discredit the women's game. They hired medical experts to make detailed public statements declaring that soccer did terrible things to women's bodies, that women were not biologically designed to play soccer, that it would inhibit their fertility, and that it was inherently dangerous. The Ladies shrugged off such ridiculous declarations and continued to play. A few months later, in 1921, the FA took their indignation as far as they could and banned all women from playing soccer in front of crowds at any professional stadiums. The ban lasted for fifty years.

The women earned nothing and asked for no compensation save travel expenses; their devotion was purely to the game and their capacity to raise money for charity. The Dick, Kerr Ladies were determined to continue. In 1922, they traveled to Canada by steamship to play a tournament, only to discover on arrival in Quebec that the Canadian Football Association had banned them from playing there, too—most likely after being contacted by the UK Football Association.

The last stop on their tour was the United States, where they were finally allowed to play. But since there were no women's teams in the United States at that time, the Dick, Kerr Ladies were forced to play against men. From the moment they kicked off their first game in Paterson, New Jersey, the women wowed the crowds. Out of nine games played, the Ladies won three, drew three, and only lost three. Paterson goalkeeper Peter Renzulli recalled, "We were national champions and we had a hell of a job beating them."

American newspapers raved about the women's abilities. Even so, once the tournament was over, the women traveled back home to England to a country where they were no longer allowed to play, and they faded into relative obscurity.

Title IX

The Dick, Kerr's Ladies may have sparked an early appreciation of women's soccer in the United States, but it took decades for the game to establish a firm foothold across the country. The sport slowly grew from schools and colleges until, in 1951, the first league was established. In 1972, Title IX legislation was passed into law, requiring mandatory gender equality in education. Women's soccer benefited. Varsity teams nurtured talent throughout the 1980s, and in 1985, the US Women's National Team (USWNT) played its first match, a 0–1 defeat away to Italy.

The First International Tournament

In 1988, the Fédération Internationale de Football Association (FIFA) held its first women's soccer tournament (delicately titled the Women's Invitation Tournament), a test run for any future World Cups, in China. Moya Dodd, who played for Australia in that tournament and is now a leading figure in the soccer world, recalled how exciting it was to take part. There was pressure to "put on a good show," but the players put everything they had into it. Norway won the tournament in front of a crowd of around thirty thousand spectators, setting the stage for what would come next.

It was a Spartan existence for women's soccer players in those early years of international competition. Australia—known as the Matildas—trained in parking lots lit by the beams of their car headlights and were often ridiculed on the field. While Dodd had to sew the national team crest onto her own tracksuit, the USWNT played in the men's team's old uniforms.

Every minute on the field had to be fought for and earned. But out there in the darkness, the first sparks had been lit.

Nettie Honeyball (standing second from left) with her teammates in 1895.

NETTIE J. HONEYBALL
ENIGMA

The young woman in the photograph has pale skin, dark eyes, and a mass of strawberry-blonde curls piled on top of her head. Her hand rests on her hip; her chin is slightly raised. She stares at the camera with a look of defiance, energy, and excitement, although there is, perhaps, a faint trace of trepidation behind her smile.

Her photograph appeared in the *Daily Sketch*, a British tabloid newspaper, on February 6, 1895, alongside an interview with "Miss Nettie J. Honeyball," one of the world's first "feminine footballers."

When she spoke of her decision to form the first British Ladies Football Club, her words appeared in shocking contrast to the deeply traditional, chauvinistic mores of Victorian-era Britain. She said, "There is nothing farcical about the British Ladies Football Club. I founded the association late last year, with the fixed resolve of proving to the world that women are not the 'ornamental and useless' creatures men have pictured. I must confess my convictions on all matters, where the sexes are so widely divided, are all on the side of emancipation, and I look forward to a time when ladies may sit in Parliament and have a voice in the direction of affairs, especially those which concern them the most."

But to her audience, the most audacious part of the article wasn't what she was saying but what she was wearing.

In 1895, Victorian Britain was a land of extremes.

Men were seen as superior in every sense—intellectually, physically, emotionally. Women were confined to domesticity, to an entirely separate sphere from their husbands, brothers, and sons, who went out to work. Increasingly, middle-class girls were encouraged to study within the home—music, singing, languages—but their skills were only being honed with a view to making them more marriageable. They were to learn nothing too intellectual, lest they intimidate a potential spouse.

And their clothing was prohibitive, cumbersome, and dangerous to wear. Women were expected to wear crinoline underskirts with steel hoops, cloth skirts that kept their legs covered down to the ankle, and corsets that squeezed their stomachs and chests. Everything, for Victorian women, was a bind. But the combination of domestic confinement and increased study gave middle-class women the impetus to take steps toward emancipation, to begin campaigning for the right to vote and the right to wear "rational dress."

For Nettie and her cohorts, rational dress was a huge part of forming the British Ladies Football Club. In the picture that had so scandalized *Daily Sketch* readers, Nettie had been wearing a men's uniform: a long-sleeved shirt, shorts, long socks, and shin guards. Nobody had seen anything like it before.

As she wrote in a letter to another newspaper, "There is no reason why football should not be played by women, and played well, too, provided they dress rationally and relegate to limbo the straight-jacket attire in which fashion delights to clothe them."

Yet while women like Nettie were fiercely advocating for great changes, ancient attitudes prevailed. The same year that the British Ladies Football Club formed, a woman named Bridget Cleary was murdered in Ireland, burned alive by her husband and several neighbors who suspected she had been replaced by a witch. The trial gained a great deal of attention in the press, serving as a stark reminder that a woman with a modicum of free will was to be feared and subjugated.

As Nettie was about to learn, the more moves women made to broach equality, the more they met with hatred and hostility.

In the early part of the year, advertisements began appearing in the English newspapers:

> The British Ladies Football Club. Ladies' Football Match, North v. South, will be played on the Maidenhead Football Ground on Easter Monday Afternoon. Kick-Off at 3.30 pm. Admission 6d. Enclosure & Pavilion 1s. extra.
>
> Ladies desirous of joining the above Club should apply to Miss Nellie J. Honeyball, "Ellesmere", 27, Weston Park, Crouch End, N.

The notices promised an esteemed guest at the match as well: Lady Florence Dixie, a well-known novelist, newspaper columnist, women's rights advocate, and member of the aristocracy. Dixie and her family were no strangers to newspaper coverage. Her father, the Marquess of Queensberry, had accused Oscar Wilde of an illegal homosexual affair with his son and was fighting slander charges in court. Dixie herself had been so forthright in her advocacy of women's suffrage that she had received a letter bomb in the mail and had allegedly been attacked and stabbed by two men dressed as women while she was out walking her dog. Dixie had been approached by Nettie to act as a spokesperson for the upcoming game, the first of many for the BLFC, Nettie hoped.

The publicity worked. The match attracted around ten thousand spectators, who poured through the single turnstile at the revised venue of Crouch End in north London before kickoff, bringing to the lush field an atmosphere of curiosity and disdain.

A little before four in the afternoon, the Ladies ran onto the field, divided into the two teams, North versus South London. In James Lee's comprehensive account, from *The Lady Footballers: Struggling to Play in Victorian Britain,* the sound that rang out around the ground was a mix of cheers and jeers. Some men fell about, laughing, at seeing the women running in shorts; others yelled out derisive comments. It made the women, who had only been playing for a few weeks, nervous, and the first three goals scored were own goals. Many of the spectators decided they had seen enough and filed out, pouring scorn on the women's abilities. The most talented player on the field, Miss Gilbert, who powered her North side to a 7–1 victory, was deemed to be a man in disguise and was subjected to shouts of "Tommy!"

Newspaper coverage widely labeled the women's efforts a "farce" and a "joke" and commonly resorted to attacks on the women's physical appearance. Their dress was unbecoming, and worse, apparently, for the male journalists reporting on the game, the women were not what the men would describe as "beauties."

It was only the beginning for Nettie. The hostility of the crowd and the press coverage served to prove her point that society still viewed women as ornamental, incapable of athletic prowess.

⚽

With the club up and running, Nettie took her teams on a tour of England in the months that followed. They played at a range of playing fields and stadiums belonging to long-established men's teams; some of local press coverage was supportive and encouraged the crowds to cheer, while some remained cynical and derogatory.

An article in the *Newcastle Daily Journal* read, "With the advent of the new woman, it was only natural that she should have a desire to compete in those games which have been looked upon as being exclusively the property of man."

Meanwhile, an editorial in the *Blackburn Times* gave the opposing view: "Woman in her place is a charming creature [but] the idea of donning football shirts, knickers, and shin-guards, and trying to ape the man is somewhat disturbing to one's peace of mind. . . . Let them look to their hop-scotch and skipping-ropes, and leave cricket and football to the boys."

The latter view began to permeate audiences, and by the end of the tour, crowds had petered out into the hundreds. Mrs. Graham, one of the club's most talented players, who played both in goal and as an outfield player, refused to give in. She organized a tour of Scotland the following year, during which Mrs. Graham's XI would take on some of Scotland's men's teams. It was a bold idea—one that ended in carnage.

If the majority of men were apathetic about seeing two teams of women playing a soccer match, seeing them play against their own gender sparked a violent reaction. During their first match at Irvine, one of the male players smashed into one of the women, giving her a black eye. The incident served as a portent of something dark and sinister brewing. The women called a halt to the game, and it was reported that the crowd had invaded the field and surrounded the women, forcing them to kick and push their way back to the clubhouse.

Nine days later, an angry mob attacked Mrs. Graham's XI after a match in Glasgow. The women were about to be taken to their hotel in horse-drawn cabs when several thousand rioters descended on their convoy, smashing windows and attacking the drivers and players, even injuring a police officer. Mrs. Graham was wounded as she tried to protect her players, her arm badly sliced up by flying glass.

Despite the occasional positive reception, the women never knew quite what to expect when they arrived for a game. As violent incidents escalated, it became clear to all that it was no longer safe for the women to play. The English FA compounded things further by banning their men's teams from playing against women. The first attempt to popularize women's soccer, a daring and death-defying effort, had come to an upsetting conclusion.

⚽

We know what Nettie Honeyball looked like and what she stood for, but we don't know exactly who she was. "Nettie" was a pseudonym, a means of protecting her real identity.

Was she Nellie Honeyball, as described in the first advertisements for the BLFC and listed in a census poll as the daughter of an upholsterer in Pimlico, London, or was she, as recent research suggests, an Irish-born woman named Mary Hutson?

The only known photographs of Nettie show her standing proudly in her BLFC uniform, kitted out in the shorts and shin guards that caused such consternation, an enigmatic pioneer of the game, fighting to show what women were capable of, if they were only given the opportunity.

LILY PARR

LILY PARR
MIDFIELDER

Augusting 1920, the tail end of an unseasonably cool summer. Ground frost speckled the fields of northern England before daylight broke and bathed the landscape in a strange blend of bright sunshine and dank fog.

Alfred Frankland, coach of the Dick, Kerr Ladies FC, stood on the sidelines of a misty cricket field in the seaside town of Morecambe. Wearing his trademark dark, tailored overcoat, he watched his charges crush a team of young women from nearby St. Helens by six goals to nothing. The chill afternoon air drifted in from the sea, filling the thousand or so spectators' lungs with briny wafts as they jostled and cheered, knowing that the proceeds from their tickets had gone toward funding a good cause: the Discharged Soldiers and Sailors Association of World War I.

Frankland, the office administrator at the Dick, Kerr munitions factory, was a natural showman, a charismatic and dapper gentleman who understood the importance of charity—and the value of publicity. He had already dubbed his team the "World's Champions," although they had never played an international game and no world championships yet existed for women's soccer. In order to raise money for the war effort, he had formed the most formidable women's soccer team in sporting history, starting with the women who worked at the factory and branching out to include talented members of opposing teams, whom he swiftly poached.

But he had never seen a player anywhere near as gifted as the athletic, deft, powerful woman weaving down the St. Helens wing while her teammates flailed.

Lily Parr was almost six feet tall and only fourteen years old. She possessed the kind of flair and natural playing talent that soccer coaches all over the world salivate over and the finesse of one who practiced her skills day in, day out. Even as her team struggled, Lily shone.

As soon as the final whistle blew and the teams jogged off, Frankland quickly grabbed the best player on his team, pacey goalscorer Alice Woods, and asked her to go and fetch Lily. The Dick, Kerr Ladies had some crucial games coming up, first against a national team representing France and then, the day after Christmas, a showcase at one of the country's greatest—and largest—stadiums, Goodison Park. Lily was the best player Frankland had ever seen; he desperately wanted her on his team.

Woods dutifully hurried into the hut beside the cricket pavilion, where the players were getting changed, only to find that Lily was nowhere to be found.

Gone, too, was the match ball.

⚽

Alice Woods had made a promise to Frankland, one she was determined to fulfill.

For several evenings, she sneaked out of her home after dark with her sister, Jane, and marched into the notoriously dangerous slums of St. Helens, looking for Lily Parr. She had been told that Lily lived in Gerrard's Bridge, an infamous part of town where pickpockets and drunks skulked under dim gaslights and the stench of livestock and sewage pervaded everything.

Just as they were about to give up and head home, they spotted a long, lean figure lurking in the shadows, cigarette in mouth, repeatedly booting a fine leather match ball against a gas lamp. Power, precision, presence. There was no mistaking her. Or the stolen ball.

As Barbara Jacobs writes in her book *The Dick, Kerr's Ladies*, Lily stopped as the young women approached, slowly removed the cigarette from her mouth, and asked, "What dost tha bloody want, Woods?"

When Woods explained that Alfred Frankland was looking to recruit Lily for his team, she led them inside to ask permission from her mother. The

Woods sisters held their breath as they squelched through the mud of the Parr family's tiny backyard, filled with pigs, chickens, and at least one horse, and into a ramshackle terraced house.

"Inside [the house] was chaotic," writes Jacobs. "There were unidentifiable children racing through the cluttered spaces, wearing less than the requisite amount of clothes, their noses, and eyes, running yellow and green."

Lily Parr was born and raised in that house. The fourth child of Sarah and George, a servicewoman and a glass laborer, she spent her childhood running around the slums with her three brothers, John, Bob, and George, playing rugby and soccer, spitting, cussing, and smoking. Joining the Dick, Kerr's would offer her a way out of the squalor, a path to somewhere better, and a chance to show the skills she'd spent her young life cultivating.

⚽

Within days, Lily had moved into the home of one her new teammates, Alice Norris, in the far more upmarket climes of Preston, Lancashire. In her book *In a League of Their Own!: The Dick, Kerr Ladies 1917–1965*, Gail Newsham quotes Norris as saying, "I had two sisters and we all lived in a three-bedroomed house, so there was enough room to take her in, but when Lily came to stay and we went upstairs to show her the bedroom we were supposed to be sharing, she threw me out and my nightclothes came out after me! I never got back in my room much after that, not while Lily was staying with us anyway."

Soon, Lily was living a life beyond anything she could have imagined back home in St. Helens. She played in front of twenty-two thousand spectators at the Pershing Stadium in Paris as the Dick, Kerr Ladies took drew 1–1 with a national team representing France. The following three exhibition matches, played around France, were resounding victories for the northern English side: 0–2, 0–6, 0–2.

Just a few weeks later, on the day after Christmas, she lined up against her old team, St. Helens, in front of a record crowd of fifty-five thousand people at Goodison Park. Lily and her Dick, Kerr teammates were becoming as well known as they were successful. The future, it seemed, was bright.

During that heady, electrifying first season, Lily scored an outstanding forty-three goals for the Dick, Kerr Ladies. Lily's reputation preceded her; everyone clamored to see this rangy, raven-haired winger whose blistering shots were too much for even the most agile of goalkeepers. A male goalkeeper in Lancashire challenged her to put a shot past him, suggesting that it was far easier for her to score against women than men. She duly obliged, striking the ball with every ounce of her strength. He put his arm up to catch it and heard an enormous crack. As Newsham writes, "Lily smiled to herself as she heard him [yell] to his teammates . . . 'Get me to hospital as quick as you can, she's broken me bloody arm.'"

In 1921, Lily and the Ladies played sixty-seven soccer games for charity in front of around nine hundred thousand people. While this gave Frankland and the Ladies' supporters cause to celebrate, key figures in the men's game were concerned about competition. They issued reports, citing "medical evidence" that playing soccer negatively affected women's health and fertility. When the players laughed them off and continued playing, they took decisive action.

On December 5, 1921, the men's Football Association issued this statement: "Complaints have been made as to [soccer] being played by women, the council feel compelled to express their strong opinion that the game of football is quite unsuitable for females and ought not to be encouraged . . . the council request clubs belonging to the association to refuse the use of their grounds for such matches."

Frankland was furious, going as far as to suggest that the FA's decision to stop the women from playing in stadiums was an act of sabotage. Lily, meanwhile, remained as determined and resilient as ever. The ban only made her and her teammates more resolute in their determination to keep playing.

A few weeks after the statement went out, the Dick, Kerr Ladies hosted a game against Fleetwood Ladies, on a playing field near the factory, which they dubbed their "home turf." They invited medical experts to watch in order to prove that there were no physical repercussions to women playing soccer. Lily wowed the crowd again and scored the opening goal of a 3–1 victory.

Thousands of spectators still turned out to watch the women play every week, and the women committed to travel to Canada by steamship to play a few games. The women were well known; several passengers asked for their autographs during the rough crossing, where many of those onboard were seasick and terrified of going under like the *Titanic* had less than a decade previously.

When the Ladies arrived in Winnipeg, they discovered that the men of the Canadian Dominion Football Association, most likely on the recommendation of London counterparts, had voted to oppose women's soccer. After their long, arduous journey, they found they had once again been deprived of their opportunities to play.

A Mr. Zelickman, of Brooklyn FC, invited the women to play in America. Since there were no official women's teams, the Ladies found that their opposition would consist of men's teams. They lost 6–3 to Paterson FC, followed by a 4–4 draw with J&P Coats FC, a game where Lily was so impressive that the entire crowd got behind her. She continued to flourish as the Ladies thrived, beating New York FC 8–4 and Baltimore SC 3–2. Newspaper reports of the tour heralded Lily as the greatest women's player in the world.

When it was over, the team returned to England and continued to play wherever they could, even though playing in front of big crowds was now no longer an option. Lily was central to everything—even as personnel changed around her, as her teammates got married and stopped playing, and as the team changed its name from Dick, Kerr to Preston Ladies. She scored five goals in an 11–2 victory over Blackpool Ladies at Leicester in 1927, after which the local newspaper report read, "Everyone who went to the game came away with one big impression: that they had seen an outside left [Parr] who if she had been a man would have gained international honors."

She continued playing until 1951, thirty years after she had made her debut for the Dick, Kerr Ladies. But she never quite let go of one old habit. As her teammate Joan Whalley put it, "Wherever she went, she used to try and take the football from the games. . . . After the match, somebody would come looking for the football. 'Where's the match ball? Where's the ball?'

But it was nearly always missing. I'd say to some of the others, 'It'll be that Parr again.' She would be . . . pretending to look for it as well. How many balls she got away with, I don't know, but she would produce them on the bus when we were miles away from the venue. We never knew what she did with them all."

Lily was quiet and reserved in public, but with close friends she showed a caustic sense of humor and a generous streak. If she heard of people who were struggling to make ends meet, she'd loan them money or bail them out. After she retired from soccer, she worked as a nurse, tending to her patients with kindness and generosity and, from time to time, regaling them with stories of her incredible sporting career.

Lily died of cancer in Preston in 1978 and was laid to rest in her hometown of St. Helens. Since her death, she has come to be recognized and celebrated as one of the greatest and most influential women's soccer players of all time.

ALICE MILLIAT

ALICE MILLIAT

COACH

Madame Alice Milliat had nothing to lose.

Widowed and childless in her midthirties, she lived alone in Paris, free from the impediments that confined women of her time to domestic life. A keen rower and swimmer, Alice had been working as a translator when she joined Femina Sport, France's first sports club for women, in 1911.

Soon, she came across her first adversary: Baron Pierre de Coubertin, founder of the International Olympic Committee (IOC) and lifelong opponent of gender equality and women playing sports. Women had begun competing in the Olympics in 1900, first in golf and tennis, later in croquet and diving, but de Coubertin didn't want them taking part in other events, notably track and field. He felt it was unfeminine for women to sweat in public. Alice and her peers saw de Coubertin's views as an affront.

By 1917, World War I was still raging, causing severe damage to France and depleting the country of a generation of young men. Just like in the United Kingdom, women stepped forward into public life and into organized sports, where Alice was at the forefront, spearheading change. That year, Femina Sport organized the first track and field championship, much to the chagrin of their male compatriots. As Leigh and Bonin note in their academic paper on Alice, "Those first sportswomen who dared to brave public opinion and to bring shame on their families were viewed as wild, emotionally disturbed, fanatic women using sport only as an occasion for a brawl."

Undeterred, they channeled the publicity surrounding the event to form the Women's Sports Federation of France. Alice began as treasurer, but by the following summer, she was general secretary and in 1919 was unanimously elected president. That year, she oversaw women's championships in field hockey, soccer, basketball, and swimming.

Over in England, Alfred Frankland, coach of the Dick, Kerr Ladies, heard about Alice's efforts. He invited her to bring a soccer team to the United Kingdom for a tournament against his team, expecting her to politely decline. She immediately agreed.

In April 1920, Alice's team sailed to England amid a flurry of publicity. The tournament fixtures appeared on the front page of the *Daily News*, alongside photographs of the French team uniforms. When the French side arrived in Preston by train, they were greeted by a brass band and thousands of people lining the streets like a parade. The atmosphere was overwhelming and lifted the French women to a surprise 2–1 victory.

Sensing change in the air, Alice returned to France with her eyes on the next goal: to convince the IOC to allow women to run track and field in the Olympics. She put in an official request and was resolutely denied. Rather than revert to protest, which she felt would fall on deaf ears, Alice decided to stage an Olympic tournament of her own—the Women's Olympiad in Monte Carlo in 1921. Despite the success of the event, the IOC rejected a further request to allow women's athletics at the Olympics.

As indefatigable as ever, Alice created the Women's Olympic Games. The event took place on a single day in Paris in 1922, with five nations competing, including the United States. Up to twenty thousand fans turned out to watch, which only succeeded in angering the IOC. They forced the women to stop using the word "Olympic."

Alice continued with the event under the banner of the Women's World Games until the IOC finally relented and allowed women's track and field to take place at the 1928 Olympics in Gothenburg, Sweden. However, women were confined to five events, compared to the men's twenty-two, leaving Alice and others to feel as aggrieved as ever. The British women's team boycotted the event entirely.

Alice achieved a great deal in her lifetime as a fierce advocate of women's sports. All of it was part of a greater cause—women's suffrage.

"Women's sports of all kinds are handicapped in my country by the lack of playing space," she said. "As we have no vote, we cannot make our needs publicly felt, or bring pressure to bear in the right quarters. I always tell my girls that the vote is one of the things they will have to work for if France is to keep its place with the other nations in the realm of feminine sport."

It wasn't until 1945 that French women were given the right to vote, provided they were literate, and restrictions on women's suffrage remained in the national constitution until 1965, six years after Alice's death.

Sylvia Gore (front row, second from right) with the first England women's team.

SYLVIA GORE
MIDFIELDER

The conditions were terrible, but the game had to go on. There was no other option for Sylvia Gore and her England teammates. Years of passion, dedication, and determination had led them to a waterlogged playing field in Greenock, Scotland, on an afternoon of torrential rain and biting wind. They were shivering, soaked to the bone, but they weren't going anywhere.

On November 19, 1972, the England women's team played their first international game, taking on the women's team of Scotland. It was also the first time women had been allowed to play on a professional field in the United Kingdom since the English Football Association had banned women from playing soccer fifty years earlier.

Sylvia had been dreaming of this moment since she had started kicking a ball around the streets of her hometown of Prescot, Lancashire, when she was four years old. At the time, the FA ban was still in place, and it was difficult for girls to find a place to play. She wasn't allowed to play for the boys' team at her school, but she found a home at a well-known women's team thirty miles away in Manchester. Sylvia joined Manchester Corinthians at the age of twelve.

Corinthians had been founded in 1949 by Peter Ashley so that his soccer-loving daughter would have somewhere to play. They played from the 1950s to the 1970s, raising money for charity and amassing large crowds, despite the continuing ban. Sylvia and her Corinthians team were forced to play on poor pitches as a consequence, with no facilities for changing or washing after the game. Often, they would dowse themselves with buckets of icy water in lieu of a warm shower or jump into the nearest duck pond to clean off.

After years of playing and training in the toughest conditions, heavy rain and sodden turf didn't faze Sylvia. Even so, in an interview with a local newspaper years later, she recalled being surprised by her own composure on the day. She said, "I picked up the ball in my own area and ran 40 yards. I thought I would slip over but I stayed on my feet and side-footed the ball past the keeper."

It was the first official goal for the England women's team, cementing Sylvia's rightful place in history. She continued playing for England until she injured her back at the age of thirty-five. After retiring, she began a career as a volunteer coach, intent on helping pave the way for future generations. "I want to keep on going and inspire kids to keep on learning," she said, adding, "[Because] I still am."

Sylvia coached the national women's team of Wales between 1982 and 1989 and was serving as ambassador to Manchester City's women's team when she passed away in 2016.

Sharon McMurtry (far left) with the Cozars team.

SHARON McMURTRY
MIDFIELDER

They say history is written by the victors. There is little record of those who come close, the ones who are just inches away from glory.

On a balmy August afternoon in 1985, in Jesolo, a tiny Italian town on the Adriatic Coast, the US women's team were playing their first-ever international match. Their opponents, Italy, conceded a penalty when a defender brought down Stacey Enos in the box.

Sharon McMurtry stepped forward to take it. If she netted, she would score the first goal in USWNT history and carve out her place in sporting history.

"[Penalty kicks] always made me nervous," Sharon said in an interview with US Soccer to mark the twentieth anniversary of the game. "In that kind of game, I was extremely nervous. It was important."

Nerves got the better of Sharon, and she missed, striking the ball wide past the left post. USA lost the game 1–0. "That feeling of missing a penalty kick just doesn't change," she said. "Every time you miss a penalty kick, same feeling."

Despite the miss, Sharon was named US Soccer Female Athlete of the Year, an accolade that was not marked with a ceremony, just a letter in the mail and a certificate. There were no frills to women's soccer back then, no acclaim, no supporters. The only two fans cheering the USWNT that day in Jesolo were Italian. According to legend, it was those Italians who began the now-famous chant of "Oooosa" that still rings out at USWNT games today.

Not much is known of Sharon's era, of those first outings as an international team. There were few records kept and barely any spectators, just a group of women who came together to play soccer, even though hardly anybody was watching.

⚽

The foundations of the USWNT grew out of Seattle in the 1980s, largely from a soccer club named the Cozars, home to several of the inaugural internationals including Sharon, alongside Denise Boyer, Lori Henry, Denise Bender, and Michelle Akers. The first national team coach was Seattle's Mike Ryan, who considered Sharon his protégée.

But when Anson Dorrance took over in 1986, he phased Sharon and most of her peers out, preferring to set his sights on a younger squad.

"Sharon McMurtry was one of [Ryan's] superstars; just classy with a remarkable skill set," Dorrance said. "If she had been young enough, she would've been one of the players in that '91 World Cup. Unfortunately, a lot of [Ryan's] players peaked a little too early to be dominant in 1991."

Sharon began her sporting career playing basketball at the University of Seattle. She left early to play for a professional team in Holland, and somewhere along the way, she returned to soccer, which she had played in high school alongside her brother.

Long and lean at five feet nine, she was strong and dominant in midfield. She took pride in creating opportunities for her teammates, setting them up with long passes and sharp crosses. But nothing gave her more satisfaction than playing for her country. She was so overcome with emotion when she stood on the pitch while the national anthem played that she could barely sing the words.

It's been more than three decades since those nebulous early days. Sharon now lives in Pahrump, Nevada, just beyond Death Valley, sixty miles west of Las Vegas, a town with stunning mountain vistas and 330 days of sunshine a year, her mind no longer on soccer. The USWNT's major tournament wins have all but passed her by.

In some ways, her hometown isn't too dissimilar to Jesolo, where she played her first international game. A little off the beaten path, a sultry and picturesque hidden gem.

"Jesolo was not even on the map," she said, harking back to the team's inaugural game. "I think the Italians didn't want the Americans to know where it was because it was just beautiful."

Like Sharon, its significance remains a well-kept secret.

FROM BARE BONES TO BARE BRAS

1990s

Let's begin in late November 1991, along the historic Maritime Silk Road on the southern coast of China.

It was a cloudy, cool month and a time of great change in the region. After several decades of communist rule, China had only recently begun opening its markets and borders. While the port cities on the southern coast were industrializing at a relatively rapid rate, the country was still somewhat closed off to overseas visitors. This was where FIFA had agreed to host the first-ever Women's World Cup, in a region far removed from public scrutiny—and interest. The heads of the international football federation weren't ready to call it a World Cup, to dignify its existence with the potency of their brand.

Many of the association's higher-ups felt that women's soccer was inferior to the men's game and that to host a women's tournament was to risk tarnishing FIFA's global reputation. A compromise was reached. The event, sponsored by Mars, was named the "First FIFA World Championship for Women's Football for the M&Ms Cup." Games were only eighty minutes long, since the executive organizers feared that the women wouldn't be able to play a full ninety like the men. Or, as team captain April Heinrichs deadpanned, "They were afraid our ovaries were going to fall out."

The relative remoteness of the region suited FIFA; the games were only shown on Chinese TV, so if the tournament was the disaster some predicted, none of it would be seen by the outside world. But while the organizers were reticent, the Chinese were eager to host a standout event. They had their sights set on an upcoming Olympic bid and wanted to demonstrate their capabilities and passion. Thousands of factory workers attended the games as fans, each assigned a team to support, and the stadiums were packed.

The competing teams had few expectations; they were used to getting by with only the most basic equipment, things their male counterparts no longer used or needed, and playing their games in front of a handful of spectators. To these women, the level of national interest in China was astounding.

The tournament comprised twelve teams, and all five of those competing from Europe made it to the quarterfinals: Sweden, Norway, Italy, Denmark, and European champions Germany. Hosts China, who had unexpectedly beat Norway in the opening fixture, also made it past the group stage, as did Chinese Taipei. In the semifinals, USA and Norway emerged victorious over Sweden and Germany respectively, to set up a fiercely contested final and a sporting rivalry that would come to dominate women's soccer throughout the decade.

"We hated Norway," Michelle Akers, USA forward and the tournament's top scorer, recalled. "We always hated them. They were good, they were tough, they were bitchy, they talked smack. We always hated them but it was fun. The more I hated them, the harder I ended up playing."

Norway's Linda Medalen admitted that her team sought to take down the USA from the beginning. "It's fun to beat the Americans," she said. "Because they get so upset, make so much noise, when they lose. This is a problem. Never be weak."

Sixty-five thousand people packed into the Guangdong stadium for the big final, creating an atmosphere unlike anything either side had ever seen. The USA were victorious—the first-ever world champions of women's soccer. Scenes of mass jubilation spilled out from the stadium and onto the streets. Chinese fans surrounded the team bus, cheering the team and waving banners and American flags. The American team traveled away from the stadium in a euphoric haze and celebrated long into the night.

Little fanfare greeted the teams as they arrived home from the tournament, even for the winners. The games had only been broadcast throughout China, and very few national or international media outlets reported the results. But a small shift had occurred. The First FIFA World Championship for Women's Football for the M&Ms Cup had demonstrated to FIFA that a real World Cup for women was a viable proposition. There was interest, support, and passion, particularly if television coverage could be increased and spread internationally.

USA's Heinrichs described 1991 as "a silent trigger."

Official FIFA World Cup

Four years after the US victory in Guangdong, Sweden played host to the second women's world soccer championships—the first official FIFA Women's World Cup. Women's soccer had long been established in Sweden; the first leagues were organized in the coastal region of Umea in the early 1950s, and the national team had been playing since the early 1970s.

The hosts faltered in their first game, losing 1–0 to Brazil, but came back to reach the quarterfinals, where they were knocked out on penalties by China. Tournament favorites Norway, meanwhile, cruised through their group, scoring a total of seventeen goals in three games against Nigeria, England, and Canada. When they met USA in the semifinal, they were out for revenge.

The Americans were keen to maintain their title but had lost their star goalscorer, Akers, to injury seven minutes into their opening game. As she prepared to come back in for the semifinal, she felt overcome with nerves. She wrote in her diary before the game, "I start tonight and, for the first time ever, I'm terrified to play. I don't know what I will be able to do. . . . I want to score goals, be a threat, be the best player out on that field. And it's killing me knowing I won't be that player."

Akers was proved right. Norway scored after ten minutes and held their rivals back for the remaining eighty minutes. The Norwegians didn't hold back in their celebrations. The team joined up to crawl around the field, hand to ankle, in a move known as the Train, lording it over their archrivals. As Akers recalls, "It was awful shaking their hands. I felt more like punching them."

Next Norway faced a strong German side, who had beaten China to reach the final. Germany had one of the youngest squads in the tournament, led by seventeen-year-old forward Birgit Prinz. The rain lashed down in Stockholm as more than seventeen thousand spectators watched from the stands and one in four Norwegians tuned in to cheer their team on from home. Two goals were enough for this outstanding Norway side, and they were deserving winners of the first official women's World Cup, having scored twenty-three times and conceded just once.

"The Norwegians were in the limelight, receiving awards, holding the trophy," wrote Akers. "The U.S. [was] in the back of the banquet room, unnoticed and forgotten. . . . We now look forward to the Olympics. This team will be ready."

Women's Soccer at the Olympics

In 1996, women's soccer was included in the Olympics for the first time, with the USA playing host.

There wasn't time to hold qualifying games, so the best eight teams in the world were automatically entered—with the exception of England, who couldn't compete unless they played under the banner of Team GB, encompassing Scotland, Northern Ireland, and Wales. There was too much contention between those regions to officially field a team, and they were replaced by Brazil. The attendances were large for women's soccer. Twenty-five thousand at the outset, they grew as the home side advanced.

Once again, the USA met Norway in the semifinal. It was a taut, tight game, as expected. Norway's captain, Medalen—who also worked part-time as a police officer—put her side ahead after eighteen minutes, and Akers leveled the scoring with a penalty in the seventy-seventh. The teams were still tied when the final whistle blew, sending the game into thirty minutes of extra time. The Golden Goal rule was in place, meaning if either team scored during those thirty extra minutes, they would immediately win and end the game, preventing penalties. Substitute Shannon Macmillan came on for Tiffeny Milbrett and scored just four minutes later to seal victory for the USA and spell heartbreak for their opponents. The Norwegian team slumped to the ground, gutted by the defeat.

From then on, there was no stopping the host team. MacMillan scored again in the final game against China, tapping in the rebound from a deflected shot by Mia Hamm in front of a crowd of over seventy-six thousand people at the University of Georgia's stadium. Although China's superstar striker, Sun Wen, equalized, Milbrett scored the historic winning goal in the sixty-eighth minute. The USA held on to claim the win—and the first gold medals in the history of women's soccer.

The '99ers

Following the USA's Olympic victory, American interest in women's soccer was piqued, especially since they were set to host again in 1999. This time, it would be the women's World Cup. The original plan had been to play the games at a few small stadiums on the East Coast, but after attracting such an immense crowd for the Olympic final and with lobbying from the players, tournament organizers made a bold decision: to go bigger.

The teams would play from coast to coast, at the enormous stadiums that had held the men's World Cup in 1994. It was a risk but one that immediately paid off. Over seventy-eight thousand fans packed into the Giants stadium in New York to watch the opening game between USA and Denmark, the largest ever to see a women-only sporting event.

For the players, it was a key moment. The world was watching; America was holding its breath. A generation of young fans began to seek the players out, waiting for autographs after training sessions, crowding into the stadiums for pretournament friendlies, and screaming support for their idols. The women understood their mission.

"I want these girls to know that they can play at the highest level," said midfielder Kristine Lilly. "[Growing up,] we didn't have anyone to look up to on the national team because there wasn't one. We didn't wait for autographs because there was no one to wait for."

It was a landmark occasion for two teams from Africa as well: Ghana made their first appearance at a major international tournament, and Nigeria became the first African team to make it to the quarterfinals of a women's World Cup. Elsewhere, North Korea pulled off a shock win over Denmark, the USA came from behind to beat Germany in the quarterfinals, and China thrashed Norway 5–0 in the semifinal, meaning that the Europeans no longer retained their dominance of the women's game.

Over ninety thousand fans packed out the Rose Bowl for the 1999 World Cup final, making it the most attended women's sporting event in history, and over forty million tuned in to watch the game on the TV.

Over the course of ninety minutes, the teams were tied at 0–0, with neither able to find a way to score. The game went into extra time. American hearts were in their mouths as China looked threatening. Liu Ying played a corner, and Fan Yunjie headed goalward. But Kristine Lilly headed the ball back off the line to take the game to penalties. Both teams scored their first two penalties, and the dead heat continued until Briana Scurry made a save and Brandi Chastain netted the decisive spot kick.

The crowd went wild, and Chastain immediately yanked her shirt off in celebration and slid to her knees in shorts and a black sports bra. She twirled the shirt around her head as her teammates mobbed her, creating a now-iconic image that encapsulated the team's triumph and the wider celebration of women's soccer across the world. The photograph appeared everywhere, from the front pages of the newspapers to the cover of *Sports Illustrated* magazine. "That picture," Chastain said, "represents someone [who] was in love with what they were doing."

American victories bookended the first decade of women's world soccer competition, as well as ensuring the first gold medals at the Olympics. The team gained iconic status, and many of the players became superstars, famous for the first time outside of their sport. They set a high standard, one that would be put to the test in years to come.

MICHELLE
AKERS

MICHELLE AKERS
FORWARD

It feels like trying to run underwater.

An overpowering tiredness seeps into her bones, her muscles, her mind. She wants to stop for a moment, to lie down, curl up in a ball, close her eyes, sleep. She doesn't know what's wrong, what's causing it. She only knows that she has to fight it.

She's the best player in the world, and she's in the middle of a game. Around the stadium, the fans are yelling her name. Across the field, her teammates are relying on her. And yet, her body won't do what she needs it to do. Everything starts to shut down.

She hangs her head for a moment, clenches her fists in frustration.

This can't be happening again.

⚽

Michelle Akers is a powerhouse, imbued with the qualities that characterize world-class forwards: strength, agility, tenacity, and fearlessness in the face of goal. The first iconic player for the USWNT, she joined the team when it formed in 1985 and scored the first-ever goal in a 2–2 tie against Denmark. From the very beginning, she wanted more: more media coverage, more competition, more game time.

In the late 1980s, Michelle flew out to Switzerland several times as part of a concerted effort to convince the heads of FIFA to host a World Cup for women. She sat in cool Zurich boardrooms, surrounded by leading and legendary figures from the men's game: Pelé, Beckenbauer, FIFA head Sepp Blatter. She listened while they discussed the prospect of a women's tournament. They were concerned that the physical challenges would be too great for what they regarded as the fragility of the female constitution. Michelle tried to convince them otherwise.

"All these men were saying, 'There's no way you can play ninety minutes, it's too demanding on a woman's body,'" she says. "I was in there by myself so I gave my opinion, but I knew it would only go so far."

The men agreed that the women could have a trial version of their own World Cup, but the games would be only eighty minutes long. There was nothing to do but accept their decision. "At the time," she says, "we were just grateful for having a tournament."

The first women's World Cup, in 1991—the First FIFA World Championship for Women's Football for the M&Ms Cup, as it was called—was a landmark event for women's soccer, even though the games were shorter, even though they weren't broadcast on TV outside of China, even though the players wore hand-me-down men's uniforms.

The food was strange and unfamiliar; many of the players couldn't stomach it. For the duration of the tournament, they mostly ate what they had brought in their suitcases from home: dry bread and packet oatmeal.

"We called it the China Diet," Michelle recalls. "We lost so much weight and had constant diarrhea."

The food, the culture, their surroundings, everything would have been startlingly unfamiliar had the team not played a tournament in the same region three years earlier, which meant they were somewhat prepared when the real thing came about.

"We knew we had to bring our own food," she says. "We brought toilet paper too because at the stadium most of the toilets were just holes in the ground. In the locker room was this kind of trough we had to share, so you had to immediately get rid of any modesty you might have had in order to survive and play."

Although the stadiums were packed full of supporters, Michelle remembers being taken aback by how quiet they were at times. "The crowds were almost silent," she says. "You could literally hear people in the stands, cracking sunflower seeds and eating them."

Despite her sense of culture shock, Michelle was outstanding on the field. USA coach Anson Dorrance played the team in a four-three-three formation, featuring a three-pronged attack that came to be known as the "triple-edged sword." With April Heinrichs and Caron Gabarra on either side, Michelle was the sharpest point, a livewire in front of goal. She was utterly dominant, scoring ten goals during the tournament, including two in the final against Norway. Her second goal came minutes before the end of the game, when she charged forward and took the ball past goalkeeper Reidun Seth before executing a cool finish to seal victory for her side and ensure that they returned home with the trophy.

But when the team landed back at JFK Airport, only about three or four people were there to greet them, one of whom was a friend of Michelle's. There were no fans, no jubilant celebrations in the airport, no paparazzi flashbulbs popping. Yet the lack of national interest didn't faze Michelle. She had already begun thinking about what lay ahead and contemplating future challenges, both collectively and individually. She wanted to figure out where the limits lay and push through them.

"Our campaign to be included in the Olympics began that moment out on the field when we were holding the trophy. My two thoughts were, one: I can't wait to get home and have a hamburger and two: I want to be better."

A little over a year passed when Michelle began to feel unwell. "I just wasn't bouncing back like I used to. I'd go out to train—I love training—but I couldn't get going. I'd push myself and feel worse and worse. The more I pushed, the worse it got. That's when I knew I had to figure out what was going on. I could hardly function."

After training sessions, she would crawl into her truck and lie down for hours before she could muster the strength to drive the few miles home. When she made it through her front door, she would collapse again and lie down on the kitchen floor, unable to go any farther. With no clues to what the problem was, she desperately sought help.

For months, Michelle saw a specialist and several researchers. She was eventually diagnosed with chronic fatigue syndrome (CFS), a debilitating condition that causes extreme exhaustion, rendering some sufferers bed bound or in wheelchairs. To compound the problem, the syndrome came with the stigma of skepticism. With so little knowledge or research into what caused CFS, cynical voices suggested it was the product of furtive imaginations, hypochondria spun out of control. It wasn't until 2017 that the condition was linked to inflammation in the gut and its virulence acknowledged.

Back in the 1990s, many assumed it was all in the mind.

One afternoon, the USWNT was holding an open session where fans could show up and watch the team train, running drills and knocking the ball around.

Michelle was sitting on a soccer ball off to one side, watching her teammates do a scrimmage. She wanted to be out there, too, but she felt horrible. Her limbs were tired and aching, as though she was suffering from a never-ending flu. She noticed a fan leaning over the railings nearby.

He called out to her, "You tired?"

She nodded. "Yeah." As if it weren't obvious.

He laughed and said, "Oh right, you got that chronic fatigue thing. *Everybody* has that."

It was the way he said it—mocking her, belittling the way she was feeling. Michelle turned away, saying nothing in response. Inside, her blood boiled.

"It burned me so bad," she says. "I wanted to punch him in the face."

The team's coaching staff were far more sympathetic. They knew her talent, her drive, her commitment. They knew how badly she wanted to continue being the best in the world. They found creative ways to use her tremendous abilities and preserve what remained of her energy. She moved from her trusted position as forward to midfield, where she had backup. Her teammates worked hard to pass the ball to her feet more, to make her run less, whenever they could.

Michelle took to the position and continued to prove her worth. She was immense in midfield, too, an imposing five-feet-ten frame with a mop of thick curls and a steely, competitive intensity. It is testament to her talent that, in spite of her illness, she played a critical role in ensuring the USA won Olympic gold in 1996. In 1999, she played for ninety-one minutes of the World Cup final before Briana Scurry inadvertently knocked her out with a stray punch. She was replaced by Sara Whalen and missed the crucial penalty shoot-out, but it didn't matter.

"It's a bummer I got knocked out, but I didn't feel cheated. My standard was always to do my best, and as long as I knew I'd done everything in my power to be my best, I was totally happy."

Michelle's mind-set is one of acceptance and positivity. She looks back on her struggles with CFS as her "best blessing." "It's funny how that works," she says. "It was tough but it led to discovery, growth, and evolvement."

⚽

Michelle's life is very different now, a world away from being voted FIFA's Player of the Century, from sweat, blood, concussions, intravenous drips after games, packed-out stadiums filled with either earsplitting cheers or sun-flower seeds and silence.

She lives on a farm in rural Georgia where she runs a sanctuary for sick horses, of which she has seven. In addition, she has four rescue dogs and, most importantly of all, a thirteen-year-old son named Cody.

"I love being a mom," she says. "Every day, even on the worst days. I always say to him, 'Cody, I love being your mom,' and he's like, 'I know.'"

She still follows soccer, though she doesn't feel the evolution of the game has been entirely positive. "I'm still like, 'What the hell?' about so many things," she admits. "The [gender] parity still isn't there. There are so many easy ways to make it the same or at least create the opportunity for the game to evolve. It's frustrating that we still have to fight, instead of having it just keep moving forward. It's super frustrating."

Sometimes she wonders about the players' commitment and compares the current work ethic to her own inimitable, relentless toil. "The whole priority was to win, to do what we needed to do, and that eliminated anything that might be a distraction. So, to see our team play when it's obvious the focus isn't always on being the best team, it's more off the field, is hard. For me, it's personal. That's my team. It makes me feel disheartened, sometimes, to see how the culture has changed."

There are hopeful signs, though, she says, that parity is slowly, slowly coming to pass, even if they don't appear wholly progressive at first glance.

"Now there are debates about who should be playing, and people are criticizing the [women's] team and bad-mouthing them and expressing opinions. All of that is positive. They're being treated like athletes."

KRISTINE LILLY

KRISTINE LILLY

MIDFIELDER

Some records may never be broken.

Joe DiMaggio's fifty-six-game hit streak. Michael Phelps's fourteen gold medals. Kristine Lilly's 352 international soccer appearances—otherwise known as caps.

A veteran of five World Cups and three Olympic games, Lil holds a host of other records: most games played for the USWNT, most games started for the USWNT, most games started consecutively, the only player in the history of international soccer to play in four successive decades. By 2010, Lil had appeared in over three-quarters of all the US women's games that had ever been played. It seemed she could, and would, go on forever.

Nobody has witnessed more changes to the fabric of women's soccer in America from within its ranks. In the beginning, no one knew what to expect. Lil recalls telling her parents, native New Yorkers who were oblivious to soccer, that she had been called up to the national squad. "I was like, 'Um, yeah, so I made the US team, and we have a trip to China. Can I go?' I mean, what were they gonna say? No? They were like, 'Okay.' It was just all new to us."

Lil was raised in Wilton, the idyllic small town in Connecticut that novelist Ira Levin fictionalized in *The Stepford Wives*. Growing up, she had only ever played soccer with boys, but when she joined the US team, she found herself in her element.

"Where I grew up, there weren't a lot of girls who wanted to tear the field up or sweat and try to win and be competitive. So when I joined the national team and I was around all these women who wanted to do that, I was like, 'Well, this is great! This is empowering. We all have the same mind-set.'"

It seemed as if each woman on the team had been the lone girl in her hometown who felt happiest with a soccer ball at her feet. Together, they formed a collective; everybody pitched in to make sure the team functioned.

"I remember our duties would be set up each morning, like, who was responsible for filling up the water, bringing the pinnies down. So, we all had our jobs to do to bring the stuff to practice. But we didn't know any different. We were like, 'Oh, all right. This is what it takes.' We didn't know that we should get paid. We didn't know any of those things until we started to understand a bit more what we were a part of."

The travel arrangements, the accommodations, none of it particularly befitted an elite sports team representing a wealthy nation. There were hotels in far-flung places where cockroaches scuttled across the floors and where hot water only came on once a day and the bathrooms flooded so that the team had to rinse off after training in the swimming pool after training.

"I remember talking about adversity all the time on trips," she says. "And it does build character. We laughed about it, and we made the best of it. And I think that's the difference between then and now. I mean, I look at my kids, and you want to give your kids everything; you know, you want them to have everything. But there's gotta be a fine line where they appreciate and work for it too."

Although the team found strength in adversity, overcoming less-than-ideal playing conditions to succeed, Lil believes that their spirit and work ethic were also helped along by smart coaching strategies instilled by Anson Dorrance.

"I think the perception of us playing in the early nineties is that we never lost," she says. "Well, that's not true. You need to lose. You need to fail. You need to make mistakes. In our games, we might've been successful, but what Anson created was constant competition. In one v. ones, every day in practice we were losing. And we realized we didn't like it. If you were on the losing four v. four team, you were miserable for half a day at least. So, I think that's how you build resilience, how you build character and grow as a team, because the down times are when you really come together."

If the USA team of the 1990s is widely regarded as the benchmark by which all future teams would be measured, then Lil is the player at the heart of it all. She is, per the description offered by teammate Julie Foudy, "the standard-bearer." In the course of her outstanding career, Lil won two World Cups, two Olympic gold medals, and one silver; scored 130 international goals; was a founding player in the Women's United Soccer Association (WUSA); and became the first player in history—male or female—to play two hundred international games.

She grew up on the team she came to embody, and it's those early years that hold the fondest memories for her. "I learned a lot from my teammates," she says. "I was on the road with girls that were in their early to midtwenties. And I was sixteen and thinking they were so old. A lot of things we did back then were the first. You know, the first World Cup, the first Olympics. So, we were a part of something that, you know, no one ever would ever be a part of again."

Lil scored her first goal when she was sixteen years and 22 days old and her last when she was thirty-eight years and 264 days old, making her both the youngest and oldest player ever to score for the USA. She was there for all the firsts, and the seconds and thirds too. By the time she retired in 2010, she was the only woman to have ever played in five World Cups. She wonders if her longevity could be a family trait; her grandmother lived to ninety-two and never had a driver's license, preferring instead to walk everywhere. But circumstances played a role too. When her teammates Foudy, Mia Hamm, and Joy Fawcett retired, Lil felt that she could keep playing. "I wasn't married; I didn't have kids yet," she says. "I was still enjoying what I was doing, still being effective at the highest level."

She returned to playing after the birth of her first daughter in 2008 but retired before the birth of her second. Her oldest, Sidney, who spent some of her infancy on the road with the USWNT, is now old enough to play soccer for a local team. It's not always easy for Lil to be on the sidelines, towing the line between coach and parent, watching rather than playing.

"It's hard to keep quiet," she admits. "I want to teach her every time I get a chance. But I gotta remember that it's too much sometimes. You've got to just be like, 'Good job,' and not worry about what you saw right before half-time or what she could've have done here or there. And then I gotta remember she's only ten years old."

Although Lil is an incredibly tough act to follow, being the daughter of a soccer legend definitely has its benefits. "The fun part is I get to bring the gold medals to their schools," Lil says. "They get really proud to show them off and show their mommy off a little bit."

JOY FAWCETT

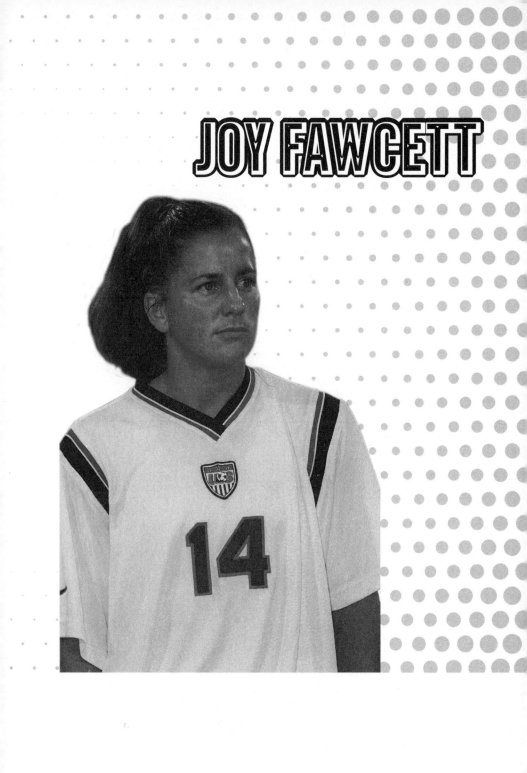

JOY FAWCETT
DEFENDER

In the fall of 1994, Joy Fawcett traveled to Minnesota to play in a soccer tournament. When she arrived at her dorm room, weighted down by bags and carrying her infant daughter, she was turned away and told she couldn't stay. Babies weren't allowed in the dorm rooms.

"I was like, 'Okay, well, I have nowhere to go. I was told I could bring her.'" The tournament organizers scrabbled around to find an alternative. Luckily, a kind family who lived nearby put Joy and her daughter up for the week. It ended up being a positive experience; the matriarch of the family was a lactation consultant who gave Joy advice on nursing the baby.

But it was still a bewildering time. Joy was a first-time mom, adapting to life with a newborn and figuring out how to combine it with her life as a soccer player. "There were so many issues that never occurred to me," she says.

Back then, being a mom and a star soccer player was unexplored territory. When she had approached USWNT coach Anson Dorrance and told him that she and her husband intended to try for a baby, he replied, "I know I won't be able to convince you otherwise, so sure."

Joy trained throughout her pregnancy, even though at the time it was highly uncommon and the perceived medical wisdom was that moms-to-be should avoid sustained exercise. "I was doing the sprints and the workouts, and then when I was three months along, I had a doctor's appointment. I remember him asking me, 'What are you doing?' and I told him. He was like, 'Oh, God, you've got to stop doing that.'"

She heeded the doctor's warnings and slowed down a little. Using the magazine *Fit Pregnancy* as her only resource, Joy continued to work out, keeping tabs on her heart rate and doing whatever exercises the publication recommended. Eight weeks after she gave birth to baby Katelyn, she was back out on the training field.

In those early days, she says, she was always worried. "I wanted to be on the team so badly and not lose that spot, but I wanted to make sure the kids were cared for and had everything they needed too. It was a balancing act, for sure, but I had a lot of help."

Joy's husband, Walter, did whatever he could to support her. "He was willing to move, willing to travel when needed. He quit his job, saying, 'I don't want to miss out on our kids' lives, so I'm going to move and relocate.' He gave a lot to it, and I couldn't have done it without that."

Her teammates on the USWNT pitched in as much as they could too. "They were really good after practice and traveling, helping me entertain and babysit and carry luggage all the time. I always had to have a car seat, a bed, and all the extra food and diaper bags. They were really helpful in making sure we were able to get it all from one place to the next."

And there was the fun stuff too. Joy's USA teammates would build houses out of boxes in hotel hallways. "They helped my girls with their school projects, building leprechaun traps and stuff. I think it gave them a little reprieve from the stress of the soccer field, to be able to play with kids."

When Katelyn was two years old, Joy was instrumental in defense when the USWNT won Olympic gold in 1996. She gave birth to her second daughter, Carli, a year later and returned to the team again to be a key figure in the World Cup–winning side of 1999. Joy was so vital to the USA back line that she played every minute of the 1995, 1999, and 2003 World Cups and the 1996 and 2000 Olympics. Her skill for dispossessing the opposition without committing a foul meant she only accrued two yellow cards—total—during the course of her 239 international games—an unparalleled feat for a defender.

Not only did Joy set an inspiring example for other players and athletes, but she also campaigned for US Soccer to support players who are also moms with paid childcare at tournaments—a precedent that remains in place today.

"US Soccer was really good about it," she says. "They didn't fight us. It was just a case of knowing what to ask for and what we needed and trying to figure out how to make it work. They were really supportive in paying for a nanny and letting the kids come along from the beginning."

There were moments along the way when Joy wavered, when she talked to other moms outside of soccer and wondered if she was doing the right thing for her girls. "I remember traveling with Katey, and I'm dragging her everywhere, and she's in airports, sleeps whenever, and I'd come home and listen to other moms, and they're like, 'My daughter sleeps at this time. She's on a very regular schedule.' I was like, 'Oh my God, what are we doing with my kids? She's not on any schedule; she falls asleep when she wants to fall asleep, wherever we are.' Now I can see how well [my kids] have done, how much they loved it all, and how they've turned out. And the soccer went well, as well. I've been blessed on both sides."

In the years since she retired as a player, Joy has turned her hand to coaching. She is the current assistant coach to the US deaf women's national soccer team (USDWNT), working alongside her former teammate and coach Amy Griffin. The experience of coaching the USDWNT, who won the 2016 Deaf World Cup, has been insightful and inspiring.

"The girls have been so inclusive and awesome. It's been a lot of fun," she says. "They're very forgiving in my attempts at communication with them through sign language. It's a great group of girls."

The challenges within the group are illuminating. There is a broad spectrum of hearing impairment and differences in how the players communicate. "Some can only hear with their implants, and they don't sign at all, so when they take the implants out, they have no way to communicate on the soccer field. Then you have others who are completely deaf, and they only sign. For me to communicate with them is hard without the interpreter, but they're very patient." She jokes, "I'm good at charades."

The USDWNT is still a new side, aiming to earn recognition on the field for their playing abilities and raise awareness of the vast capabilities of deaf athletes.

Joy is constantly working to understand the nuances of deaf culture. "It is very interesting," she says. "There's some that think that sign language is the way to go, and there's others that are, 'I don't want my kid to sign at all because I don't want them to be different.' They have so many struggles in such a small community, but they're overcoming them. It's neat to see because the younger ones, when they get together, they're more accepting than I think the older generations are."

And there are similarities, Joy says, to the team she joined as a player back in 1986.

"This team reminds me of our team when we first started as the women's national team," she says. "We were just trying to get funding and acceptance in the soccer community, to fight to be funded by US Soccer, to be supported by them. I enjoy imparting my experiences and what I've learned to help them grow and move forward. It's neat to see them do that."

CARLA OVERBECK

CARLA OVERBECK

DEFENDER

The Water Carrier.

That's how Sam Walker classifies Carla Overbeck in his book *The Captain Class: The Hidden Force That Creates the World's Greatest Teams*. "The Luggage Carrier" might have been more apt, since this was the additional role she took on as captain: whenever the USA team traveled and checked into a hotel, Carla would carry each team member's bags up to the room. It was a discreet, thoughtful gesture that showed the players that their captain was always looking out for them. Walker's theory is this: the most successful teams usually boast an industrious authority figure leading them quietly and without fanfare. In the case of the '99ers, this was Carla.

During a playing career in which she amassed 168 caps, two World Cups, an Olympic gold, and an Olympic silver medal, Carla might have been tempted to court the limelight. But she freely admitted that it wasn't in her nature.

While her USA teammates were partying at a victory rally in Manhattan to celebrate the 1999 World Cup, Carla was home doing laundry. "I've never cared about getting my name in the paper," she said. "As long as my team wins, I'm happy. I don't care about all the TV shows. I was glad I wasn't the one they were asking for."

By then, Carla had a son, Jackson, who was almost two years old. Like Joy Fawcett, she had trained throughout her pregnancy, even lifting weights on the day she gave birth. Seven weeks later, she was back playing. Before

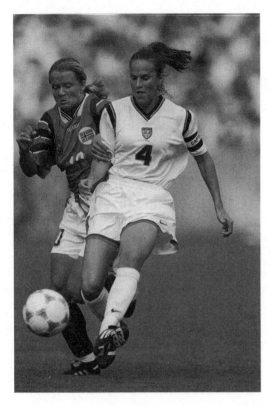

the 1999 World Cup, she and Faw-cett negotiated a breakthrough deal to have the US Soccer Federation pay for a nanny to travel with the team and help care for their young children.

The hallmarks of Carla's char-acter and playing style were that she was dogged, tenacious, and generous, qualities she has carried into her work as assistant coach to the women's soccer team at Duke. As one of her young charges wrote, "She laughs, she jokes, and she makes fun of all of us, making our relationship with her not one of intimidation, but respect. She is goofy and fun, but come game time she is intelligent, inspiring and one of the most passionate people on the sideline. If you do not know Carla's story, you would have no idea how much she has accomplished and how tough she is because she is incredibly humble."

But Carla's competitiveness is never far from the surface. Her old team-mates often joked about their captain's frequent swearing. "She could be very blunt and up front and to the point," says Fawcett.

Coach Anson Dorrance said he thought she carried her teammates' luggage just so that she could "say anything she wanted."

Nevertheless, many of them credit her with being the heartbeat of the team. "She made us laugh when we needed it, whenever times were hard or we were struggling," Fawcett adds. "She was a great leader."

HEGE
RIISE

HEGE RIISE
FORWARD

It has been referred to as one of the greatest goals in World Cup history.

Norway's Hege Riise picks up the ball just inside the German half, skips around one defender, then another, wrong-foots a third, and fires the ball into the far corner of the net from outside the penalty box.

For a brilliant individual goal like that to come at any stage of the tournament is impressive, but this was the World Cup final: time for the dazzling Norway team of the 1990s to earn the trophy that had eluded them.

"Some moments you just can't forget and that goal in the final is one for me," she told FIFA.com. "But although we were so clearly on top, we always knew [we were playing against] Germany, who never give up, so we didn't relax until the final whistle. Then we really had a party. We even had two military planes flying alongside ours to give us a special escort back to Norway, where there was a big celebration at the airport."

The Norway team had an outstanding tournament in 1995, beating their soccer rivals and nemeses, the USA, before powering past Germany in the final. Hege came home with the majority of plaudits, as well as the Golden Ball award for best player. Hege was born in Lørenskog, a village surrounded by lush forests, to the east of Norway's capital, Oslo. She grew up playing soccer and skiing, forsaking the latter when it became clear just how proficient she was with a soccer ball. Even then, she wasn't sure she could make the national team until her chance came in 1990. She made her debut at the age of twenty and became an immediate fixture on the international circuit.

Even more than skill, Hege played with intuition, an innate knowledge of where her teammates were at all times. She parlayed her visionary abilities into helping the Norway team win trophies, and she remains one of

only three women in the world to win the Olympics, the World Cup, and the European Championship.

When she retired in 1994, she held 188 caps, the record for all Norwegian soccer players. She assisted Pia Sundhage as a coach for the USWNT from 2007 to 2012, helping the Americans to win Olympic gold at the 2012 London games. At some point, Hege hopes to coach the Norway women's team, to be at the helm of the team she led for so long as a player.

But when Hege looks back on her career so far, it is that sublime goal she celebrates. "That was the best moment of my career without any doubt. Winning the Olympics was wonderful, but the flow of the tournament wasn't the same. That '95 World Cup was my best experience, and the Golden Ball is something I'm still really so proud of. I did feel like I had a fantastic tournament, and I enjoyed every minute of being out there. I was in such good shape; I just felt like nothing could stop me out there."

JULIE FOUDY

JULIE FOUDY
MIDFIELDER

P resence. Ease. Confidence. Charisma. Volume.

Julie Foudy was an obvious choice to captain the USWNT and, later, to join ESPN as a reporter, commentator, and analyst. Dubbed "Loudy Foudy" by her USA teammates, she has a warmth that seems to transmit through the screen. With a huge smile, affable demeanor, and sharp intellect that earned her a degree in biology from Stanford, she is forthright in expressing herself and rails against injustice and unsporting behavior.

Julie was in Pyeongchang in 2018, reporting on the Winter Olympics, when downhill skier Lindsey Vonn was subjected to online abuse for saying, "I hope to represent the people of the United States, not the president," prior to the games.

The barrage of abuse that came Vonn's way willed her to fail—and worse. Some hoped she would break her leg or "fall off a cliff." It was too much for Julie, who admitted that the incident had "sent [her] over the edge." She wrote on her Twitter account that she was "sickened and disgusted once again by the lack of humanity that engulfs our country."

Such abuse leaves a particularly bitter taste for Julie, who recalls the reverential treatment the USA women's soccer team received when they competed in their first Olympic Games in 1996.

"When we used to play with the national team, people would ask, 'What team are you?' and we'd say, 'We're the US soccer team.' They'd be like, 'Oh, that's phenomenal.' But when we said, 'We're the US Olympic team,' they would literally stand up and start singing the national anthem."

It even happened in midair, on a flight carrying the USWNT to their opening game in Orlando, Florida.

"The whole plane started singing the national anthem to us, because we said, 'We're the US Olympic team.' There's something about the Olympics, and that patriotism is something I've always loved about our country. So, to see people celebrating an athlete's failures and wishing her harm just took me over the edge. It's like, 'Come on. Is this who we've become as a country?'"

Born in San Diego and raised in the leafy suburban idyll of Mission Viejo in Orange County, Julie discovered a passion and a talent for soccer at middle school. She continued playing through her teens and was named First Team All-American twice, Player of the Year for Southern California three years in a row, and High School Player of the Decade for the 1980s.

Just two years later, Julie was in China, competing in the First FIFA World Championship for Women's Football for the M&Ms Cup. "I remember thinking, 'Well, at least I like M&Ms! Good thing it's not the Almond Joy Cup.'"

Although it had been her passion throughout her youth and adolescence, her parents, she says, were not soccer people. "I had to beg my dad to go [to the 1991 World Cup] because it was a busy time of the year for his business. I said, 'You will really will want to go to this, Dad. You're not gonna want to miss this one.'"

Julie was right; the experience was unforgettable. The Chinese officials looked after all the players' parents, organized sightseeing tours, and showed them great hospitality. "They created a lot of hype around the event," Julie says, recalling the crowds of people lining the streets, cheering. "And then we got home, and literally no one in the States knew about it. We had just won a World Cup, and my professor at Stanford was like, 'Yeah, whatever.

Sit down. You have a test to take.' There was no ticker-tape parade, that's for sure."

And yet Julie was hooked on the game. She secured a place in medical school but decided to pursue soccer instead. As she looks back now, it seems a clear and obvious choice for the star midfielder, but back then, it was hazy. "There really was no path. I didn't ever grow up thinking, 'Oh, I want to be a professional soccer player,' because there wasn't anyone professional doing it."

But Julie has helped forge that path for future generations. In 2002, she participated in a Commission on Opportunity in Athletics and was vehement in her assessment that gender-based discrimination still persisted in school sports, despite the implementation of Title IX legislation. In 2006, she and her husband, Ian Sawyers, established the Julie Foudy Sports Leadership Academy to foster the sporting and leadership abilities of young girls. And in 2017, she wrote *Choose to Matter*, a book aimed at inspiring young women to find their own leadership style and make a positive impact.

Julie is one of those women who has helped lay the groundwork for change. Her decades-long mission to empower young girls and women must count as part of a vast cultural process of incrementalism, the slow but steady pace of change that has led to progressive movements such as #TimesUp and #MeToo.

"I don't think it's coincidence that all these things are colliding together," she says. "In soccer, you're seeing women from national teams all over the world stand up and say, 'This isn't right.' Which is, sadly, the only thing that causes change to happen."

Equality, parity, equal pay: these are the things Julie wants to see the next generation fighting for.

"You wish it wasn't the case, that players are having to risk World Cup qualifiers like Denmark did, or international games or salaries. But that's what they're doing.

"The good news is we're seeing a shift—these federations are having to say, 'Okay, we'll reassess and redo these contracts.' We thought that would be the by-product of '99, that globally people would see the potential in this women's [sports] market. They'd say, 'Ah, okay, there's dollar signs now attached to my women's team if I just put a small investment in.' And that hasn't been the case. It's been too slow. So, now you have players having to do it. My hope is we continue to get courage in numbers."

Although change has been slow, standards are being set. In 2017, the Football Association of Norway announced a historic deal to pay their international women's soccer team as much as they pay the men. Other associations may be forced to follow suit, especially when teams such as Denmark feel forced to go on strike, missing important games in order to make themselves heard.

More work from the organizing bodies is needed, of course. And that begins with more coverage. Julie recalls being told in the early 1990s that nobody came to their games because nobody cared about the team. "We'd say, 'Well, how do you know that? They don't know we're here. If you don't tell people we're in town or spend the money to market the news that we're in town, then how can you make the argument that they didn't show up because they don't care?'"

The team would go out for postgame meals at local restaurants, and the servers and customers would often approach them, saying, "Oh, we didn't know you guys were in town."

"Before the '99 World Cup happened, we had a local organizing committee that for four years marketed the heck out of it and took it to the grassroots level, to organizing clubs, and sold tickets. The result was, we had these huge crowds. So, we said to them, 'See what happens when you put a little energy and investment into this program? This is what we've been saying for ten years.'"

⚽

They still hang out together, the group of women who won the World Cup, who played as a team in the first Olympics that allowed them, whose professional and personal lives were entwined for decades.

"It's a very close group," says Julie. "I think that's the really neat thing, too; it's something I always talk to my kids about. These teammates, they're stuck with me forever. It's a neat group of women who really enjoyed each other. And I think that enjoyment came through in a lot of what we did."

Theirs is an everlasting friendship and camaraderie, the bonds of which won't be broken by time or distance.

"We don't see each other as much because of the kids [we have] and the craziness, but we're gonna do a reunion for the twentieth anniversary of 1999. That will be the time to get everyone together."

SUN WEN

SUN WEN

FORWARD

Time seems to stand still.

It's a cool night in November 1991, and Sun Wen's skin prickles against the bright-red uniform she's wearing. She is only eighteen years old, and yet she's standing under the lights on the field in Guangdong, lining up for China at the opening game in the first-ever women's world soccer championships. There's a running track around the field, creating a little distance between the teams and the crowd. But there is a crowd. Twenty-six thousand at least.

There are video cameras, too, beaming this game across China. She thinks of her parents back home in their apartment, hundreds of miles away in Shanghai. They will be surprised to see her on TV; she didn't tell them she'd been picked to play. She had kept it secret.

They know she was in contention; they know she's good. Her father has been encouraging her to play since she was a kid, kicking a ball around in the park beside the Huangpu River. He encouraged her to play even when others in the neighborhood looked down on her, a little girl playing a man's game. They said she was a "fake boy."

Her mother—well, that's more complicated. Her mother isn't all that supportive of this. She doesn't see soccer as a profession, and it isn't right now. Her mother thinks soccer is something Wen should play in her spare time while she concentrates on her academic future. So Wen has made her a promise: if soccer doesn't work out, she will go to college.

It will be tough to give it up, if that's what she has to do. She has put all her energies into playing soccer. At thirteen, she was accepted into the elite Shanghai Sports School, one of six pupils out of the hundreds who tried out. It was a boarding school, attended by outstanding child athletes from around China who had left their families to enter into a rigorous training regime. She endured those first lonely weeks away from home. She dreamed she had a bicycle and could ride back to her parents after the school day was over, away from the dormitory filled with girls she didn't know. But after a while, she got used to it, even though the fitness regime was grueling and her young body was pushed to its limits with three-thousand-meter runs, even though she wanted to stop running and cry.

At fifteen, Wen tried out for a soccer team, but the coach laughed at her and told her that she had no future. Undeterred, she tried out for another team, and that coach saw her potential. Soon she was playing for a team in the Chinese women's league, although she was mostly riding the bench. One game changed everything; Wen came on as a substitute for the last thirty minutes and made a huge impact. A scout for the national team happened to be watching.

Now here she is in Guangdong, impossibly nervous and impossibly proud. The Chinese national anthem begins to boom out of the stadium loudspeakers. Sun puts her hand on her heart, and for this brief moment, she has to remind herself to breathe.

China won that game, the opener for the inaugural women's world soccer championships, by thrashing Norway, one of the tournament favorites, 4–0. Although they lost to Sweden in the quarterfinals, the team had performed impressively. Wen was its most promising player, a forward with great control of the ball, excellent vision, and the ability to pass and finish with precision.

While her parents were proud, they didn't shower Wen with praise when she returned home from the tournament. "They were happy to see me progressing," she says and then laughs at the idea they would tell her they were proud of her. "Chinese parents don't say anything."

As the thin, untrodden path to professional women's soccer began to form, Wen's mother began to accept her decision to become a soccer player. In 1996, China made it to the Olympic soccer final in 1996, and Wen brought home a silver medal. But Wen's star really shone at the 1999 World Cup. At that watershed tournament for women's soccer, Wen won both the Golden Ball for best player and the Golden Boot for scoring six goals in seven games. China lost the final on penalties to the USA, but she looks back on it as the greatest game of her life, even though the memories are hazy.

"I remember it was really hot," she says. "But I can't remember any details about the game. Everything was like a dream."

You can imagine it feeling that way at the time, let alone in retrospect: the Rose Bowl, a searing heatwave, ninety thousand fans, and a historic occasion for women's soccer.

"For us, we didn't lose, because women's soccer was played in front of that number [of people]. That was the most important part. It was meaningful."

When the first professional league, the Women's United Soccer Association, was established, Wen was the first pick of the draft, recruited to Atlanta. It seemed like fate at the time. Wen is an avid reader, and one of her favorite books was *Gone with the Wind*, which she had read in Chinese. She smiles at the memory of finding herself in Atlanta. "That's how life can be. You never know what will happen."

Wen's departure from the constricted, rigidly disciplined world of Chinese athletics and her move to America at the turn of the new millennium were a huge culture shock. She had come of age under the communist regime, where everything was carefully managed and controlled, her days and weeks planned out by other people.

"We didn't have to think about a lot of things," she says. "But in the US, it's totally different. There's a lot of things you have to learn. You have to face a lot of new challenges: how to drive, how to rent a car, how to rent a house, everything."

She made friends with other players and developed a close-knit circle of other Chinese transplants. When they weren't playing, they would organize trips to Florida to go deep-sea fishing and crab trapping. It was a different life but one that Wen came to love too. Seeing the US game from the inside gave her a different perspective on her own mind-set.

After team training sessions, she watched many of the American players stay behind to work out by themselves. They worked far harder than she had imagined. But what impressed her most was how much they loved playing soccer.

"In China, most of us would think about winning. Winning was what made us happy. But for the American players, they enjoyed the playing. Whatever happened, they just tried their best, and they could accept whatever happened, win or lose."

Wen was the first woman to win Asian Football Player of the Year, and she shared the FIFA award for Women's Player of the Twentieth Century with Michelle Akers, a player she much admired.

"Giant opponents [like her] make you greater," she says. "I read her book, and in it, she said, 'One for all, all for one.' I think that's the meaning of soccer. We two together made a lot of difference for the women's game."

Wen now coaches the youth team in China, working with a number of talented young players, like midfielder Wang Shuang. While Wen is happy to pass on her knowledge and experience, she's aware that the world has changed a great deal since she first started playing soccer.

"Things are different now," she says. "Players have many, many distractions. I was more tough. I had one hundred percent concentration."

This, Wen says, is the key to everything. Her advice to young players is to "devote yourself one hundred percent. Concentration is very, very important. If you love it and you want to make something happen, it will happen."

BRIANA SCURRY

BRIANA SCURRY

GOALKEEPER

Picture this: you're the third kicker in a penalty shoot-out to decide the World Cup final. The crowd around you, all ninety thousand of them, is hushed, clinging to one another, chewing on fingernails, watching through the gaps in their fingers—a sea of bodies rigid with tension.

You walk forward and set the ball on the spot. As you do, you glance up. There, facing you down, is Briana Scurry.

Nobody has a game face like Briana. Her brow is furrowed; she scowls as she skulks along the goal line. In Briana's mind, she is a "female tiger, waiting, waiting, waiting, ready to pounce." She lifts her head and stares right at you. She is saying something under her breath, although it's not loud enough for you to hear. Later, you will find out it was what you both already knew.

"This is the one."

🜨

In rural Minnesota, twenty miles north of Minneapolis, where the Mississippi River converges with the Crow, is the small city of Dayton. As cities go, Dayton is sedate; it is home to just five thousand people, a historic Catholic church, several golf courses, and a couple of car repair shops.

Briana Scurry was five years old when her family set up home there in the mid-1970s. "There were no streetlights," she recalls. "Just stop signs."

More bewildering for Briana, coming from the Twin Cities, was that she and her family were the sole African American residents in the area. "It was tricky," she admits. "It was a little tricky at times. I got name-called every once in a while, stuff like 'chocolate' and 'blackie' and that kind of thing."

It didn't happen at school as much as around town, by cruel boys loitering at the bus stop. Briana was an easy target; she was always there early. "My dad used to say, 'Always be first. I don't care if you're getting on the bus; try to be the first one there.' At first I didn't want to, because I didn't want to get picked on." Then her sister stepped in, and the boys left her alone. Briana, the youngest of nine and nine years younger than her nearest sibling, had no shortage of protectors.

Even with eight other children to care for, Briana's parents spotted her potential and encouraged her burgeoning athletic prowess. She ran track and played basketball, soccer, and tackle football with her parents ever present and enthusiastic. "If I got a knock, they'd say, 'Okay, get back in there.' They didn't treat me like I was fragile, so I never believed I was fragile."

Others did. At twelve, she was the only girl on her soccer team when the coach decided to put her in goal, thinking she would be safer. It was there that Briana shone, employing her pace, strength, and agility, as well as her experience on the basketball court, to handle and parry the ball with precision.

Her goalkeeping ability won her a scholarship to the University of Massachusetts, where the awards and accolades kept flooding in. Three years after graduating, she was standing on a podium at the Sanford Stadium in Georgia, wearing Olympic gold as the USA goalkeeper. She had played every minute of every game and conceded only three goals. Briana's parents were in the crowd, grinning down at her, knowing they had witnessed the realization of a long-standing ambition.

"My Olympic dream began when I was watching Miracle on Ice, the 1980 Olympic hockey team," she says. "I remember sitting on the couch with my mom and dad when Jim Craig was spinning on his head against the Soviet Union. I said, 'I want to be an Olympian.' They both heard me, and they both supported me in that dream. Anything I ever wanted to do, they both firmly believed that I could. I feel like I'm very lucky in that regard; they never once doubted me."

The team's sponsors rented out a sorority house on the University of Georgia campus for their gold-medal-winning after-party. Briana's parents, who were quite a bit older than her teammates' parents, gamely came along to celebrate. As the night progressed, she recalls seeing them sitting on the couch in the corner of the room, so tired, yet so determined to be there for their daughter's big moment. She hugged them both and told them they could go back to their hotel for some much-needed rest.

With the Olympics over, Briana and her teammates set their sights on the 1999 World Cup. USA were hosting the tournament, and the team took it upon themselves to drum up interest and enthusiasm.

"We did barnstorming events with clubs all over the country to get the word out. A lot of people made a huge effort to make that World Cup the way it was. It helped that we were accessible, that we were willing to do the extra work. It's not like the men's game where you just show up and play; we had to promote the heck out of ourselves."

The women's promotional efforts were so successful that their surging popularity prompted the organizing committee to move the tournament from small stadiums to the biggest arenas in the country. But with the increase in attention came an increase in expectation. As the World Cup loomed, there were a few jitters within the USA camp.

"You're promoting and promoting, and all of a sudden, we're looking around, thinking, 'Oh, gosh, we've actually got to go and win this thing now.'"

They came out strong, crushing Denmark in their opening fixture. A tricky game against Germany followed, and the USA had to come from behind twice to see them off. Briana played the game of her life against Brazil, making five or six full-stretch dives to keep a clean sheet. Going into the final, it seemed the whole country had woken up to the women's incredible journey and indefatigable spirit.

"Everybody was paying attention," says Briana. "It was crazy. *Good Morning America* showed up to film our practice; the Rose Bowl sold out in, like, two seconds. But China was playing really, really well. They were killing on their side of the bracket. They whooped Norway in their semifinal, and we were excited to take them on but there was a little anxiety about it."

Their fears were diminished when they saw the team lineups. "The interesting thing about China is that they were as afraid of us as we were worried about them. They completely changed how they were playing to play against us—they went defensive."

The heat on the day of the World Cup final was oppressive. Some readouts put pitch-side temperatures at around 107 degrees Fahrenheit. Briana thought about her parents up in the stands, sweltering in the midafternoon sun, and felt even more determined to leave it all out on the field. Even so, play began at a deliberate, defensive pace.

"It was fairly even," she says. "It was goal box to goal box. There wasn't a whole lot of action in my goal box; there wasn't a whole lot of action in Gao's box either. Then in overtime, they were all over us. It was crazy."

Briana inadvertently took the USA's star midfielder, Michelle Akers, out of the game with a stray fist, leaving a defensive void in the middle of the park. As the game edged toward the final whistle, China's Fan Yunjie sent a looping header toward goal that had Briana beaten, but Kristine Lilly made a last-ditch clearance to keep it out.

Then came the penalties.

USA coach Tony DiCicco took Briana aside after the full-time whistle. "All you need to do is save one," he said. "If you save one, you'll be a hero. If you save two, they'll make a statue of you and put it up in your hometown."

Briana stood with her back to goal while her teammates took their kicks. She watched for the crowd's reaction to see whether they scored or not. Her goal was to remain focused on what she had to do, to save that one penalty. China scored their first two, and so did the USA.

Kicker number three for China was Liu Ying, a diminutive midfielder who wore the number thirteen on her shirt. She trudged up to the penalty spot and placed the ball down. Briana watched and paced and muttered.

"Usually I don't even look at them," Briana says. "I just look at my cues like their body, their approach, right or left foot, how far away are they from the ball. I don't guess at all; I go by instinct and feeling, but I also go by their approach and other cues.

"But this particular kicker, that third kicker, for whatever reason, as I was walking into the goal, something in my mind said, 'Look.' And I looked at her. I saw her walking up there, head down, shoulders down, fussing with the ball, and I'm like, 'This is the one.' I just knew it."

Ying struck the ball. Briana dived forward and down to her left. The crowd watched with bated breath. Briana pushed the ball to safety, and the stadium erupted in jubilation.

That save made the difference. All the remaining players from both sides scored their penalties. Brandi Chastain converted hers to win the World Cup for the USA.

"Going into that game we were really confident, but we were very much aware of what we needed to do," says Briana. "It had to be a perfect performance for us to beat China, and it was."

⚽

A little more than a decade after her World Cup heroics, Briana's career was over.

She took a knee to the temple in a club match for the Washington Freedom—a hit that, as Briana puts it, at first glance seemed "unremarkable." While play continued, Briana's vision worsened. She could barely read the names and numbers on her teammates' shirts. Everything was swirling in front of her eyes, multiplied and unfocused.

Halftime came ten minutes later, and as a trainer helped her off the pitch, Briana said, "I'm not okay." It was a phrase she'd keep having to repeat for the next three years.

A couple of weeks in the reserves stretched into a couple of months. Still Briana wasn't recovering. When the season drew to a close, she began to panic.

"I totally switched from, 'I want to play; I can't believe I'm not healing enough to play,' to, 'What the heck is happening to my life?' I was able to achieve great success, in part because of my mentality and my knowledge and my belief and my understanding of myself, my mental toughness. After the concussion, I totally changed."

In 2010, concussion awareness was limited. Briana's doctors kept telling her that she should be healing, that she should be recovering, that she was— in their eyes—okay. "And I'm like no, there's something wrong. My vision is weird. I don't feel like myself. I've got this headache in the same spot every day, and it keeps coming back, and I have this weird anxiety, which I never had before, and all these weird feelings and thoughts and ways that I'm going about my day that are not me. This is not who I am at all."

She compared the feeling to being suddenly unplugged, "having the cord pulled out of the wall." Finally, she was paired up with a brain injury specialist in Baltimore, who took her concerns seriously and operated. After extensive surgery, two pea-sized clumps of damaged tissue were removed from her brain. She immediately began to recover.

In the years since, Briana has become a leading advocate for concussion awareness. "I couldn't let those three years of my life just disappear. I had to make it mean something."

Her concern for the next generation of players is clear. "Those of us who've suffered and understand it are just trying to keep the sport safer.

I'm all for soccer. I want every little girl who ever thought about kicking a soccer ball to play. Every single one of them. I also want their administrators and their coaches to be intelligent about it. That's all."

⚽

Dayton, Minnesota, isn't home to a Briana Scurry statue yet, but it is home to the Briana Scurry Soccer Field, where young Daytonites dive around on the turf in attempts to play like their local hero.

Briana, though, isn't easy to emulate. In 2017, she became the first African American woman elected to the National Soccer Hall of Fame. A case bearing her photograph after the famous penalty save and her goalkeeping gloves is on display at the National Museum of African American History and Culture in Washington, DC. Right beside Michael Jordan, right across from the Williams' sisters, her place in sporting history assured.

Her only regret is that her beloved parents passed away before they could see her honored. "It would have been really cool for them to see that," she says. "Whatever belief or confidence I needed, it came from them."

SISSI

SISSI
FORWARD

A trailblazer with a shorn head and a sweet left foot, Sissi burst onto the international soccer scene during the 1999 World Cup.

An extremely popular and talented player for Brazil, she scored seven goals during the tournament, tying with Sun Wen for the Golden Boot—the award for most goals scored during a World Cup. Her most impressive strike came in the quarterfinals against Nigeria, when she scored a stunning free kick from twenty-five yards to send her team into the semis.

Sissi was born Sisleide Lima do Amor in the Brazilian state of Bahia, and her family initially discouraged her from playing soccer. Her father had hoped Sissi's brother might grow to be a soccer player, but he didn't have the ability or the interest. Sissi did. But she was a girl, and in Brazil, women were banned from playing until 1979, when Sissi turned twelve.

She found ways to sneak in a practice, crafting soccer balls out of socks stuffed with toilet paper or using her dolls' heads. Eventually, her family took note, and her father bought her a soccer ball. From there, Sissi flourished.

At fourteen, she left home to play for a team in Salvador. Two years later, she made her international debut for Brazil and was included in the team for the 1988 World Invitational Tournament in China, a precursor to the 1991 world championships. She had to wait more than a decade to make her mark in a real World Cup, and for a time, it looked as if she might miss the 1999 tournament. Before it began, she suffered a facial injury playing indoor soccer, or futsal, and had to have surgery. She played the tournament anyway, with broken bones in her cheeks. Her deft footwork marked her out as a fan favorite, and her shaved head made her unmistakable.

At club level, Sissi played in the WUSA and the Women's Professional Soccer league (WPS). She now coaches a girls' team in San Francisco, her adopted home. In 2017, she was included in Chelsea Clinton's book *She Persisted Around the World: 13 Women Who Changed History*.

An icon who paved the way for her predecessors, Sissi was delighted to see her compatriot, Marta, continuing what she started. Sissi described her as "different class." According to Sissi, "The fans think that there's competition between the two of us, but that couldn't be further from the truth. Our styles are totally different. She was born with a gift and I respect her hugely. Every generation has its icons, and Marta is the best possible standard-bearer for Brazilian women's football right now."

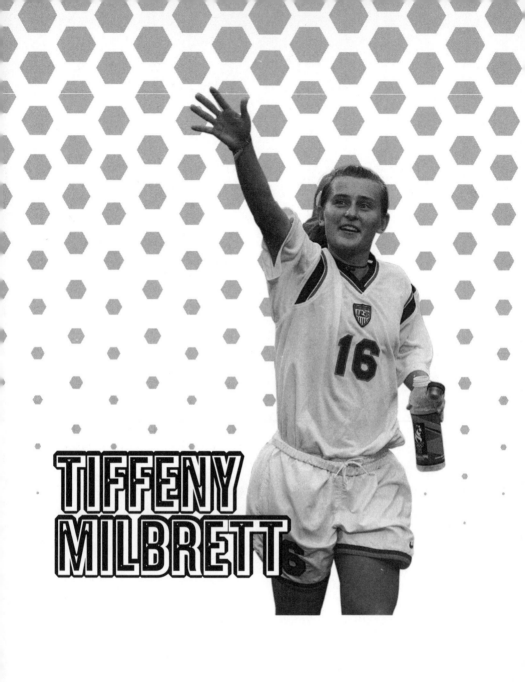

TIFFENY MILBRETT

TIFFENY MILBRETT
FORWARD

In the winter of 2001, Tiffeny Milbrett was sitting on a stage in Zurich, Switzerland. For the first time, the FIFA World Player of the Year Award included women, and Tiffeny was nominated, as were her USWNT teammate Mia Hamm and China's Sun Wen. For the men, it was Spain's Raul, England's David Beckham, and Portugal's Luis Figo, all sitting against the backdrop of a giant screen. As the players were introduced, footage of their greatest moments that year played to a sea of journalists, who were poised to ask questions. For Tiffeny, it was surreal, even though by then she was already a World Cup winner and Olympic gold medalist.

Her clips showed just what she was capable of—the rampaging runs, the sublime finishes, the chips, and the dinks. When it was over, Raul leaned over to her and said, "Man, you're good!" She grinned and thanked him.

Then the lights came up, and the questions began. On and on, for a long stretch of time, the journalists only addressed the male players. Tiffeny sat there, listening, waiting, wondering whether she was going to be asked anything at all. Finally, a FIFA representative spoke up and said, "Let's have a question for the women."

There was a long silence. Then a journalist put up his hand.

"Okay," he said. "Who do you think will win the men's award?"

⚽

Gender inequality was something of a foreign concept to Tiffeny when she was young. Raised by a single mom who worked long hours on an assembly line to provide for her kids, she didn't have to look far to find a sporting role model. "My mom was an athlete," she says. "But she grew up in a small town at a time when there were no organized women's sports teams."

There were no college scholarships and no varsity sports for girls either, but Tiffeny's mother, Elsie, kept pushing, kept trying to squeeze her way onto a team. First, she joined a men's softball league, with young Tiffeny accompanying her as a spectator. Then she established a women's league. When the chance came to play women's soccer, Elsie jumped at it, playing for more than twenty years in a Portland adult league.

"I grew up on the sidelines of her practices and games," says Tiffeny. "There were very few other moms who were that active and that athletically driven. She really was the very first person who inspired me to discover sports and find out that it's what I wanted to do."

Tiffeny didn't have to wait long. When she was eight years old, she caught the eye of Clive Charles, a former soccer player from England who became a legendary figure in the Portland soccer scene and Tiffeny's mentor. "He was the first male to absolutely give full respect to female soccer players," she says. "He trained you and coached you, but all that started with believing that, first of all, the female gender deserves one hundred percent respect, let alone that the female athlete deserves one hundred percent respect. And how you're treated is very, very important."

As she was afforded such respect as a youngster by Coach Charles, it was difficult for Tiffeny to expect anything less. Under his stewardship, Tiffeny thrived, going on to become a three-time All-American with 103 goals in seventy-four games at the University of Portland.

"I wouldn't change that experience for the world," she says. "But you have to understand that it's a great source of pain too, moving forward, because whenever I encounter something that isn't that quality, that isn't giving me respect, I know immediately. I know right away because I've been seen the difference, I've been given the highest level of it."

Under Charles, Tiffeny got used to a level of freedom in her game that she wanted to replicate as a player for the USWNT. When she found it, there was nobody better or more entertaining to watch. In 1996, it was Milbrett who scored the decisive goal to give the USWNT their first gold medals in the Olympics. She was the USA's leading goalscorer at the 1999 World Cup, and over the course of her international career, she earned 206 caps, scored one hundred goals, and made sixty-four assists. Yet, shockingly, it took until 2018 for her to be inducted into the National Soccer Hall of Fame. Because when she wasn't given free rein as a player, she spoke out about it.

Feeling hamstrung by the style and tactical rigors of certain USWNT coaches, Tiffeny quit the team twice, in 2003 and 2007. Her refusal to be stifled, or to accept less than she felt was worth, marked her out as a "difficult woman."

"I've thought about that for years," she says. "And not just the Hall of Fame thing, but through the course of my career. I believe my playing spoke for itself. And then outside of that, you need people to support you, you need people to stand up for you, you need to be thought of as great."

In a 2017 article for soccer magazine *FourFourTwo*, journalist Scott French called it "absolutely criminal" that Tiffeny hadn't yet been awarded her rightful place among the country's acclaimed soccer stars: "[She] was among the Americans' most entertaining, skilled, and cerebral players, and her accomplishments are more impressive considering that she never really fit into the US program."

Tiffeny's nonconformity was what made her so special, so fearless, and difficult to predict. She constantly surprised the opposition, weaving out of tight spaces, scoring goals from unexpected angles. In the run-up to the 1999 World Cup, she was the team's leading scorer, and her strike partner Hamm sang her praises: "I can't say enough about her. We all end up standing and watching her and saying, 'Wow.'" But while Hamm became a superstar, gracing magazine covers and cereal boxes, Tiffeny's talents were largely overlooked. For years after, she was the team's unsung star.

"Do I believe that at times I should have had more support?" she wonders. "Sure. Do I believe that at times I should have been more valued in various ways? Sure. Absolutely. All I ask now is, at the end of the day, people make their decisions about me based on what I did on the soccer field, not on my personality. Well, sorry, but it's not a popularity contest, is it?"

Tiffeny didn't hold back her opinions or try to fit a mold that she knew wouldn't play to her strengths, contrary to the way women are expected to obey and conform. She is the kind of person who makes you want to strive for better.

"Tiffeny was her own person, for sure," says her former USWNT teammate Joy Fawcett. "She had her opinions and wasn't afraid to express them, even at the cost of whatever it may be. She was not afraid to express herself. She was an amazing player on the field, quick, and she could slice through a defense really well. And off the field, she was her own person. Maybe she rubbed some people the wrong way, but I loved her."

She may not have won all the plaudits—or that first FIFA Player of the Year Award—but Tiffeny Milbrett remains one of the all-time greats, indispensable to the USA's dominance of world soccer in the 1990s. At last, two decades later, she is finally getting her due.

BRANDI CHASTAIN
FORWARD

The heat.

Thick and oppressive, it bears down on the field, thermometers reading 104 degrees Fahrenheit. Vapors trickle up from the ground, and everything is hazy, sweltering, the Rose Bowl broiling like a furnace. It won't shift, won't give them any respite.

Brandi Chastain is ready for this to be over. She's exhausted. She's played 120 minutes of soccer against a tough, gritty China team with the sun scorching over Pasadena, and now there are penalties to be taken. She has one last job to do—one last kick, and they can all go inside, cool down, rest.

She stands on the sideline, rubbing a cold towel over her bare arms and face. All around her, players are stretching out their tired limbs, hoping not to cramp. It's the World Cup final, and somehow, after all those elapsed minutes, there is still everything to play for. Lauren Gray, the USWNT assistant coach, runs over to her and asks if she wants to take a penalty kick.

It's an odd question, Brandi thinks, because if the USA had won a penalty during the game, she would have been the one to take it—especially with Michelle Akers knocked out, back in the locker room recovering from a head injury.

She doesn't hesitate. "Yes, of course," she says.

Gray runs back to the bench. Moments later, head coach Tony DiCicco approaches her to confirm. "You're going to take a penalty," he says.

"Yes," she says again. "I already talked to Lauren."

She wonders why they keep going over this. Maybe it's the heat, making this feel like a feverish dream.

DiCicco looks at her square on. "You're going to take it with your left foot," he says.

Before Brandi can argue, he's on his way back to the sidelines. She has never taken a penalty with her left foot in a game before. Sure, she plays on the left; she's as comfortable with her left foot as her right, and she's taken plenty of left-footed penalties in practice. But that's practice; she's never taken one in a game before. And as games go, this is the biggest.

"We had spent a lot of time practicing taking penalty kicks and free kicks to multiple areas in the goal," she says. "But here's the thing: our practices were open to the public. I think Tony was a little bit nervous that China had been watching us practice penalty kicks, and he didn't want to give them any kind of advantage."

Arms linked, mouths dry, the teams gather in the center circle to watch the penalties unfold. Suddenly, Brandi realizes she doesn't know what number she is in the order of kickers. *Gosh, Brandi,* she thinks. *That wouldn't be a sign of confidence to your teammates, not knowing what number you are. So just wait it out quietly and see where you fall in the lineup.*

The first kicker goes, then the second, then the third. It turns out Brandi is last. By the time she starts to walk toward the penalty spot, tiredness has seeped into her bones. She tells herself, "You have one more job to do, and it's to kick the ball into the net. It's not that hard; you've practiced it your whole life. Just do it."

Briana Scurry has already saved one of China's penalties, ensuring that the advantage is firmly with the US women. All that's left for Brandi to do is score. Then she remembers what happened the last time she played against China, in a tournament a few months earlier.

"During the game, we got a penalty kick. I stepped up to take it. I put the ball down on the spot, and as I looked up, there in front of me stood the goalkeeper, Gao Hong. She's a very good goalkeeper, a super quirky character, as most goalkeepers are, and she was just smiling. She winked and she kinda laughed and she got into my head. She unnerved me, and I was really uncomfortable. When the whistle blew, I took the kick with my right foot; it hit the crossbar, came out, and we ended up losing the game two to one."

As Brandi places the ball down on the spot, she's only thinking one thing: don't look at the goalkeeper.

Head down, uniform drenched in sweat, Brandi takes her run up. She makes contact with the ball, striking it cleanly with her left foot. It sails into the top corner of the net, past Gao Hung's outstretched fingertips. GOAL! They've done it! They've won the World Cup! A wall of sound erupts. Screams of joy and relief ring out, and her USA teammates sprint up the field to leap all over her. Brandi wheels away from goal, yanks off her shirt, and swings it over her head, sliding to her knees in front of the crowd.

Behind the touchline, a pitch-side photographer snaps a shot, capturing an immediately iconic image, one that has defined women's soccer for the past twenty years.

Euphoric grin, golden tan, black sports bra.

⚽

When Brandi Chastain first began playing soccer, she was hooked. Without considering where it might lead her or how she might pursue it, her love for the game was immediate and all-encompassing. As an eight-year-old, she wore her full uniform and cleats to bed and slept in them the night before a game. She has maintained that kind of enthusiasm for it ever since.

Brandi lives in San Jose, California, where she works as a volunteer coach at her alma mater, Santa Clara, alongside her husband, Jerry Smith, who was once her soccer coach. In addition, she coaches a varsity team of high school boys and a team of eighth grade girls. From this vantage point, Brandi can see the impact of that win in 1999 still unfurling at the grassroots.

"The farther we get away from it, the more I realize how that moment really helped influence girls' participation in soccer in a positive way," she says. "The beauty is that it's a positive environment. It gives them an opportunity to be as courageous and as confident and as awesome as they possibly can be. If they have good people around them, like I did with my teammates, telling them, 'Hey, you got this,' then, well, what is there to be nervous about? They can just go and have fun. That's why we're out there."

But success brings with it the burden of expectation. Opportunities for female soccer players in the USA are now abundant, and consequently, the pressure can be immense. Sometimes that worries her.

"For young girls especially, with college scholarships being so important, it has created an environment where soccer is not just for fun; it's for earning your next place," she says. "In some ways, I think it has become really stressful for kids and parents alike because they're paying a lot of money for their kids to participate in leagues and go to tournaments and travel and stay in hotels. They worry that if they don't do those things, they won't get the next opportunity. That part has changed dramatically."

Brandi remembers traveling to her first tournament, riding in the family car as her parents drove her across the Golden Gate Bridge. It felt like they had gone hundreds of miles, but it was only a couple of hours away.

"Kids are getting on planes and crossing state lines and playing in tournaments against kids from different regions and international games. The world is a much bigger place now, as it relates to soccer."

⚽

Known as "the Most Famous Sports Bra in the World," the photograph of Brandi's celebration made the covers of *Newsweek*, *Sports Illustrated*, and

Time magazines that summer. By that time, she had been playing for the USWNT for nearly eleven years, having earned her first cap in 1988 and scored her first international goal in 1991. She had played club soccer out in Japan, been a founding player in the WUSA, and battled through a serious knee injury to play every minute of the USA's gold-medal-winning Olympic games in Atlanta. Yet it is the one moment, the celebration, that still follows Brandi around.

"It's not embarrassing [as such]" she says. "That it's still looked upon as a wonderful sports memory is humbling. The intention was never for it to be a highlight; it was just a celebration of a wonderful moment. That's what sports allow us to do, and I think that's why most people play, to have that moment of joy. It just so happened that it was seen by millions of people and, now with social media, millions more."

Although Brandi became the face of that momentous victory, there was always so much more to it than that split-second click of a camera shutter. "I wouldn't have been there had the team not existed," she says. "Maybe it was fate. It was a lot of things happening at the right time. I wish I could put whatever it was in a bottle. It was special."

MIA HAMM

MIA HAMM
FORWARD

Springtime in Seattle.

A crowd of Californians clad in black and gold stands in the away supporters' section of the CenturyLink Field. Anticipation hangs in the air over the artificial turf, where their team will play its first-ever competitive game.

It has taken years to bring Los Angeles Football Club to this moment, built from nothing into a thriving brand with an impressive following and a well-known coach, Bob Bradley, at the helm. There are promising players too, like Diego Rossi, the young Uruguayan everyone is excited about.

But the real soccer legend, twice a World Cup winner, Olympic gold medalist, and FIFA World Player of the Year, is watching her new team from the co-owners' box. She's the poster on the wall that launched entire generations of soccer careers. She's one of the most recognizable names and faces in the global game and the benchmark for all the women's players who came after. Every talented goalscorer in the USA will vie to be named the next her, even though there is only one.

Mia.

⚽

Mariel Margaret Hamm was born in Selma, Alabama, with a partial club-foot. To correct it, she wore casts on her feet. So the legend goes, once they were removed, she was blazing trails like a rocket, swift and unstoppable. As her sister, Caroline Cruickshank, put it, "You could not stop her."

Mia got used to life on the road early; her father was in the US Air Force, and the family moved frequently. She discovered soccer as a preschooler living in Italy, watching the local kids play in the park, running into the mix in her purple dress and lace tights so that she could see how it felt to kick the ball herself. The Hamm family then moved to Wichita Falls, Texas, where they adopted a son from Thailand, eight-year-old Garrett.

Mia was besotted. Everything Garrett did, Mia wanted to do too. He loved sports, so Mia began playing sports. At five years old, she joined a local soccer team, cut her hair short like her brother, and discovered a love for the game. She practiced every day so that Garrett's friends wouldn't make fun of her, so that she could hang with her beloved brother without embarrassing him.

When Garrett was sixteen, he was playing quarterback for the high school football team when a fellow parent noticed he bruised rapidly and easily. He was diagnosed with a rare blood disease, aplastic anemia, a condition almost unheard of in mid-1980s suburban America. From there, the family desperately tried to seek out more information and provide him with treatment. Garrett had been heading for college, most likely on an athletic scholarship, and suddenly he was battling a chronic illness.

The diagnosis cast a long shadow over Mia. She was fast becoming an outstanding soccer player while watching her brother's sporting dreams fall apart. It gave her the impetus to try even harder, to fight for every ball.

A natural goalscorer, Mia was just fifteen when she was called up to the USWNT, the youngest player ever to make the squad. At college, she shone, helping the North Carolina Tar Heels to four NCAA Championship wins in five years. She took time out to play in the first world soccer championships in China in 1991, when she was still only nineteen and the youngest player on the team. She scored the deciding goal in the USA's first game of the tournament, helping them to a 3–2 victory over Sweden.

Four years later, she led the USA to the 1995 World Cup in Sweden, scoring once again in the opening game. Although the team lost in the final, there was plenty to be excited about. Women's soccer would be included in the Olympic games for the first time the following year, in a tournament held on home soil for Mia and her teammates: Atlanta 1996.

It was a sign of progress, women being given more respect in the sporting sphere, but archaic attitudes are slow to change. An awful incident in Mia's home life underscored an essential truth of chauvinism: how it's woven into the fabric of our world, how it can have deadly repercussions. Not long before the Atlanta games, Garrett's health declined, and he was taken to the emergency room. Mia's mother, Stephanie, was by Garrett's side, but when she described his rare condition to an ER doctor, she was rebuffed. "The only problem this guy has," the doctor told Stephanie, "is that he's twenty-seven years old and his mommy's still taking care of him." He was treated for flu-like symptoms and suffered a life-threatening complication.

It was clear to Mia that there were bigger things outside of soccer, and that knowledge took some of the pressure off the game. As the Olympic tournament began, she was fired up, determined, darting around the field from the kickoff. She scored the USA's second goal in the opening game, a 3–0 win over Denmark. Then midway through the second half, she sprained her ankle and had to be subbed off. She missed the next game, a scoreless draw against China, and came back in for the semifinal against Norway, but she was still hampered, dropping back to midfield when the strain on her ankle was too much.

Nothing was going to keep Mia from playing in the final, a defining moment for women's soccer, played in front of more than seventy-six thousand spectators at the Sanford Stadium. Even though NBC declined to televise the game, the public's interest in the team was piqued. Mia set up the team's first goal; her deflected shot parried onto the post and into the path of Shannon MacMillan, who slotted it home. China equalized through Sun Wen but couldn't hold on. Mia was instrumental in setting up the USA's winning goal, passing to Joy Fawcett, who set up Tiffeny Milbrett to finish. Mia gave her all and was being carried from the field on a stretcher when the final whistle blew and jubilant screams rang out—the USA had beaten China to win gold.

When Mia stepped off the team bus back at the hotel that night, Garrett was the first person she saw. He was still very unwell but had made it to the games to support his little sister. He had tears streaming down his face as he pulled Mia in for a hug. "I'm so proud of you," he told her. That moment meant everything to her.

For the next eight months, Mia's life was a blur. The USA team had captured public hearts, and none more so than her. She was eminently marketable, looking like the archetype of an American girl next door. She was advertising Nike and doing shampoo commercials; she made *People* magazine's most beautiful list and was fast becoming a household name. Then, less than a year after the greatest moment of her life, came the worst. Garrett passed away from complications arising from a bone marrow transplant. And, as Mia said, "Everything just stopped."

A week later, the USWNT were on a victory tour to celebrate the team's success in Atlanta. Mia watched on TV at home as her teammates took to the field; they were all wearing black armbands in memory of her brother. Seeing that gave her something to focus on, motivation to "get back out there." She rejoined the team after Garrett's funeral and said later, "Playing in that first

game, being around them, I knew I was going to be okay."

Garrett's story is as integral to Mia's story as it is to the story of the USWNT, the bonds that arose between the players of the 1990s, and the philanthropy that is inextricably linked to the role of professional women's soccer player. In 1999, she levied her fame to launch the Mia Hamm Foundation, raising awareness for bone marrow and cord blood transplants while increasing opportunities for young women in sports.

"She set the standard," says Dan Levy, who helped establish the foundation and later became her agent. "She understood that she needed to be a role model for the next generation, for women in general. She understood that it was gonna take some hard work with her marketing partners to move the needle not just for her, but for the sport itself."

⚽

In 1999, Mia went stellar.

She was a recognizable face and name beyond the world of soccer, even though she didn't particularly enjoy the limelight. Her teammates saw her discomfort and turned it into levity. When Nike named a building after her at their Oregon headquarters, Mia returned to camp to find the team equipment room covered with tape, labeling everything: the "Mia Hamm Lamp," the "Mia Hamm Air Conditioner," the "Mia Hamm Table." The team kept her grounded and safe while the Mia Hamm commercial juggernaut rolled on, unimpeded.

There was the Gatorade commercial where she went one-on-one with Michael Jordan, the Soccer Barbie with her face on the packaging, the Wheaties cereal box, the cover of *Sports Illustrated* that dubbed her "the Reluctant Superstar." The accompanying article named her as the world's greatest female soccer player and provided an astute description: Mia had a "divided soul" in which the "shy, self-critical athlete [was] locked in mortal combat with the relentlessly driven superstar."

Mia wanted to be outstanding, but in being outstanding, she lost her privacy, something that was clearly very important to her. Of all the great soccer players' autobiographies, Mia's is the one that reads more like a tactical manual, with diagrams of skills games and training exercises. "I have always been uncomfortable talking about my personal accomplishments," it reads. "But I must say that scoring my one hundredth career international goal was surprisingly emotional for me."

By the time she retired after the 2004 Olympics, Mia had scored 158 goals and made 142 assists, making her the leading scorer in the game at that time. Although her on-field record has since been surpassed, her influence on the global game has not.

Search the internet for Mia Hamm, and you will find a wealth of inspirational quotes, some of which have been illustrated and turned into art:

"Somewhere behind the athlete you've become and the hours of practice and the coaches who have pushed you is a little girl who fell in love with the game and never looked back . . . play for her."

"Take your victories, whatever they may be, cherish them, use them, but don't settle for them."

"I am building a fire, and every day I train, I add more fuel. At just the right moment, I light the match."

Fifteen years after she stopped playing, she is still inspiring, still leading, still a poster on the wall.

A LEAGUE OF THEIR OWN

2000s

Expectations were immense, and as it all began, it seemed as though they would be met.

The Women's United Soccer Association—the first professional women's soccer league in the United States—kicked off on April 14, 2001, in front of a sellout crowd at the RFK Stadium in Washington, DC. Ticket booths were so overwhelmed by the numbers that some of the 34,148 fans didn't make it to their seats until just before halftime.

The atmosphere was electric; the stands were filled with fans who had been glued to the 1999 World Cup and were excited to see two of its biggest names lining up against each other: Mia Hamm for the Washington Freedom and Brandi Chastain for the Bay Area CyberRays. The matchup didn't disappoint. Late in the game, Chastain was called for a foul on Hamm in the penalty area. Delma Goncalves, known as Pretinha, Freedom's Brazilian standout, made the kick and secured a 1–0 win for her side. The result left Chastain in tears.

After the game, reporters grilled Chastain about her reaction. "My emotions go both ways," she said. "The referee is the person who ultimately makes the call. And, unfortunately, today, the call went against me and there's nothing I can do to change that. . . . It's hard to stand up here in defeat, but it doesn't change the pride I have in my heart."

The drama was inbuilt; the characters were strong, and the stage was set for all those associated with WUSA to capture. At the same time, the players were thrust into the limelight, requiring them to adapt to growing levels of public interest and to hone their public personas as women's professional soccer began in earnest.

Founded by the chairman and chief executive officer of Discovery Communications, John Hendricks, with funding from major investors like Time Warner Cable and Comcast, the league had accrued over $40 million to secure the first five years of its existence. Structured like Major League Soccer (MLS), with the league owning the players' contracts, it consisted of eight teams across the country: Atlanta Beat, Boston Breakers, Bay Area Cyber-Rays, Carolina Courage, New York Power, Philadelphia Charge, San Diego Spirit, and Washington Freedom. All twenty members of the 1999 USWNT squad had a team to play for and were considered to be the league's founding players.

Hendricks felt that the women's soccer market had huge, untapped potential. He had been trying to start a professional league for years and capitalized on the popularity of the '99 World Cup to see his vision to fruition.

There was so much hype surrounding the building and branding of the WUSA—in commercials, the best-known players were cast as animated superheroes—that some executives at the MLS began to worry for their own league's popularity. There were even rumors of the MLS launching their own women's league in order to compete, but after establishing talks, they decided to partner with WUSA instead.

World Cup–winning coach Tony DiCicco, who passed away in 2017, joined WUSA as the league's commissioner. Soon the best women's players from around the world began signing contracts with WUSA teams.

"It's not like they're going to get rich coming here," DiCicco said at the time. "But they want to come here because they'll be respected as top athletes here. Women's soccer is way down the priority list overseas, but in this country, women's soccer has a following and a respect. They saw that last summer, and they want to play where the game is respected, just like our men's national team members want to play in Europe."

The business model was geared to a modest attendance of sixty-five hundred fans at each game, but the league's founders felt they would soon surpass that. The players shared their enthusiasm. As DiCicco noted, "The members of the US national team really bought into the idea that they were missionaries for the sport. It wasn't a labor for them; they wanted to be role models, to tie in with their fans. I think that's the phenomenon that happened [in 1999]. It wasn't just sport, there was a connection between the fans and players. Our job is to recreate that connection, not just with one team, but a league of players."

The signs were undoubtedly promising, and it seemed that interest and support were there in abundance. So where and how did it all go wrong?

The Fall of WUSA

WUSA began struggling not long into its first season.

Attendances and ratings began to decline at a steady pace from that exhilarating opening game in DC. The initial $40 million investment—predicted to last five seasons—was gone after just one. Corporate sponsorship didn't materialize the way it had during and after the '99 World Cup. But more than anything, the league suffered from a lack of consistent coverage.

WUSA games weren't broadcast on network TV after a deal was struck to show twenty-two games on TNT and CNN/SI. By the end of the 2003 season, there was no TV contract in place at all for the following year. Despite the difficulties, the women's game in the USA grew exponentially. Julie Foudy told the *New York Times* that she had seen the evidence for herself: "Where once the pool of [USWNT] players was 25, now the pool is 125 who are training and playing at the highest level. There's more depth, and it's not a coincidence—it's a product of the league."

Players like Shannon Boxx, a midfielder for San Diego Spirit in the WUSA's inaugural season, broke through the international ranks thanks to her time in the WUSA. Boxx went on to win 195 caps for the USA over the next twelve years. University of Florida forward Abby Wambach was an up-and-coming player in the early days of WUSA; she joined Washington Freedom in the draft before the 2002 season and scored twenty-three goals in just 37 appearances during that campaign. Internationals like Birgit Prinz, Homare Sawa, Kelly Smith, and Sun Wen brought their star power and gained greater exposure with WUSA teams. Outwardly, at least, the signs were positive leading up to the 2003 World Cup.

But all was not well behind the scenes. During the 2003 season, WUSA players had already agreed to a 30 percent pay cut to help keep things going. The 2003 World Cup was to begin when the season was over, and it was having problems of its own. The tournament was hastily relocated from China due to the outbreak of the SARS virus, and the USA were unexpectedly due to host again. What might have been an opportunity to rekindle the home fires of '99 looked bleaker than it had four years earlier, with dark clouds brewing on the horizon. Just five days before the World Cup was to kick off, WUSA announced that the league was to be "suspended."

"It's a sad day for all of us who have labored in all of this," Hendricks, the league's chairman, said when the news broke. "My singular disappointment, as we witnessed with all the sponsorship support off the '99 World Cup, the financial support and the creative commercials you all remember that introduced America to the players, was we felt that kind of support would be shifted to a league that would operate full time. Unfortunately, that has not materialized."

Shannon MacMillan, one of the founding players and a member of the 1999 World Cup–winning team, described the league's closure as "heartbreaking." She said, "It's hard in the sense that it is the last thing you want to be focusing on, but at the same time we can use this to roll into the World Cup. We can be ambassadors and say, 'Hey, we need help.' We're not ashamed to ask for help. We need more big-time investors to step up, and fuel our dream by believing in us."

The Limelight Dims

The WUSA players would be going into the 2003 World Cup game-fit, having played a full season of professional soccer. Julie Foudy admitted that the league's failure might serve as a distraction to the USWNT going into the World Cup. But she insisted, "We are genetically predisposed to not give up."

In a much-feted semifinal match, Germany—led by Birgit Prinz of WU-SA's Carolina Courage—swept the USA aside 3–0, thanks to two late goals. For Hamm and Foudy and several other members of the '99 team, it was the end of an era, the swan song of their World Cup careers ending on a low. It was insult added to the injury of WUSA's demise.

Yet hope remained for the league to be revived. As Hamm said, "We are not giving up, by any means."

Since the World Cup had been rescheduled at such short notice, tickets were sold late and attendances were significantly lower than they had been in 1999. That, in tandem with the demise of the WUSA, caused some commentators to suggest that the heyday of women's soccer had already been and gone. A crowd of around twenty-five thousand watched Germany play Sweden in the final at the Home Depot Center in California. Sweden went 1–0 up before halftime through Hanna Ljungberg, but Germany's Maren Meinert leveled the score. In the ninety-eighth minute, Nia Kunzer headed in the winner—a Golden Goal—to claim Germany's first World Cup trophy.

Ending on a High

In the 2004 Olympics, the USWNT returned to global dominance.

It was the last international tournament for Julie Foudy, Mia Hamm, and Joy Fawcett, and there was pressure for such a gilded era to end with gold medals. In the final, Brazil looked more threatening—with the precocious talents of a young player named Marta in attack—but the USA had a new secret weapon: Abby Wambach. The prodigious forward headed Kristine Lilly's corner kick into the goal in extra time to secure the win.

"I don't like to lose," Foudy said afterward. "And I really didn't want to lose our last game."

She thanked Wambach for sending them out on a high.

"It's a fabulous way to win an Olympic gold medal," Wambach said, "and it's an even better way to send off these women, because they're what this is about. This is not about me, or the younger players. It's about them."

China Plays Host

Following the crisis around the SARS outbreak and the hasty change of host country in 2003, China was given another chance to put on the World Cup four years later. The tournament began with a record win as Germany thrashed Argentina 11–0.

Brazil's Marta was the tournament's standout player and won the Golden Boot with seven goals, two of which came against USA in the semifinal. Around fifty thousand fans packed out the Hangzhou Dragon Stadium that night and ended up watching Greg Ryan's USA team lose 4–0, a catastrophic defeat by the standards they had set. The game became notorious for Hope Solo's postgame comments to a reporter, when she publicly called out Ryan's decision to bench her for the game and underscored a period of turmoil for the former world champions.

Brazil took their momentum into the final, but even Marta's world-class talent wasn't enough to win the tournament. Two goals—from Prinz and Simone Laudehr—sealed victory for Germany as they became the first team in women's soccer history to secure back-to-back World Cups.

Doubt Sets In

In 2008, a new US league came into existence: the Women's Professional Soccer league. This time ten teams were part of the league's makeup: Atlanta Beat, Boston Breakers, Chicago Red Stars, FC Gold Pride, Los Angeles Sol, Florida's magicjack, Philadelphia Independence, Sky Blue FC of New Jersey, Saint Louis Athletica, and Western New York Flash. The plan was to grow the league slowly, to learn from the mistakes of WUSA, the overconfidence and overspending, and to secure wider media coverage.

But as the decade drew to a close, things weren't looking good, and some reports predicted the demise of women's pro soccer altogether.

MARTA

FORWARD

"Get on the bus."

So begins a poignant letter from Marta Vieira da Silva to her four-teen-year-old self, published in the *Players' Tribune* in 2017. An internation-ally renowned player of such caliber that she is known simply by her first name—Marta—it would be easy to presume from watching her delicate footwork, pace, trickery, and confidence on the field that soccer came easy. But in the beginning, that wasn't the case.

The letter harks back to a pivotal moment in Marta's life. Standing at a bus station near her hometown of Dois Riachos in Brazil, she was about to undertake a three-day bus journey alone to Rio de Janeiro. With only a minute to say goodbye to her family, before venturing into the unknown to pursue an opportunity to do what she loved, she wavered. At home, she could stay with her family and grow up in familiar surroundings. But the bus was about to take her alone into the unknown.

What she couldn't have known—but might have hoped—was that it would take her to far-flung places where she would become a soccer leg-end. She would take part in World Cups and Olympics, and she would win more FIFA World Player of the Year awards than any other player—male or female—in history. She would excite crowds and inspire a whole new gener-ation of girls both abroad and at home in Brazil. Perhaps in that moment of hesitation, she could sense her future self willing her on in the letter:

"It seems like a difficult decision to get on the bus. You don't even know for sure what will happen when you get to Rio. But trust me when I say that after everything you've already gone through, you can do this.

"You've already fought, Marta. You're stronger than you realize."

⚽

In Brazil, soccer is often compared to a religion. From Garrincha to Pelé, Ronaldhino to Neymar, the Latin American nation has long been regarded as soccer's spiritual home. But only as far as the men's game is concerned. For forty years, women weren't even allowed to play. And it all came down to a very different kind of letter in the mail.

In the 1940s, several women's teams were playing in tournaments in Rio de Janeiro. But a disgruntled citizen named José Fuzeira wrote to then-president Getulio Vargas to suggest that playing soccer was harmful to women's reproductive health and femininity. The letter worked; the seeds of doubt were planted in the minds of the male establishment, and women were banned from playing, just as they had been in England several years earlier.

The ban lasted until the mid-1970s, when feminist leaders like Rose Filardis campaigned against Brazil's National Sports Council to ensure the ruling was overturned. But the country's soccer culture was slow to catch up. In 1986, when Marta was born into an impoverished community and to parents on the brink of separation, the notion of girls or women playing soccer was still frowned upon.

As a child, with her mom and brother out working, Marta spent long days at her grandparents' home. She would join in with the neighborhood boys who played soccer in the streets, the only girl in the area brave enough to try. From the moment she started playing, she loved it, even though she suffered daily taunts for being a girl who loved soccer. For a while, it was lonely. But still, she kept playing.

⚽

Three years after boarding that bus, Marta was playing for Brazil in the 2003 women's World Cup. Brazil made it to the quarterfinals but narrowly lost 2–1 to Sweden. Marta's extraordinary talents caught the attention of everyone watching and proved her worth when she scored from the penalty spot for Brazil's only goal of the game.

When the tournament was over, Sweden came calling: Umea IK persuaded Marta to leave her home country and come play for them. In her first season at Umea—a region where the first women's soccer leagues in Sweden began—the team won the UEFA Cup, beating Frankfurt 8–0 over two legs. Marta scored three of those goals and twenty-two in the league overall. In her second season, Umea went undefeated, Marta having scored twenty-one times as they won the domestic league.

Marta announced that she was leaving Sweden in 2009 on the same day she was named FIFA World Player of the Year—a title she retained for four more consecutive years—and would be joining Los Angeles Sol in the newly established WPS.

Sol had a successful first season on the field with Marta as their talisman, narrowly losing the championship to Sky Blue FC in a 1–0 defeat. But despite good crowds at all their home games, they were plagued by financial

issues, and the team folded after only one season. Marta and her teammates were entered into the draft; she joined Gold Pride and won the championship with them that season. But once again, the team folded. She joined her third team in the three years, the Western New York Flash, and this time, after a year, the entire WPS league ceased operations.

Along with hundreds of other players in the United States, Marta still needed a professional league to serve as a fitting showcase for her talents. On the world stage, however, she continued to wow the crowds. So far, she has played in four World Cups and three Olympic Games, winning a silver medal twice. She has scored more goals in the World Cup than anyone else, having played every game for her country.

Marta has since found a home for her pace and flair at Orlando Pride in the National Women's Soccer League (NWSL). With such an outstanding career to date, it's hard to believe she will only be thirty-three when the 2019 World Cup kicks off.

⚽

Although she has had to overcome a number of obstacles in her career—clubs shuttering, leagues folding, living abroad, and not being able to communicate in her mother tongue—Marta has always shared a common language with her teammates: soccer. Her advice to young girls who long to play soccer but struggle for acceptance and against prejudice, is this:

"All over the world, there are other girls who feel the same. Girls who get stares, girls who get asked why they're out there, girls who get pulled from tournaments and called names. But that loneliness, it won't last. And it won't be long before you're all playing together."

Marta's is a story of triumph over doubters and naysayers, over the boys in her neighborhood who called her names for playing soccer, over the girls in the big cities who thought she was poor and unsophisticated. The sweetest moments come to those who fight for them.

When she returned to Brazil a soccer superstar, huge crowds welcomed her home. She laughed as she saw the people who had once called her names and told her that she could never be a professional player applaud her as she passed by.

How satisfying she must find it now, to see that the Wikipedia entry for her tiny hometown states only four things: its location, its population, its size, and the fact that it is the birthplace of Marta, "maybe the most notable woman soccer player in the world."

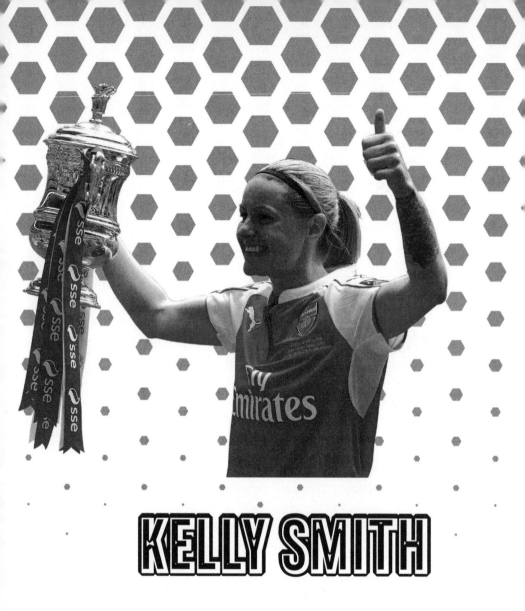

KELLY SMITH

KELLY SMITH
FORWARD

O ut there on the field, Kelly Smith exuded the rare, knowing confidence that comes with being a world-class center-forward.

There was the goal she scored for England at Euro 2009, an outlandish volley from the halfway line that sailed over the hapless Russia goalkeeper. Or the celebration at the 2007 World Cup after she scored with a deft flick to draw England level with Japan: she peeled off her left cleat, held it to her lips, and kissed it theatrically for the cameras.

From the moment Kelly left Watford, a small town just outside London, and slotted into the prestigious US college system, she stood out. The system was still in its infancy, and much of the play was geared toward speed and strength, while Kelly possessed the added dimension of exceptionally well-honed skill. Her ability to dribble past players and deftly score left many onlookers in awe. She was the complete package. Jim Harrison, the assistant coach of her college side, Seton Hall, described her as a "genius."

As a youngster playing on a boys' team, Kelly had been so precociously talented that the parents of opposing players complained about her and forced the team to let her go. Reflecting on that early drawback, she said, "It was a problem for them to see a girl like me dominating a game featuring their sons."

Kelly had a flair that wowed crowds, an innate awareness of the space on which she played, an ease with which she picked out teammates and found top corners. While playing for her beloved Arsenal, the team she grew up supporting, she won twenty major trophies—including the FA Women's Cup, the Women's UEFA Cup, the FA Women's Premier League, the FA Women's Premier League Cup, and the Community Shield in the span of one incredible season.

All in all, you'd be forgiven for thinking Kelly was just as confident off the field, a person who moved through life with the kind of effortless self-assurance she perfected as a player. And you'd be wrong.

⚽

"Kelly Smith?"

The announcer at the Big East Awards dinner stood on stage repeating her name. The crowd turned their heads, but nobody stepped forward. An awkward silence settled over the banquet hall. Finally, Seton Hall coach Betty Ann Kempf walked up to the stage, collecting Smith's Offensive Player of the Year award on her behalf. Kempf was puzzled. Smith had been seated at the table just a short while earlier. Where had she gone?

Later on in the evening, one of the other Seton Hall players found her hiding in a toilet cubicle, crying. Kelly was painfully shy, terrified of public speaking, and had bolted for the restrooms before her award was announced. Her fear of giving an acceptance speech to a roomful of strangers was palpable.

She described the incident in her autobiography, *Footballer: My Story*, adding, "I felt so inadequate because I knew I couldn't do what was expected of me at such an occasion."

Although a move to the United States had seemed ideal for a young player whose skills surpassed the infrastructure that could develop them in her home country, for Kelly it was an unsettling transition. She was a homebody and an introvert. In America, self-confidence is a prized asset in any sphere but especially in sports. Kelly was plunged into a soccer scene on the rise, where the best players needed to acquire a public persona and become at ease with media interest.

"I hated my life out there in those first weeks," she said. "I couldn't play soccer [due to administrative issues] and because of that, I couldn't fit in."

Soccer, she admitted, was how she communicated. "That was where my personality came out—on the field."

Without it, she was unmoored. She searched for other ways to feign confidence and soon discovered alcohol. Cheap beer at college parties quickly morphed into habitual binge drinking.

"When I was sober, I was back to being the person who couldn't cope, and I struggled, particularly when somebody came up to me and wanted to talk about [soccer], or wanted to get to know me. When I was drunk, you couldn't shut me up. I spent my life being two different people."

Although alcohol remained a part of her life, as time passed, she used it less as she began to feel more settled in America. After graduating from Seton Hall, Kelly found herself in the "epicenter of the explosion" of women's soccer after 1999. She joined the Philadelphia Charge in the inaugural season of the WUSA and made an immediate impact, scoring on her debut live on TV and in front of a sellout crowd of fifteen thousand. Playing professional soccer, letting her feet do the talking, it all felt so right.

"At long last, I was where I wanted to be."

Then came the first of several debilitating injuries. In a game against the Bay Area CyberRays, Smith tore the ACL on her right knee. For the next five months, she was laid up, missing her beloved soccer, desperately waiting until she had healed enough to start running. In only her second game back for Philadelphia, her right knee popped again, this time from a torn meniscus. She fought back to fitness again, only to be felled by a leg-breaking tackle while playing for the New Jersey Wildcats against Delaware.

It was her fourth major injury in four seasons, and the impact left her both physically and psychologically shattered. She began drinking vodka alone, using it to blot out her pain and frustration.

"Increasingly, I withdrew myself from life," she said. "When you are out of the game for up to six months, what can you do with all your time? I had gone through the whole process twice, and for what? It seemed like for nothing. So I hit the bottle."

The lowest point came when Kelly drove herself to an England training camp, drunk. Her coaches stepped in and staged an immediate intervention. It was, she admits, "unacceptable" and forced her to face up to her problems. Getting sober was the greatest challenge she had faced.

Kelly checked into rehab and focused on managing her depression and the overwhelming urge to drink. With her newfound sobriety, she shone on the field again. She was named Player of the Year two seasons running in England while playing for Arsenal and became England's all-time highest goalscorer. She returned to the United States for a spell with the Boston Breakers, during which she was more accustomed to life overseas, and she finished her career with four more seasons at Arsenal, culminating in an FA Cup victory.

Meanwhile, Kelly found that opening up about her struggles with substance abuse gave her strength. The public persona she had been required to cultivate became more comfortable, once she realized she could use it to speak honestly and help bring those issues to the fore.

In retirement, Kelly has made it her mission not only to advocate for the women's game but also to speak frankly about mental health. She revealed that it took her thirty-eight years to "feel comfortable in [her] own skin," but now she is there. In 2017, she married her partner, DeAnna, and they welcomed a son soon after.

There is little trace of the young woman who once hid in the toilets rather than speak to a crowd. In the summer of 2018, she was a regular pundit for the men's World Cup on the Fox Soccer network, bringing her insights and affable charm into millions of households across the United States.

Looking back on her darker days, she said, "I wouldn't change it, even though I went through the struggles that I did. That was part of my journey."

HOPE POWELL
COACH

From the outside, dictatorships appear to collapse quickly.

Symbolic monuments are swept to rubble, statues toppled, cheers of jubilant relief ring out in the streets. But though such downfalls seem sudden, they have usually been brewing for a long time.

When it drew to a close, Hope Powell's fifteen-year tenure as England coach was referred to as "the dictatorship"—such was her influence and stronghold on the women's game. In that time, she transformed its fortunes. Under Hope, England qualified for their first World Cup, reaching the quarterfinal stages twice, and made it as far as the European Championship final in 2009. It was then—and remains now—rare to find a woman of color coaching a soccer team. She had to be that much better than everybody else, that much more determined and, without question, tougher too.

When Hope was born in south London in 1966, the year the England men's team won the World Cup on home soil, women were still banned from playing soccer in the United Kingdom. She recalled being told by relatives that her birth father had been violent toward her mother before he abandoned the family when she was a toddler. When her mother got together with a new partner, they moved to a housing project where they were one of the only black families. There were occasions of racist abuse, piles of dog feces left on their doorstep, and insults yelled and muttered by prejudiced neighbors. She tried to shut it out and just get by.

Hope adored her mother but found her strict and intimidating. A traditional woman, she enforced gender stereotypes within the home: girls did the housework; boys didn't. In her autobiography, *Hope: My Life in Football*, she describes her stepfather as a bully who was brutal with his fists. She recalled being a young girl of eight or nine, scrappy and thin, and standing in front of her mother while her stepfather was throwing punches, trying desperately to protect her. It was deeply scarring, as Hope noted, "I'd often stay awake at night, listening for telltale noises, shouting and [arguments]. I found it increasingly hard to sleep, worrying what might happen next."

She escaped when she could. Down the street from the housing project where she lived was a disused industrial storage site, walled off with wire fencing, where the local boys would slip through a hole in the fence and play soccer. They called it "the cage." Hope used to stand behind the fence, watching, hoping for a turn.

One afternoon, the boys were a player down, and she was finally invited to join. Hope was small, skinny, and quick, and she immediately took to the game. "I was better than all of the boys in the cage. It was easy."

From there, her passion grew. She watched every soccer game she could on TV, studying the way the men played the ball, every turn, tackle, and pass. Then she would attempt to replicate them over and over when she returned to the cage.

At high school, Hope had her first brush with the English Football Association (FA), the organization that would one day hire her to coach their women's team. It was an inauspicious introduction. She had been playing with her school's boys' team when the FA found out and banned her: girls weren't permitted to play in the boys' competitions. By that time, Hope had made her debut for the England women's team (the country-wide ban on women's soccer was lifted in the 1970s), so she was in the strange position of being allowed to represent her country at the highest level but not her high school.

As a player, Hope found herself constantly battling negative attitudes to women's soccer. When England made it to the final of the 1984 European Competition (what later came to be called the European Championships),

they couldn't find a London venue; none of the men's teams would let them play in their stadiums.

Everything seemed like a fight, but Hope was used to that. From her difficult childhood, she had acquired resilience, self-reliance, and a lack of patience for those who thought things came easily. Hope's fighting spirit gave her an edge, pushing her to achieve. As England coach, she broke down barriers and brought the game kicking and screaming into the foreground of national sport. While she was head coach of the national side, the FA launched the first women's league in the United Kingdom, the Women's Super League (WSL).

She also gained a fearsome reputation, a disagree-with-me-and-you're-out style of coaching that led key players to retire prematurely from international soccer rather than play for her. She took over all aspects of the national setup, even down to contracts and legal disputes, meaning if you had a problem with Hope, there was nowhere to turn.

One of England's best players, Leanne Sanderson, retired from the international game at twenty-two, citing "personal issues" with Hope, while star midfielder Katie Chapman said she didn't feel supported when her England contract was canceled after she took a break to be with her children.

"I feel like it's personal and it's got to the point where I can't take it anymore," Sanderson said at the time. "I don't want to turn my back on my country but as long as Hope Powell is in charge I don't see myself going back and I don't think she would want me there."

Hope began criticizing her players in public, apparently lambasting their "cowardice" after England lost to France in the 2011 World Cup, when she told the press that some of her players were too scared to take penalties in the crucial shoot-out. Her comments drew ire from other prominent English players. Everton midfielder Leanne Duffy, who was not involved with the national team, took to social media to criticize Hope using the hashtag #getrid.

The end came two years later, when Hope was fired by the FA. Still the dichotomy remained. England captain Casey Stoney thanked Powell for "making her dreams come true" by making her team captain while simultaneously describing her as "ruthless."

For the woman who became known for transforming the women's game in England, a period of obscurity ensued. It took Hope four years to return to coaching. In 2017, she took over as team coach of Brighton in the Women's Super League 2, the second tier of club soccer in the United Kingdom. "I just wanted and needed some time out," she said. "I think it was the right decision and I've come back refreshed."

Even with a fresh start, it can be hard to shake off the baggage of a battered reputation, so it's good to be reminded of all that Hope achieved.

"She was a strong-minded boss," one of her England charges, Fara Williams, recalls. "She knew what she needed to get out of her players. When she was my coach, you have to remember that Hope had nothing. When she took over, there weren't any full-time professionals; they all had had nine-to-five jobs, and she had to try to get them to understand that they had to do extra training if they wanted to compete on the world stage. She did her upmost to get us a part-time contract with the FA, so we could get by work-ing part-time while training. She did so much for our game."

Williams would encourage Hope to let her guard down more so that people could see her soft, kindhearted side. But Hope wouldn't entertain it; her view was that leaders needed to be tough and maintain their boundaries.

"You can talk about her as manager, and at times you could say she was horrible," Williams admits. "But she had a heart of gold outside of [soccer]."

Hope recently acknowledged that her time as England coach changed her perspective on women coaches. Before Phil Neville was given the En-gland job, she said, "If you'd have asked me [who should get the job] 20 years ago I'd have said 'best person' but now I think it's important that there are women role models and that people have someone to aspire to. I think that's really important."

It is a great shame that when discussing role models in the English game, Hope's legacy is tinged with acrimony.

FARA
WILLIAMS

FARA WILLIAMS
FORWARD

Three long peeps of the referee's whistle, and England's dream is over.

Fara Williams sinks down to her haunches, her head hanging low, and stares at the turf. She listens to the applause as it rings out around Ewood Park, one of England's oldest and most beloved stadiums, and tries to let it lift her. Twenty-six thousand fans, almost full capacity, are showing their appreciation, yet it doesn't feel like enough. The team wanted, more than anything, to go further than the group stage of Euro 2005, but they've been undone tonight by a strong Sweden side, by a single goal in the third minute.

For a few hours more, at least, she is still Fara the international soccer player. In a moment, she will pick herself up and trudge back to the locker room. She will peel off her white England shirt, sit back on the bench, and listen to what Hope Powell, the England coach, has to say, even though it won't be pretty. After she's showered, she'll change back into her regular clothes and pick up her backpack, the one she carries everywhere.

Then she will go back to being the other Fara, the one none of her teammates knows. Tomorrow she will return to the homeless hostel where she lives in a room with three single beds, sleeping near two virtual strangers, in a room where the walls are bare, the air is dank, and the furniture is sparse, with just three small closets and a sink. She has learned the hard way not to leave her stuff in the closets.

This Fara won't tell anyone at the hostel where she's been either. She won't tell them that she was representing her country in a major international soccer tournament, playing at the highest level in front of tens of thousands of fans. They won't ask, anyway; it's none of their business.

When night falls, this Fara will climb into her sleeping bag, grateful to the person who bought it for her: Powell, her England coach, the only one who knows the truth. She will tuck her backpack inside too before she zips it up. It holds all her clothes for the week; she has to keep them with her always, or they'll get stolen.

When this Fara closes her eyes, she'll see the floodlights again, the field all lit up, the crowd on their feet, cheering. And she'll know she has a purpose.

⚽

The Surrey Lane Estate is a housing project in Battersea, a grouping of grey, high-rise tower blocks looming over the London skyline. It's never been an easy place to live—too many people with too few resources, a stifled atmosphere that veers toward frustration and anger. Known as "social housing," projects like this were built in the early twentieth century to house low-income families, but over the years, they have been underfunded and poorly maintained. Closed off from the wealthier surrounding neighborhoods, it's easy to get trapped in a cycle of poverty here and hard to see a way out. The kids on the estate tend to get into trouble. Outdoor space is minimal, but there are patches of grass, concrete playing courts, and a playground of sorts. This is where Fara grew up, where she learned how to play soccer, scrapping for every kick.

At twelve, she joined the Chelsea Ladies Under 14s team. She broke into the first team, where she began gaining momentum as a forward. In 2001, the year she made her England debut, she scored thirty goals. Things were looking peachy in her playing career, but her life away from soccer was another story.

Fara had survived a tumultuous upbringing in an overcrowded apartment on the estate, turning to soccer when she needed an outlet. "There were a lot of things my mum had to go through with my dad and my stepdad," she says. "It was something no young child should grow up seeing. When I saw those things as a young girl, it was just easier to run out and go play [soccer], pretending nothing was happening at home."

Not long after her England debut, Fara had a huge bust-up with a family member, one that caused her to leave home. "People assume I fell out with my mum," she says. "But I didn't. She's been my hero from day one and my motivation when I was growing up. I wanted a better life for her."

But at the time, Fara felt she couldn't turn to her for help. Everything at home was too fraught, too messy, and she couldn't make contact again or go back. She didn't know where to turn, so she spent a night wandering the streets. It was a frightening experience, hunkering down in the darkened doorways of south London. With no small amount of determination, she found her way to a homeless shelter in the center of the city, a shelter with the look and feel of a concrete bunker.

"Basically, you were put in a room underground. They'd give you a bed, but you weren't allowed in until 6:30 p.m. and you had to be out by 8:00 a.m. That was for health and safety, because there were no windows in the rooms. You could only stay there for a maximum of two weeks; then you had to find a hostel."

She moved into the hostel and soon found herself sidelined from soccer with a back injury. She looked on in pain while England missed out on qualifying for the 2003 World Cup. Such was the lack of infrastructure and funding in women's soccer in the United Kingdom that all the players had full-time jobs aside from their playing careers. Powell, the England coach, helped Fara find work as a skills coach for the FA. Although Fara was intensely grateful for Powell's support in her personal life, it shifted the power dynamics of their professional relationship.

"It was hard," Fara says, "because she was our national team coach. We probably had a different relationship to what the other players had because she was someone I could go to, someone who would check in on me. I think it made our relationship more difficult than others. I never wanted to let her down in any way in football. And sometimes I did. Sometimes I made mistakes."

Coming from a broken home, Fara was eager to please the people who looked out for her and wounded enough to wall herself away from emotional connection. She kept her head down and focused on her soccer.

"When things got difficult in my life, I knew I could just get a ball and go out and play. I guess that remained from when I was young. Even now, you know, with the way things are in life, when things are hard I always know I have [soccer]."

That's why, Fara says, she was luckier than most. "It wasn't too hard for me," she insists. "Most people who live in hostels, young homeless people, find it really hard because they don't have jobs, they don't have any direction or any focus. I was on the England team. That was my focus, remaining there pushing on and maybe keeping the other part of my life a secret, not allowing it to be a distraction. It was home to me; it was where I slept and was able to eat, but I didn't feel afraid. I was in a good position. From the outside looking in, people might say, 'But you were in a hostel.' Well, I saw people in some difficult positions in the hostel, but mine certainly wasn't."

Fara doesn't want pity, and she doesn't want her life reduced to a sound-bite either: Fara Williams, the "homeless soccer star." You can imagine her rolling her eyes. It's reductive, simplifying the circumstances of her life. But that, she says, is how we tend to view homelessness: as a state of being rather than the by-product of numerous, complex misfortunes.

"There is a perception of what homelessness is and what it should look like. There are many different stories. Many people had everything, had businesses and houses, and it came to an end. They found themselves unable to afford their mortgage, lost their business, and found themselves on the street in hostels trying to rebuild. Most young people are homeless because of family breakdowns. They can't deal with the issues at home."

Before her own family breakdown, Fara shared the same perceptions of homelessness. She was frightened of people who lived on the streets and did her best to avoid them. "It's sad," she says. "They're human beings. They like to be spoken to; they like to have conversations, and people often just walk past them. I was one of those people who probably would have walked past them on the street and not given them the time of day. But when you find yourself in a similar position, you understand. Everybody is there for different reasons."

It was during her years in the hostel that her playing career blossomed. At club level, she left Chelsea and moved to Charlton Athletic. There followed spells at Everton—where the fans nicknamed her "Queen" Fara—then Liverpool and Arsenal, by which time she had reconciled with her family. Fara is a natural goalscorer, occasionally given to moments of audaciousness; at her current club, Reading, she scored a goal directly from kickoff with a long lob from the halfway line. Such moments are a sign of confidence, of a woman enjoying her game and her life. But they are also the mark of a woman who has taken the hardships of her past and turned them into assets.

During the years Fara lived in hostels, when she didn't have contact with her family, she channeled her mother's tenacity.

"I'm definitely like my mum," she says. "I have the same character. People have role models; she was mine. She was the one person who showed so much strength through so many things. If I have one trait of hers, it's that."

It's a trait that has served her well in soccer; Fara has an unusual affinity for taking penalties. Uncannily relaxed and calm under pressure, she is the one to trust when the ball is placed on the spot.

⚽

Here is another story.

It's the 108th minute of a scoreless game. Germany versus England, old foes on the soccer field. The former is always claiming victory over the latter in the men's and women's games. This is the World Cup playoff, the contest to decide who finishes third in 2015. England want this so bad—a victory over their sporting nemesis, a bronze medal to galvanize the game back home.

Then Lianne Sanderson is brought down in the box. England has a penalty. Who else could possibly step forward to take it but Queen Fara? She places the ball on the spot. In front of her, Germany's Nadine Angerer is poised on the goal line. Here we have a forward who loves taking penalties and a goalkeeper who loves saving them.

Others might balk at the pressure, but not Fara. There are no doubts, no mistakes. She coolly slots the ball into the back of the net. And the victory belongs to England.

As Fara runs to her teammates to celebrate, she glances up at the stands. Her mum is here tonight, at the Commonwealth Stadium in Edmonton, Canada. She is here cheering for her daughter, the England international, the match winner.

Tonight, it couldn't be clearer that Fara has done what she set out to do: she has given her mum a better life. And at the same time, she has carved out an incredible one for herself.

NADINE
ANGERER

NADINE ANGERER
GOALKEEPER

There is a saying in Germany that "the ball is round"—no matter how much planning you do, anything can happen. Even so, this much is certain: with Nadine Angerer in goal, far less is left to chance.

Nadine was born into a sporting family in a small village near Frankfurt. Her mother was a professional triathlete, while her father played handball. Her parents encouraged her to take part in various sports and were pleased to see her kicking a soccer ball around with the boys in her village. When the boys asked if she'd be willing to join their local team, her parents were open and accepting. Nadine was such a talent that her teammates did what they could to accommodate her; they even subbed her out five minutes before the end of each game so that she could use the locker room showers before the boys came off the field.

Back then, Nadine played as a forward. It was only when she stepped in to goal to relieve an injured teammate that her shot-stopping talent came to the fore. She made her debut for the German national side when she was seventeen, but she quickly found herself stuck on the sidelines while Silke Rottenberg cemented her place as the team's number one. Ten years passed while Nadine sat by and waited and watched. She won medals and trophies by virtue of being part of the squad but not as a first-team player: the World Cup in 2003, two Olympic bronze medals, and three UEFA Championships. Immense frustration could have clouded her career, but Nadine took it in her stride and remained focused on her role as the backup keeper.

When Rottenberg tore her ACL, Nadine stepped into the starting lineup. She came into the German side just before the 2007 World Cup and quickly channeled that decade of patience into performances. Germany progressed through the World Cup without conceding a single goal, thanks largely to Nadine's safe hands.

The toughest test came in the final against Brazil. Linda Bresonik brought Christiane down in the box, and Brazil was awarded a penalty. Nadine needed to keep a cool head in order to keep a clean sheet.

"I remember everything was really hectic," she said. "But I was completely calm."

Marta stepped forward to take the kick, blasting the ball low. Nadine dived and parried the ball to safety. Germany won the World Cup, and Nadine hadn't let a single goal get past her.

Over the next few years, Nadine came to be recognized as one of the world's greatest. In 2013, she became the first goalkeeper to win the FIFA World Player of the Year. She hadn't planned a speech, so she simply ad-libbed her way through what she wanted to say. It was an honor, sure, but to Nadine it felt strange to win an individual award for playing a team sport.

As well as her shot stopping, it was this indefatigable blend of camaraderie and composure that made her indispensable. When Birgit Prinz retired, Nadine became Germany's team captain. She remained at the top of her game until she retired after the 2015 World Cup, after which she made the progression into coaching. She now trains the keepers at her former club, the Portland Thorns.

"I always had the passion to become a goalkeeper coach," she said. "Even when I was a more experienced goalkeeper and a younger goalkeeper came in, I always had this feeling that I needed to do whatever I could to help them."

PIA SUNDHAGE

PIA SUNDHAGE

COACH

I t's an unconventional tactic, singing and playing guitar to a room full of soccer players. But it works for Pia Sundhage. And in 2008, when she took over the USA team, it was a canny way to usher in a new era.

Team spirit had been eroded by recent events, and the camp was fractious after a contentious episode at the tail end of the 2007 World Cup in China. Goalkeeper Hope Solo, who had performed well throughout the tournament, was benched for the semifinal game against Brazil in favor of Briana Scurry. When the team lost by 4–0, Solo criticized the decision and famously told a reporter in the postgame mixed zone, "There's no doubt in my mind I would have made those saves."

The fallout was immense, and Solo was ostracized; she flew home from China alone. Pia was brought in to replace Coach Greg Ryan and restore some unity to the group. She sat down with the players individually, and she listened. Then she gathered them all together and serenaded them: a guitar-strummed version of Bob Dylan's "The Times They Are a-Changin." It was quirky, endearing, and it broke the tension. Then she told them all to forgive Solo. "You don't have to forget," she said. "But you do have to forgive."

So began the most successful coaching run in women's soccer history, culminating in Olympic gold—twice—and a World Cup runners-up spot. Of the 107 games for which Pia was in charge of the USWNT, there were only six defeats.

⚽

To say she is an unconventional character is something of an understatement. Pia is full of contradictions. She is both hyperorganized and laid-back, relentlessly positive and scathing in her criticism, jovial and friendly in the locker room, yet apathetic about cultivating deep relationships with her players.

"You know," she once said, "I talk to them about their mom, their dad, their boyfriend, their girlfriend or whatever, and you know what? It goes in one ear and out the other."

But this is also part of her sensibility—a dry humor that can read as harsh in print when the intonation is lost. She is offbeat and fearless. As USA coach, she endeared herself to the fans firstly with her coaching expertise, creating a system in which the team thrived; they became more skilled in possession, incisive in attack, and solid in defense. As a character, too, she seemed to be the breath of fresh air the US team needed.

Pia turned down two official visits to the White House, saying, "Showing off and meeting important old men and women doesn't particularly fascinate me. I'm at my happiest on the pitch in a pair of football shoes."

When a reporter asked her whether a woman could coach a men's team, she responded, "Let me ask you a question: does it work with a female chancellor in Germany? Angela Merkel runs a whole fucking country. Clearly it works."

But her outspokenness could be harmful too. In a 2015 press conference, in her new role as Sweden coach, Pia described Carli Lloyd, whose two goals in the Olympic women's soccer final helped win gold for her side, as "difficult to coach." She added, "When she felt that we had faith in her, she could be one of the best players. But if she began to question that faith, she could be one of the worst."

Hearing her former coach talk that way must have been bruising for Lloyd, but Pia didn't seem concerned about causing offense. Perhaps she felt she had earned the right to speak plainly, after four extremely successful decades in the game.

On the field, she was outstanding, a utility player who was exceptional going forward but also strong in midfield and defense. She was the first woman to score at London's Wembley Stadium in a competitive international. In 146 international games, she made it onto the score sheet seventy-one times. She was so good that the Swedes put her on a postage stamp.

Coaching felt like a natural progression to Pia. She began as a player coach at Hammerby in Sweden, moving to the Philadelphia Charge and then the Boston Breakers, with whom she won the WUSA. When she returned to Sweden to coach after the league folded, Kristine Lilly followed because the lure of Pia's coaching was so great.

When she took over the USWNT in 2007, she was

the seventh coach and only the third woman to take charge. When she left five years later, everyone knew she would be hard to replace. After her last game in charge of the USA, a 6–2 victory over Australia, she did a lap of honor in front of a sellout crowd of twenty thousand emotional supporters, during which—of course—she sang.

Pia returned to Sweden once more, taking up the post of national team coach. But this time when she introduced herself by way of singing and playing guitar to the players, the reaction was muted. As veteran midfielder Caroline Seger said, "I think in America, when she sang, they would cheer for her. But we are more laid-back. So it must be completely different for her to sing to us, because we just sort of sit there."

At the Rio Olympics, Pia returned to haunt her old charges, leading Sweden to beat the USA in the quarterfinals. In an ironic twist, the victory caused the very issue she had helped diffuse as USWNT coach to flare up again within the American ranks. After the game, Solo expressed her frustration to a reporter, calling the Swedish team "a bunch of cowards" for their defensive play. This time US Soccer reacted by banning Solo from playing for six months, proving they weren't willing to forget or forgive the second time.

The following year, Pia retired from her post as Sweden national team coach; her last game in charge was her side's Euro 2017 quarterfinal defeat to the Netherlands. She seemed ready for a quieter life on home soil, but she couldn't stay away from soccer for long. She soon announced that she would be coaching Sweden's Under 17s, helping inspire and develop the skills of another generation of talented youngsters.

For a woman whose musical repertoire includes "Leaving on a Jet Plane" and who loves living in hotel rooms, it seems the pull of home has finally kept her grounded.

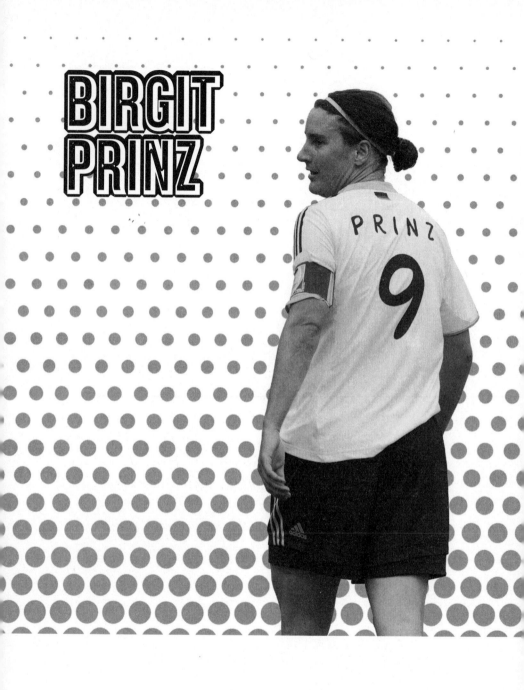

BIRGIT PRINZ

BIRGIT PRINZ
FORWARD

Dusk settled over the Volksbank Stadium in Frankfurt on a brisk March evening in 2012.

Stefan Prinz sat in the stands, looking down on the familiar sight of his tall, muscular daughter, her dark hair tied back, darting around the field below with the ball at her feet. He watched her play as he always had, the exceptionally talented soccer star he had coached from girlhood, who made her league debut at the age of fifteen and was called up to the German national team at sixteen, who had won Olympic medals and World Cups and the reverence of soccer fans the world over. Only this time, he fought back tears.

The exhibition game was Birgit Prinz's last, and it was a fitting tribute to the trailblazing striker, who played for both teams over the course of ninety minutes: her beloved league side FC Frankfurt, where she had spent the majority of her career, and the German national team, for whom she had scored over 128 times. Notable figures from the world of women's soccer were there to watch and cheer her on. Her name rang out in loud chants across the stadium.

As the final whistle sounded, she clapped and waved, thanking everyone for being there, humbled by the sight and sound of so much support.

The stadium announcer seemed to speak for everyone when he leaned into the loudspeaker and said, "The sun may go down, but Birgit Prinz will remain forever."

There was a time when Birgit thought the 2011 World Cup would be her swan song, the perfect way to finish out her glittering playing career. A legend of the game and the leading goalscorer in World Cup history with fourteen goals, she would be playing her final World Cup for Germany in Germany, where it all began for her.

But before the tournament began, there were signs of a cultural shift within the German squad. Birgit, the veteran, who once described herself as "not some happy hippo who speaks at the push of a button," is a no-nonsense, no-frills character.

Meanwhile, the young players on the team were not so publicity shy. Several members of the Under 20 team posed together in a seminude spread for *Playboy* in the run-up to the World Cup. The tournament itself was taglined, "The beautiful side of 2011." Toy manufacturer Mattel brought out a range of Barbie dolls representing the German team. Pretournament publicity shots showed the team and their coach, Silvia Neid, superimposed in front of the Brandenburg Gate, wearing only beige trench coats, belted at the waist. When the German camp released their team brochure to the press, the young players took up the majority of column inches while the older players were given short shrift. In the midst of such perky marketing, Birgit must have felt a little out of place. She had been playing in tournaments long before fanfare or fashionable attire or branded Barbie dolls.

Still, Birgit was feeling positive as the opening game drew closer, telling FIFA.com that her "enthusiasm was growing constantly." But reading between the lines, there was a trace of apprehension in some of her other responses. When asked whether team spirit was the key to success, she said, "I think you can have differences of opinion, but it's very important to trust one another and know that you can rely on your teammates. Only then can you be successful."

When the World Cup began and the time came for Birgit to show her prowess on the field, she faltered. The German press criticized her performances in Germany's two opening games, against Canada and Nigeria, as lackluster. She was substituted early in the second half in both games and stalked toward the bench with a thunderous look on her face.

"This isn't just about having fun," she told a reporter from *Der Spiegel* after the Nigeria game. "This is about success."

The headlines were cutting. "Prinz Steams," said the *Süddeutsche Zeitung*, suggesting that the forward was "furious" about being taken out of the game. Local newspaper *Augsburger Allgemeine* asked, "What will become of Birgit Prinz?" and the *Frankfurter* put Prinz on its front cover under the headline, "*Vom symbol zum problem*" or "From symbol to problem."

She didn't play in Germany's next game, against France, and instead watched from the dugout as her side put four past their opponents. As the French routed, the TV cameras cut to Birgit. The commentator described her as "looking longingly at the field."

"What is she thinking?" he continued. "Will she get a chance to play again over the course of the tournament, this player who has done so much for women's football in Germany?"

The answer was no. Birgit didn't play again, and Germany lost in the quarterfinals to Japan, who went on to win the tournament. If Birgit was angry, so was her father. Stefan criticized Coach Neid on German radio, saying, "From the beginning, she tried—even in preparation—to play young and old against each other. It made the players very insecure."

Neid didn't respond to the criticism. She, too, was a leading figure in German football, having been part of the first German national side in 1982. For Prinz, whose sublime talent and physical fortitude had led the Germans to victories in two prior World Cups, it was an inauspicious way to leave the international game.

When asked what she had learned from the experience, Birgit said, "That not everything is like a Hollywood script, although I knew that before. . . . In hindsight, I think that this can definitely help me for my future career path [as a coach]. But did I really need it that way? I cannot say."

At her tribute game, that night in Frankfurt, things had returned to a more celebratory tone. German Football Association (DFB) president Wolfgang Niersbach called her "one of the greatest ambassadors the DFB has ever had."

"What Birgit Prinz has done for women's football is unparalleled," he said. "She has put her stamp on the sport far beyond the borders of Germany. She's a mark of quality throughout the world. She has set new benchmarks with her success which are going to be very difficult to emulate."

FIGHTING FOR EQUALITY
2010s

In the 2010s, it became far clearer just how integral women's soccer is to the women's movement, social justice, and positive change.

The tone of triumph over adversity was set at the World Cup in 2011, when Japan won for the first time in the wake of the devastating tsunami that year. The team instantly became heroes both at home and around the world, as a global audience appeared to be waking up to the emotive narratives at play in the women's game.

London 2012 was host to "the greatest women's soccer game ever played" in the fierce, physical, high-scoring Olympic semifinal between Canada and the USA, who went on to win gold. Canada took bronze and proved themselves worthy hosts when the World Cup kicked off three years later. Expectations, as always, were high for the USA in 2015, even though they hadn't won the tournament for fifteen years. Jill Ellis came under fire for the way the team was playing at the beginning of the tournament, but she led them to a resounding win in the final against Japan, thanks in large part to an unforgettable Carli Lloyd hat trick. Meanwhile, England enjoyed a successful tournament and finished in third place for the first time.

The following year, Germany won gold in Rio's Olympic final, seeing off an excellent Sweden side by 2–1 in the final. USA, however, went out in the quarterfinals, the only time they hadn't progressed to the semis in a major tournament.

Farwell WPS, Hello NWSL

As the decade began, the pro soccer league in the United States was faltering once more. Women's Professional Soccer (WPS) league teams were struggling financially, attendances were dropping, and there was a major legal battle underway between the league and the controversial owner of the Boca Raton–based team magicJack, Dan Borislow. Several players had filed grievances against Borislow with the players' union, alleging bullying and intimidation. In response, the WPS moved to have Borislow's contract terminated. Borislow counterpunched and forced the matter into a lengthy, drawn-out arbitration process. There was widespread feeling that the magicJack debacle tarnished the league's reputation and business relationships. In 2012, again after just three seasons of existence, the WPS folded.

Former USWNT player Cat Whitehill said, "This was a difficult task to start with, considering it involved building a women's sports league during such difficult economic times. I am sure there will be plenty of blame scattered around in the coming months for why we were unsuccessful. . . . I suppose the saddest part is that the selfishness and ugliness of this [magicJack] lawsuit has been the final nail to end the dreams of many young women hoping for a chance to play the sport they love in the U.S."

Headlines predicted doom for the women's game, suggesting that the league's demise signaled the impossibility of establishing a world-class professional soccer league. But women's soccer players had been here before. As Julie Foudy often remarked, quitting wasn't in their DNA. In 2012, another league was formed—a third attempt—named the National Women's Soccer League. Things began tentatively but grew steadily. In 2016, the NWSL became the first women's pro soccer league in the United States to make it through their elusive fourth season. The league's commissioner, Jeff Plush, spoke for all women's soccer players and fans on the eve of that campaign, when he said, "We are around, we're not going anywhere."

A year later, the league launched a successful partnership with the Lifetime TV network, and in 2018, things were still going strong. Players like Crystal Dunn, Alex Morgan, and Carli Lloyd, who had been playing club soccer abroad, returned to the league. Yet adequate media coverage is an essential part of maintaining the success of the NWSL, and there is still a long way to go before parity is achieved.

The Demand for Equal Pay

When prominent members of the USWNT began publicly campaigning for equal pay in 2016, they couldn't have known it would have a domino effect around the world. The national women's teams of Ireland and Denmark threatened to strike; Australia did strike, and Nigerian players marched on Parliament to demand their unpaid salaries and win bonuses. Norway, meanwhile, secured a historic equal pay deal with the men's team.

In 2018, when the USA men's team failed to qualify for the men's World Cup, it only served to bolster the women's argument. The USWNT has won three World Cups and four Olympic golds. They are consistently first in the world rankings, only ever having fallen as far as second place, while the men have won nothing and in 2018 were ranked at twenty-eight. Yet the men are still paid more than the women.

Such bald statistics shine a light on the pay gap and the warped logic of gender discrimination. If this elite sports team, the world's greatest, still aren't paid equally to their far-less-successful male counterparts—for playing the exact same sport—it is indicative of the depths of institutionalized sexism. Thanks to their public campaign, the USWNT is part of a global movement to end pay disparity.

As Abby Wambach put it in her 2018 Barnard commencement speech, "We talk a lot about the pay gap. . . . What we need to talk about more is the aggregate and compounding effects of the pay gap on women's lives. Over time, the pay gap means women are able to invest less and save less so they have to work longer. When we talk about what the pay gap costs us, let's be clear. It costs us our very lives."

A Matter of Life or Death

The most famous soccer quote of all time was uttered with dry sarcasm by the legendary coach of the Liverpool men's team, Bill Shankly: "Some people believe football is a matter of life and death. I can assure you it is much, much more important than that."

Yet for many women, this is a reality. In the 2010s, stories emerged from around the world highlighting the risks women take to do something as simple as play the game they love. Few are more tragic—or elucidating—than the fate of Fatim Jawara.

In October 2016, Fatim stepped onto a ship in the port of Garabulli, Libya. The vessel was sky blue and sea worn, and Fatim was 1 of 126 people packed aboard in the muggy, north African heat. All of them were seeking a way out, of poverty or oppression, and hoping the journey to Europe would be swift and safe.

Fatim grew up in the Gambia, a country ruled by an oppressive regime and mired in extreme poverty. As a child, she fell in love with soccer and took every opportunity to play whenever she could. Her upper-body strength and agility made her stand out as a goalkeeper, and she settled into the position as she embarked on her playing career. Soccer was her passion and her path to a brighter future, one that was only just beginning to unfold.

A year before she stood on the docks in Garabulli, Fatim made her debut for the Gambian national team, the Scorpions, in a friendly against a team from Scotland. She was eighteen years old and a promising prospect from the moment she stepped onto the field. Her shot stopping was impressive, culminating in a saved penalty. There was talk of progression, of potential contracts with big European teams—if only she could get there. She paid an agent to facilitate her passage, albeit through the treacherous route known as "the back way." It is a route many thousands of migrants attempt each year, crossing miles of unforgiving desert and unpredictable seas in search of a better life.

By the time Fatim boarded the boat in Libya, she had already survived a perilous trek across the Sahara. Her family were in contact with her throughout; they begged her to return home, but she refused, telling them she was "following her destiny."

Fatim never made it to Europe. She and almost every other passenger perished when the boat capsized in high seas. Her death underscored both the tragic, desperate struggle of refugees and migrants, and the dearth of opportunities for young women in certain regions.

In Afghanistan, the women who play for the national team must contend with constant threats of violence, even death, from Taliban operatives. In Turkey, Egypt, Saudi Arabia, India, and elsewhere, women are often forbidden from playing by family members or religious clerics. Iranian women have been banned from watching soccer in stadiums for the past four decades. For many women around the world, the prospect of simply playing or watching soccer remains an impossible dream.

Those who find a way regardless are risking everything. Their defiance in the face of oppression, violence, and adversity is stunning. Many of the stories from this decade are an ode to those whose courage leads the way.

Activism and Social Media

From equal pay to equal rights, women's soccer stars have used their platform to enact change. Megan Rapinoe was the first white athlete to kneel with Colin Kaepernick back in 2016 and is one of several notable players to publicly come out as gay. Sweden's Nilla Fischer wore a rainbow-colored captain's armband for a Bundesliga fixture and had to contend with vicious online comments as a result.

While women have been targeted with vitriol and death threats online, the internet has also become a valuable tool for pursuing progressive change. Players have used social media to champion causes, campaign for charities, and raise their own profiles. The results have been largely positive although strange at times, as when the Venezuelan soccer player Deyna Castellanos—who has over a million Instagram followers—was nominated for FIFA's 2017 World Player of the Year award, despite never having played professionally.

In the latter part of the decade, the #MeToo movement brought sexual harassment to the fore, exposing instances where men have abused powerful positions to enact predatory behavior. In global sports, similar incidents have come to light everywhere from gymnastics to swimming.

Nancy Hogshead-Makar, a former swimmer who won Olympic gold in 1984 and who now leads the advocacy organization Champion Women, said, "I think the consequences of having an overwhelming male coaching staff and leadership is a lot of sexual abuse."

In soccer, American midfielder Kelly Conheeney, who plays for Hammarby in the Swedish league, published a blog in which she shared her harrowing story of suffering sexual abuse at the hands of a soccer coach.

The coach groomed Conheeney from a young and influential age, controlling her movements down to her choice of clothing and makeup. When he had gained her trust and the trust of her family, he began to molest her. Conheeney's story is powerful and essential reading. Awareness of such potential dangers is vital in bringing them to the fore. In Conheeney's case, some justice was meted out after she was able to confide in a family member. When the coach was arrested, two other victims came forward. The case went to trial, and he was convicted of endangering the welfare of a child.

This is what's important to remember, according to Conheeney: sex offenders don't lurk in the bushes waiting to attack. They are most often close to the family. They slowly work their way in until they have complete control and trust of all people involved to reach their prey.

A culture of silence protects such predators, and it's a by-product of a culture that automatically places men on a pedestal. When girls grow up believing that they must impress men in order to succeed in their chosen field, there is more than just inequality at stake. What's at risk is safety and selfhood.

The Long-Awaited Rise of the Female Coach

There are plenty of successful examples of men coaching women's soccer teams. Tony DiCicco led the USWNT to memorable Olympic and World Cup victories in the 1990s. John Herdman helped change the landscape of women's soccer in Canada, increasing its popularity inexorably. But many women feel the entire system favors male coaches. Indeed, there are no female coaches of men's soccer, for no discernable reason other than institutional sexism.

In England, former Manchester United defender Phil Neville was appointed coach of the women's national team in 2018. But several female candidates who were in contention for the job felt that his recruitment was unfair. Neville had no managerial experience at senior or international level, while many of the other candidates had both. Vera Pauw, one of the leading applicants, had been coach of the Netherlands, Scotland, South Africa, and Russia.

"Qualified women were interested in the England job," said Pauw. "Some of the most experienced women in our game did apply. They had done very well in lifting teams up the rankings but were not deemed good enough. Some with huge international experience did not even get interviews."

For years, Seattle Reign's Laura Harvey was the sole female head coach in the NWSL, but in 2018, Pauw and Denise Reddy bolstered the ranks, signing for Houston Dash and Sky Blue FC respectively. Yet there is still a long way to go, and women are still being shut out of major coaching roles. Says Pauw, "There are too many male coaches who can't get jobs in the men's game but are then given chances with women's teams."

Soon after he was appointed, Neville took the FA to task over the way the England women's team traveled. The Lionesses flew economy and took multiple flights to reach the United States and take part in the 2018 She Believes Cup. "We need to give ourselves the best opportunity to do well," he said when asked about the long-haul travel. "We were made to travel through three or four different cities just to get here and I had one training session with the team before the first game, after a nine-hour flight."

His comments made national headlines and gained attention. "If that was said by a woman coaching a women's team, no one would listen," says former Afghanistan national coach Kelly Lindsey. "They would just say, 'Ha-ha, yeah, that's how it is.' Every woman in soccer that read that comment said, 'Exactly. That's how we operate.' No one will pay attention, and no one will help us, and no one will put us at the same level as the men and pay for first class and get us to the game in three hours."

At the very least, Neville had drawn attention to the inequality. It seemed that he was surprised by it and that it wasn't what he was expecting.

"There can be some positives that come out of having somebody like that lead a women's team, because he can say what really needs to be said and people will listen," Lindsey adds. "If he does it for the right reason, there's positives. If he does it for three years so he can get a men's job, well, you know, that's a little different."

While there are still far too few female coaches in the game, the ones who break through—like Pauw, Lindsey, Sundhage, and Ellis—are winning recognition. That can only mean a shift is beginning to occur.

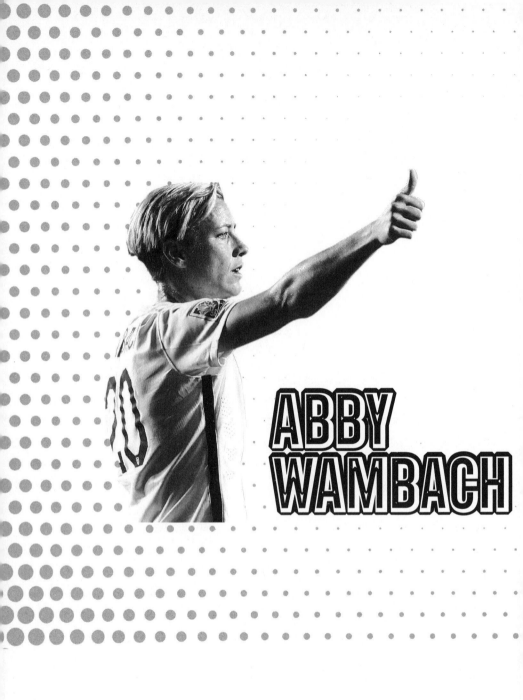

ABBY
WAMBACH

ABBY WAMBACH
FORWARD

Beneath the spotlight glare, the lectern stands empty on stage for a moment.

A hush descends on Radio City Music Hall as Abby Wambach approaches. Out there in the darkness, rows and rows of young women in caps and gowns are watching and waiting to hear her speak. This commencement ceremony marks the transition to adulthood for these young women, the Barnard College class of 2018, to be guided by the words of a soccer superstar, the leading international goalscorer of all time.

She wears a long gown, black and formal and buttoned up to the neck, where her shock of short blonde hair is buzzed, and it skims low at the laces of her glittery hi-tops. If ever there were an antidote to pomp and ceremony, it is Abby. Years ago, she stopped speaking to crowds with the methodical, bullet-pointed preparedness of a technically proficient athlete and began trusting herself. Of course, she's prepared, just as she would be for a big game, but she isn't about to tell these young women what she thinks they want to hear. Now when she speaks, it's a rallying call, from the truest version of herself.

Gone are the days when it felt like her sporting prowess defined her, gone are the near-militarized regimens of professional soccer, the terrifying prospect of life in its absence, the depression and the substance abuse, the DUI and the wake-up call, the years of blotting out difficult feelings and big transitions and physical pain. Somehow, just a few years after she retired from being one of the greatest soccer players in the world, something even better has evolved. Abby now lives in a "beautiful space between being this working mother/parent, business woman, speaker, activist, book-writer, speech-giver sort of person." She is authentic, passionate, powerful. All the assets she brought to her playing career parlayed into a new one, exemplifying the credo that there is, indeed, life after soccer.

She looks out from behind the lectern and grins.

"How's it going?"

Out there in the darkness, the young women cheer.

It didn't take long for Mary Abigail Wambach, named after the Virgin Mary, to break free from the ruffles and bows she was trussed up in for much of her childhood. Rebellion soon settled in her psyche, exhibiting itself in ways both positive and self-destructive. The youngest of seven children raised in Rochester, New York, Abby was reared on competition and fight. Her four older brothers would take her to the neighborhood cul-de-sac, wrap her in goalie pads, and blast shots at her until they were called home for dinner. She soon discovered that soccer was her "secret weapon," a way to command respect, and scored so many goals for her girls' team that they sent her to join the boys' league. At night, she went to sleep beneath a signed poster of Mia Hamm.

But when her parents insisted she attend soccer camp the summer she turned fourteen, Abby felt constrained by their demands. As soccer took over her high school career, she began acting out, reclaiming the territory of her body by consuming junk food, sometimes slurping a dozen sodas a day, chomping a whole stick of butter on a dare. Once, she rode a Jet Ski into a lightning storm. Abby's willingness to throw herself in harm's way was both her greatest strength and her most perilous trait.

From the beginning of her college career, Abby's physicality and scoring prowess were exceptional. Before she graduated, she had been drafted to the WUSA, to play for the Washington Freedom alongside her idol, Mia.

That first season she was named Rookie of the Year and earned a call to the USWNT camp.

A looming threat up front, she was the extra dimension the USA team needed as they moved into a different, more physical and technically complex era of gameplay. In 2003, April Heinrichs included her in the roster for the 2003 World Cup, one of the only major changes to the team of 1999.

Meanwhile, she was as forthright in her personal life as she was on the field; she pushed through the difficulty and awkwardness of coming out to her Catholic parents in her early twenties. In her memoir, *Forward*, she notes that there were two sides to her persona, Chill Abby and Intense Abby, and that she was locked in combat between the hard-battling soccer star and the hard-partying joker.

When the USA team lost the World Cup semifinal to Germany, Abby stood on the field and watched her opponents celebrate, refusing to return to the dressing room until she had taken it all in and fully registered the burn of defeat. A year later, in 2004, she set a new record for most goals scored by a player at an Olympic tournament. Along the way to winning gold in Athens, she scored four times, including one of the most important goals in USWNT history. The final game against Brazil was deadlocked in extra time when Abby rose and headed the ball into the net to ensure the team took home gold. That game marked a transition from the old guard of Hamm, Julie Foudy, and Joy Fawcett, who retired after the tournament, to a new era, with Abby leading the charge.

But as Abby would tell you, transitions are never easy, and the Greg Ryan era proved tricky for the team. The USWNT went into the 2007 World Cup as favorites but lost 4–0 in the semifinal to Brazil. The fallout from the defeat had huge repercussions, but the team emerged from the embers with a new coach and a new tournament to compete in. Abby had her sights set on Beijing 2008.

Then, catastrophe. A matter of days before the games began, she broke her leg in an exhibition game. It was a devastating blow, both to her and the USA's hopes of winning gold. She wrote a powerful e-mail to the team, telling them they had all the capabilities to win without her. But she struggled with the feeling of behind left behind, of missing out on her dreams. She watched the Olympic tournament on TV while in a "Vicodin haze." When her teammates won gold, she was watching from a diner in upstate New York. The team's equipment manager called her from the field so that she could hear the celebrations for herself, the cheers and screams, but it left her feeling raw. She was overjoyed for her team and depressed for herself, worried that if they could win without her, they might not need her after all.

Abby harnessed the doubts and the pain and powered through. She regained her fitness and, in only her second international game after returning from injury, scored her one hundredth international goal during a friendly with Canada in her hometown. She went into the 2011 World Cup in blistering form.

⚽

When you've scored more goals than any other professional soccer player on the planet, it's hard to pick a favorite. But on balance, Abby goes with this one.

July 10, 2011. USA v. Brazil. The World Cup quarterfinal.

Brazil's Daiane Rodrigues scores an own goal inside two minutes to give the USA a lead it carries into halftime. Then, in the sixty-eighth minute, Rachel Buehler gets a red card for a foul on Marta in the box. With the USA a player down, the referee awards Brazil a penalty. Hope Solo saves Cristiane Rozeira's spot kick, but the referee orders a retake and Marta makes no mistake. The game moves into extra time, and Marta puts Brazil in front just after the kickoff. The minutes tick by, and it looks as though the USA is going out. Brazil is stalling, trying to run down the clock and edge toward victory.

Abby feels the energy shift toward her, the way it always does when things get rough in games. The team looks to her to shoulder them, to lead them, to score big goals in crucial moments. As she runs up the field, she's doing a lot of internal self-talk. *This is your time. This is what you've been called upon to do. Everybody else has done her job; now it's on you to deliver.*

Then Megan Rapinoe plays a forty-five-yard cross with pinpoint precision. Abby leaps into the air, and in the millisecond before the ball hits her head, she thinks, *Don't fuck this up*. As soon as the ball comes off her head, she thinks that she's missed, that she's somehow hit the outside of the net. When she looks out at the crowd, she sees them going completely berserk. And she realizes, *Oh my God, that actually went in.*

Her mind goes blank. She celebrates in a way she won't remember, except from the vantage point of television replays. Then the whistle blows again, and Brazil is kicking off and she has to come back around fast.

Focus. See it through.

⚽

So crucial was Abby's extra-time equalizer that it was voted as one of the top eight moments in Women's World Cup history by *Time* magazine. It was described by ESPN as the "header heard 'round the world."

From there, the USA beat Brazil on penalties and made it all the way to the World Cup final, where they were edged out in another penalty shoot-out by Japan. The goal signaled a "mind-set shift in our country," says Abby.

"We had gone through a couple of years where we weren't playing as well as we could. It was the post–Mia Hamm generation, and we'd struggled to find the podium. Even though we ended up not winning that World Cup, it felt like a win because of that goal."

In 2012, Abby was at the top of her game, leading the USA to win gold at the 2012 Olympics. She scored in every game of the tournament except the final. Finally, after the heartbreak of sitting out the Beijing games, she had her second gold medal. She was named FIFA World Player of the Year.

Abby's rise to prominence was an important one. "We have had women who have been the faces of the game like, Mia Hamm and Julie Foudy and now Alex Morgan, and you know, for a while I was a face of the game, which was kind of an interesting dynamic, right? It wasn't what you would have expected. I had short hair and I was gay, and still I was able to play the game."

While at her peak as a player and star sportsperson, Chill Abby was doing some hard partying; one night she was caught on camera by gossip website TMZ out late one night, chugging beers. Later she would reflect that it was a product of knowing she didn't have many years left to play. The fear of retirement was creeping up on her.

But there were opportunities too. In 2015, she joined her teammates in fighting for equal pay, using her powerful voice to become an advocate. "When I started playing soccer, I had no vision for this becoming part of our social fabric of a resistance to the patriarchy," she says. "But our women's national team, we're like a cool, unique science experiment. Our women's national team has had so much more success than our men's national team and is making quite a bit of money. You compare the two and say, 'Wait, this doesn't make any sense.' We're selling a lot of tickets at the gate, so why aren't the women getting paid the same? We're not asking for more than the men; we are asking to be paid as equals."

Advocacy suited her. Abby's agent noted it, presciently telling her, "You have more to offer the world than just soccer."

In her swan song, she finally won that elusive World Cup in 2015, knowing it would be her last competition. That year, she met President Barack Obama when the team was invited to the White House. With her political interest piqued, she joined Hillary Clinton's presidential campaign and spent much of the year meeting with the country's business leaders and thinkers, honing a burgeoning talent for public speaking.

Yet retirement was hard. Her romantic life was in turmoil as her marriage to Sarah Huffman came to an end. And there was still the drink. It was only a matter of time before it caught up with her. In April 2016, she was arrested for a DUI.

It proved to be a turning point for Abby, the jolt she needed to begin the path to sobriety. She put out a statement on social media, taking full responsibility, apologizing for her mistake, and vowing to change. "Retirement is hard," she admitted later. "People don't talk about the hard transitions enough."

But Abby did. She was candid about her struggles. She discovered that "true activism is born in heartbreak." And she did what scared her most; she embraced life after soccer and found that her powers off the field were even greater than she had hoped.

"You create this persona, this soccer player person, and you make all your decisions as that person. And you find yourself thinking that you are then only a soccer player. I had to learn that soccer didn't make me who I was; I made the game what it was because of what I brought to it as a person."

This is Abby 3.0. Neither intense nor chill, she is more than that. Profound. Inspiring. True.

In the years since retirement, she met and married best-selling author Glennon Doyle, another powerful feminist, activist, philanthropist, speaker, and all-round go-getter. Together they are the power couple the world needs right now: politically active, influential, goofy. Abby is coparent/Abby to Doyle's kids, Chase, Tish, and Amma, and she is bringing everything she learned in her playing career to the family table.

"I've learned a lot from the relationships I've had with my teammates. Figuring out how to unify different mentalities, different personalities, to deal with drama inside of a locker room, to deal with people who don't necessarily think the way you think. There's so many things that you go up against when you are in a team environment, like dealing with hurt feelings, dealing with people who aren't playing as many minutes as they want to play, dealing with heartbreak, dealing with getting cut.

"I think all that's helping me be a better parent. It has helped me be patient when they're just wanting to be kids and be sad about their parents' divorce. It helps me not take things too personally."

Although Abby doesn't care for the term "stepparent," she describes it as the highest version of love she's ever experienced. "It's one of the hardest gigs out there because, oftentimes, you're putting in so much effort to make sure these kids have all they need, to make sure they know that you're there for them. And then, of course, in the end, when the going gets rough, they're still going to go to their mom and dad first."

There is no doubting Abby's place in the world, in the fight for equality, as a voice for the LGBTQ+ community and as a spokesperson for inclusivity, openness, and solidarity.

Here is what she tells the class of 2018 as she stands at the lectern:

"As you go out into the world, amplify each other's voices. Demand seats for women, people of color, and all marginalized people at every table where decisions are made. Call out each other's wins, and just like we do on the field, claim the success of one woman as a collective success for all women."

This generation can be grateful that the Abby who always led with her head now leads with her heart.

HOMARE
SAWA

HOMARE SAWA
MIDFIELDER

The first time she kicked a ball, Homare Sawa scored a goal.

She was six years old, standing on the sidelines, watching her older brother play soccer, when his coach beckoned her onto the pitch. Without hesitating, she walked straight over to the ball and toe punted it into the net.

Even that kind of early aplomb on the field couldn't foretell the kind of soccer career Homare would go on to have. Six years after that first kick, at the age of twelve, she made her debut in the Japanese women's league, and at fifteen, she played her first game for the national team—Nadeshiko Japan, as they're known. She went on to play in four Olympics and six World Cups and was awarded the FIFA World Player of the Year in 2011.

When she retired at the end of 2015, Homare was inundated with offers of employment: as a sports analyst, as a member of the organizing committee for Japan's 2023 World Cup bid, and even as a politician. But Homare wanted to slow things down, spend some time with her new husband, former soccer player Hiroaki Tsujikami, and think about coaching a generation of young Japanese girls.

At the press conference announcing her retirement, she looked businesslike in a dark-blue blazer and white shirt, yet relaxed and hopeful. She spoke into the microphone, thanking her audience for their support.

"I've never made a bigger decision in my life," she said. "But I've had the greatest career anyone could ask for."

Those present and those watching across Japan were grateful to her. Homare, a national hero, had helped uplift her homeland at a time when the country was devastated and all seemed lost.

⚽

At 2:46 p.m. on March 11, 2011, a magnitude 9.0 earthquake struck off the east coast of Japan, triggering a devastating tsunami. When the giant wave thundered ashore, it tore down buildings and washed away homes, cars, and thousands of people. It overwhelmed the Fukushima Daiichi nuclear power plant, causing radiation to spill from three reactors into the surrounding area, rendering the region immediately unsafe and unlivable for generations.

The tsunami affected all of the Japanese players personally and profoundly. Just four months later, still mourning the mass devastation and loss of life at home, the team was in Germany, poised to compete in a World Cup. Homare, who had left the national side four years earlier, returned to the squad just weeks before the tournament to reclaim the team captaincy. With their icon leading the charge again, the Japanese team were determined to deliver.

They beat New Zealand 2–1 in their opening game and then went on to put four past Mexico in their second. But they stumbled in their final game of the group stage, losing 2–0 to England and finishing second in their group.

In the locker room, Coach Norio Sasaki held up photographs of the devastation the tsunami had wrought back home to motivate his players, to remind them: *This is what our country is trying to overcome. This is who we're doing it for.*

The team heeded the message. In the quarterfinals, they narrowly squeaked past Germany, wining 1–0 after extra time. Sweden were next in the semis, and the Japanese women saw them off with a 3–1 victory, setting up a thrilling World Cup final against the USA in Frankfurt.

As Homare led her team onto the pitch, the trophy stood there on display, glinting under the lights. "When I got into the stadium, I looked at it and thought that I would like to have it," she said.

It wasn't going to be easy for Japan, facing a USA side on top of their game. Their opponents looked thoroughly dangerous throughout. Abby Wambach missed by inches, her attempt hitting the crossbar; Alex Morgan had a shot ping back off the goalpost; and Japan goalkeeper Ayumi Kaihori produced an incredible save to tip a looping header from Wambach over the bar.

Morgan finally capitalized on the relentless pressure and fired the USA ahead with just over twenty minutes left to play. But Japan fought back, and Aya Miyama rolled a scrappy equalizer past Hope Solo to level the scoring ten minutes from time.

It looked as though the USA had done it when Wambach scored with her head in extra time, but again, Japan would not be beaten. Minutes before the final whistle, Miyama swung in a corner, and there was Homare, in the right place at the right time, with a glorious flick to divert the ball home and take the final to penalties.

Kaihori saved two of the USA's three opening spot kicks, from Shannon Boxx and Tobin Heath, while Carli Lloyd blasted hers over the bar. Saki Kumagai stepped forward to take the final penalty and fired past Solo to claim victory. Her teammates rushed to celebrate with her, elated to be bringing home the first World Cup for Japan, for an Asian side, and for Homare, the team talisman.

Gold ticker tape rained down on the Nadeshiko team as they lifted the golden trophy aloft. Moments later, they unfurled a banner to show their appreciation for the tsunami relief efforts, which read, "To our friends around the world, thank you for your support." Back home in Japan, celebrations spilled into the streets with people hugging, crying, and cheering for their women's soccer team in a way they never had before.

"In a year with very little cheerful news, we were able to give our supporters in Japan this victory," Homare said. "Their support and power was the backbone in our win. I've been playing for thirty years and have been a player in the national team for almost 20 years. It was a trophy full of laughter and pain and just so many memories."

⚽

During her playing career, Homare remarked in interviews that her life would have been easier had she been born a boy. By the time she became a mother, in 2017, her success had helped ensure her daughter's generation would have more opportunities. In becoming a sporting icon, Homare challenged the patriarchal culture in Japan, showing what women can achieve under immense pressure, with little investment or attention, even in the aftermath of catastrophe.

A generation of young Japanese women will remain forever inspired by Homare, whose words they know by heart. This the phrase that resonates most, something she once said to her teammates before a big game: "If you're having a tough time, watch my back. I will be there, playing with everything I've got to lead you."

To Nadeshiko Japan fans, she always will be.

CHRISTINE SINCLAIR

CHRISTINE SINCLAIR
FORWARD

They call it the Theatre of Dreams.

Old Trafford, Manchester. A hallowed turf, one of the oldest and most historic soccer stadiums in the world. Christine Sinclair is in the dressing room, beginning her prematch routine. She pulls on her uniform, left side first. She reaches for her headphones and cues up her customary prematch song. The opening strains of Michael Jackson's "Man in the Mirror" chime through. She closes her eyes, rolls her neck, gets in the zone.

It's a brisk summer evening in 2012. Outside in the stands, more than twenty-six thousand fans have taken their seats. In a few moments, she'll line up with her teammates in the tunnel and march out onto the field. An Olympic medal is within touching distance for these old foes, Canada and their opponents tonight, USA.

Sinc is ready. She is focused.

She is about to play the game of her life.

⚽

There is a story that Sandi Sinclair likes to tell.

She had just given birth to a daughter and was preparing to bring her home from the hospital. Exhausted and overwhelmed, Sandi strapped baby Christine into her little car seat, put a blanket over her lap, and drove straight to soccer practice. After all, she needed to check on the team she was coaching.

It was a fitting first day out in the world for a future soccer icon.

"I don't really remember it," Sinc deadpans. "My family, especially on my mom's side, are soccer nuts. She's one of six kids, and all her siblings played soccer. Two of my uncles played professionally, one played for our [national] men's team, so it doesn't surprise me that that would happen. Priorities, you know?"

Sinc exudes warmth and humility. When asked about her numerous achievements, she deftly deflects the praise onto somebody else, a teammate or coach. She was recently awarded the Order of Canada, the highest honor her country can bestow on its citizens, but when asked about it, she says, "I think it goes to show that the progress that our team has made and the impact that our team has made over the course of the past few years. The country has fallen in love with us."

For a player who has transcended her sport, appeared on postage stamps, and been revered as an ambassador for the game, she credits the people around her. Her modesty, too, she says, was instilled in her by her family.

"The way my family is, there was no way of growing up with a big head. It's a very balanced family, like, 'So what? You scored a hat trick, who cares? Go do your homework.' They made sure I kept my head on straight and kept my perspective, which I think has helped me tremendously as my career's progressed. Not getting too high or too low. Because sports are fickle and they can change from one day to the next, but they shouldn't change how you view yourself."

This is part of what makes Sinc such a consistently brilliant player and a galvanizing team captain: her unwavering sense of self. She possesses a quiet fortitude, a self-belief that never strays into arrogance. The notion that she is too private, too reserved, has been leveled at her, but Sinc remains constant. When she lets somebody in, she is fiercely loyal and devoted. To hear her talk about Canada's former coach, John Herdman, is to hear her talk about a loved one. She is still reeling from his departure, even if his new role is coaching Canada's men.

"He's the best coach I've ever had, soccer-wise and also off the field," she says. "We've joked that we've been through the highest highs together and the lowest of lows."

Sinc and Herdman forged a rare connection, the kind that goes beyond the game. When her father passed away, Herdman spoke at his funeral. Together, they possessed a symbiotic sense, not only of what the team needed but also of what the country needed from its team.

Herdman's attitude, according to Sinc, is, "If you win and you don't enjoy it and it doesn't mean anything to you, have you really won?"

"He'd say, 'I'd rather coach a team where maybe we don't win the gold medal or the World Cup but twenty years from now I can call up any one of you and go to dinner.' That's the type of team he wanted to create, and he did. He had a massive impact on my life, and he still does."

But here is Sinc again deflecting credit, sending it to those she loves most. It's only in a rare moment, when asked what tips she can share with those seeking to emulate her success, that she is forthright about her own qualities.

"I pride myself on being one of the hardest workers, whether it's on my national team or my club team," she says. "I'm always asking to do more, always pushing the limit with our coaches. I'm always like, 'Can I do extra?' I think that's just born in me. I'm not gonna do anything just partially. If I'm doing it, I'm going all the way."

And what a way she has come. Under Sinc's stewardship, Canada has won Olympic bronze twice and finished fourth in the World Cup. They hosted the tournament in 2015, drawing vast crowds and helping grow the game exponentially across the country. At club level, Sinc won the WPS championship twice and the NWSL with her current team, the Portland Thorns. She is Canada's all-time leading scorer and is second only to Abby Wambach in all-time international goals scored. She has been shortlisted for FIFA Player of the Year seven times and is Canada's Soccer Player of the Year twelve times over. All this, yet Sinc's Twitter bio reads, "still striving for better."

"I think the day I stop pushing myself to be better is the day that I have to retire," she says. "Now that I've won two Olympic medals, winning's contagious, and I don't want to leave the national team without having won a major tournament. That's the goal now, and we have the team built for that. I can't say that we've had that before, especially earlier in my career. But we have it now."

At the same time, Sinc says she tries not to "put too much pressure" on herself. "Obviously, I care dearly about my professional team. I wouldn't be where I am if I didn't care about winning. But at the end of the day it's a game, and I care more about the impression you leave with people outside of what you do between the lines for ninety minutes. Leaving a legacy and inspiring the youngsters across Canada is a very important part of who I am and what I do."

That part of her job, at least, is done.

⚽

The first goal is a peach.

Canada plays the ball up the field park with ease and fluidity. It's reminiscent of the style trademarked by Sinc's favorite men's team, Liverpool: pass and move. Just over twenty minutes on the clock, and Marie-Eve Nault picks up the ball on the halfway line. She darts forward and plays it long to Melissa Tancredi, who knocks it square to Sinc. Unleashed, she cuts inside, wrong-footing Kelly O'Hara, and drives it low past Hope Solo. One–nil to Canada, a goal that signals their quality *and* their intent.

Megan Rapinoe equalizes early in the second half, but the Canada team responds quickly. Tancredi turns provider again, this time sending in a cross from the left flank. Sinc rises and heads into the net. Canada is back in the lead.

Rapinoe draws the USA level again, sending the Old Trafford crowd to their feet. They're unable to look away from this fierce contest, which is becoming more physical by the minute—tackles are flying in, and things are getting ugly. If any spectator doubted the ferocity and physicality of the women's game, this match is proving them wrong. But here Sinc is again, heading a Sophie Schmidt corner back across goal, past Solo's outstretched arm: 3–2. Bursting with adrenaline, Sinc runs over to the crowd, her brow furrowed.

"Let's go!" she screams, throwing her arms up to enlist their support. This is Canada's night; it has to be.

Except that it isn't.

Referee Christine Pederson is the foil; she penalizes goalkeeper Erin McLeod for time wasting in the dying moments of the game and awards the USA an indirect free kick—an unusually strict and controversial implementation of the rules. Tobin Heath takes the kick and finds Carli Lloyd, whose shot ricochets off Tancredi's arm. Pederson awards the USA a penalty for handball, and the Canadian players are absolutely incandescent. Two huge, divisive refereeing decisions in two minutes that will surely cost them the win. And it does. Abby Wambach makes no mistake from the spot: 3–3.

With the scoring tied at the final whistle, the game edges into thirty minutes of extra time, hard fought and tense. As those minutes tick by, it's looking likely that the winner will be decided by penalty shoot-out. Then, Alex Morgan does what Alex Morgan does best: scores with a moment of brilliance when the USA needs it most, right at the death. Canada crashes out of the tournament. The USA is through to the gold medal match.

Sinc is devastated and angry. After the final whistle, she accuses Pederson of bias, stating that "the ref decided the result before the game started." For this comment, Sinc receives a four-game suspension from FIFA.

Even the most passionate USA fan can understand her ire. Sinc deserved to be on the winning side for her performance. And yet, despite the heartbreak and the debatable officiating, she looks back on it as her greatest game. Not only for the hat trick, of course, because she is always thinking of the bigger picture—for the tenacity, the drama, the competitiveness.

"That's the game that everyone remembers," she says. "And they're like, 'That's when we fell in love with your team. In that instant, we became women's soccer fans.'"

Spoken like a true ambassador.

HOPE SOLO

GOALKEEPER

Maybe there's no point reading this, because you already know what you think about Hope Solo.

She's fiery, difficult, dangerous. A troublemaker. Sharp-tongued. Tightly wound. A lit fuse. She's a hero. She's a legend. She's meticulous, fearless, outspoken. She's not afraid to challenge the status quo. No player in the history of women's soccer has been more controversial—or more disparaged—than Hope.

Here's one thing everyone can agree on: she's one of the greatest goalkeepers of all time.

⚽

It is, in many ways, the hardest position on the field.

Goalkeepers live by their ability to keep others from achieving their goals, and they die by their mistakes. It requires a state of constant alertness, even during long periods of inaction. You are always watching your defense, relying on them, but you are also alone out there. For at least forty-five minutes, you are in enemy territory, standing with your back to the opposing fans. These are the kinds of things Hope heard:

"Hey, Hope, where's your dad?"

"Go beat up your nephew!"

"You should never have kids."

In an overly polarized world, it is difficult to accept more than one truth about a person. Here is a woman who has had her share of outbursts and yet is capable of remarkable restraint and focus. But complex feelings have been one of the few constant fixtures in Hope's life.

She was conceived in prison, during a conjugal visit her mother made to her father while he was serving time for embezzlement. In her autobiography, *Solo: A Memoir of Hope*, she describes him as "a con man, a ladies' man, unreliable at best and a criminal at worst." Yet he also "showered [her] with love."

Hope was born and raised in Richland, Washington, a town known for its nuclear reactors and active role in creating the atom bomb the United States dropped on Nagasaki during World War II. One of her high school's favorite cheers during sporting events was "Nuke 'em till they glow!"

Hope didn't set out to play in goal. She was originally a forward with a love and a knack for scoring goals, but when she covered for an injured teammate at fifteen, she showed even greater abilities as a shot stopper. It was the least glamorous of roles on the team, and she was often embarrassed to admit she played there. Even her grandparents wondered what on earth she was doing back there, "twiddling her thumbs."

Her childhood was tumultuous in the extreme, her home a place of latent anger and diminished boundaries. When she was seven, Hope's father picked her and her older brother up, ostensibly to take them to a baseball game, and drove them all the way to Seattle in what turned out to be a parental kidnapping. After the police returned them to their mother, she didn't see her father again until she was in middle school. By that time, he was homeless, a fact she discovered when she came across him one afternoon, shuffling across a parking lot on his way to a blue tarp shelter he had constructed in a local park.

⚽

Hope sought solace from her chaotic home life and found it in soccer. Following an impressive playing career in high school, she was courted by colleges across the country. She opted to stay in state and join Coaches Amy Griffin and Lesle Gallimore at the University of Washington. It was there that her affinity for the position came to the fore. She dedicated herself to learning at every opportunity, studying the opposition, taking detailed notes, asking questions of her coaches, and training as hard as she could.

Her efforts were repaid by a call to the USWNT team camp in late 1999. She found it hard to break into the "inner circle" of players, who had already been through so much together and set a high bar for future players both on and off the field. It seems she felt more comfortable being an outsider than trying to contort herself into a mold she would never fit. "Truthfully, I didn't do much to win over the veteran group," she said. "The longer I was on the national team, the more I realized that my personality was different from many of my teammates."

Hope was away with the national team when she found out that her father had died. They rallied around her, offering her love and support, and fellow goalkeeper Briana Scurry told her to be strong. "You can do this," she told Hope.

Her first major controversy came when she was still reeling from his death and had barely cemented her place in the USA's starting lineup. She performed well in the 2007 World Cup, posting three shutouts, but she was benched for the semifinal game against Brazil by Coach Greg Ryan. The decision cut deeper when she discovered that a few of her teammates had instigated the switch. USA lost 4–0, and Hope let her feelings out in a postgame interview. "I would have made those saves," she told a reporter.

It was intended as a criticism of Ryan and an expression of anger at being left out, but it sounded to the team like a shot at Scurry, who had played. Hope was frozen out by her fellow players, barred from practice, and flew home from China alone.

First, she needed to earn redemption on the field. When she returned to China the following year for the 2008 Olympics, she started every game, only conceding five times on the way to the final, where the USWNT won gold and Hope kept a clean sheet. She came up big again in the 2011 World Cup. In the quarterfinal against Brazil, she made an excellent penalty save after Marta was judged to have been fouled in the box, but the kick was retaken after the referee deemed there had been an encroachment. Hope was yellow-carded for dissent, and Brazil scored the retake. There were more penalties to come when the game ended in a tie and a shoot-out was needed to decide the winner. Hope saved Daiane's kick—Brazil's third penalty—and it proved to be the slender margin of victory that pushed USA through to the semifinal.

Although they progressed to the final, with Hope earning her one hundredth cap in the semi against France, USA lost to Japan in another penalty shoot-out. She was desperately disappointed but said, "The outcome felt like fate," given that Japan were playing in the wake of the 2011 tsunami.

"Despite our loss, I knew what had happened was good for women's soccer. We had built up the game." Hope came away from the tournament with the Golden Glove, the award for best keeper at the World Cup.

That year she became more well known outside of soccer, appearing on the thirteenth season of *Dancing with the Stars*. Greater exposure comes with greater scrutiny, and soon her personal life was making headlines. In 2012, she married NFL tight end Jerramy Stevens, and their relationship became immediate tabloid fodder, portrayed as dramatic and volatile.

While intrigue and notoriety swirled around her, Hope produced the goods on the field. She was excellent throughout the 2012 Olympics, producing one of her best saves in the eighty-second minute of the gold medal game against Japan. Mana Iwabuchi took advantage of a Christie Rampone error and blasted the ball at Hope's goal from twelve yards away. Hope dived and punched the ball clear, ensuring she went on to claim a second gold medal.

In 2014, she was arrested on domestic violence charges following an altercation between her and her sister and nephew. Though the charges would be dropped years later, they clung to Hope's persona, carrying the weight of brutality. Given the allegations, there were doubts as to whether she would compete in the 2015 World Cup, but there Hope was. She made several crucial saves in the USA's opening game of the tournament against Australia and then recorded five consecutive shutouts. Coach Jill Ellis praised her focus both on and off the field.

With the World Cup win under her belt, Hope joined her teammates in fighting for equal pay. It looked as though she might be coming through the dark times, showing her maturity and strength. Then, the following year, the pendulum swung back again. When Sweden defeated the USWNT in the quarterfinals of the Rio Olympics, Hope spoke out angrily to a reporter again. She called the Swedish team, led by her former USA coach Pia Sundhage, a "bunch of cowards." US Soccer had had enough. The federation responded by suspending her from the game for six months and terminating her contract. They were quick to suggest it was more than just the comment, giving the impression that Hope had been a difficult presence and negative influence on the team.

United States Soccer Federation (USSF) president Sunil Gulati stated, "Taking into consideration the past incidents involving Hope, as well as the private conversations we've had requiring her to conduct herself in a manner befitting a U.S. national team member, U.S. Soccer determined this is the appropriate disciplinary action."

Solo responded, "I could not be the player I am without being the person I am, even when I haven't made the best choices or said the right things."

Rich Nichols, the general counsel for the women's national team's players' association, noted that she was "fired for making comments that a man never would have been fired for."

Indeed, it seems that the women's game holds its players to a higher standard than the men's, where competitiveness and unsporting conduct are largely considered par for the course. And in terms of off-the-field behavior, several men have returned to high-level playing careers even after serving jail time for serious crimes like rape and manslaughter.

You could argue that a higher standard has been set within the women's game and it is a separate entity from the men. Or you could argue that it isn't hard to bring the women's game into disrepute because women are expected to behave with the utmost decorum, to fit the mold of hardworking professional, brand ambassador, and glossy-haired beauty while withholding any complicated feelings from public view. According to a psychological study published in 2015, angry women are seen as untrustworthy and regarded as

more emotional than men. Women are often referred to as "role models"—a term Hope has publicly derided because it carries the weight of perfection along with the notion that young girls are more impressionable than boys and can be led astray by wayward icons.

When Gulati stepped down as USSF president in 2018, Hope was one of eight candidates running in his place. She brought a number of issues to the fore while she campaigned, including the importance of making soccer in the United States accessible for all, not just "rich, white kids." She is often referred to as outspoken, like most women with strong opinions.

"I'm the only candidate who has a track record where you can see I continue to push against the status quo, where I continue to fight for equality, where I continue to hold the federation accountable," she said, adding that she had been told while playing to "basically shut your mouth and play soccer." She did not win the election, but she got her point across.

Later that year, when the domestic violence charges from 2014 were dropped, Hope felt aggrieved by the lack of coverage. She wrote on Facebook, "For the last four years, members of the media have published thousands of headlines about me, helping spread false allegations that have been extremely damaging to me, my family and my career. Last week the case was dismissed, yet many of those same reporters have been silent. Why?"

Perhaps it didn't fit the narrative; it's easier to write up bad news. Perhaps, with Hope no longer playing, the saga was no longer newsworthy. Or perhaps it's simply that tumult can be tiresome.

Whatever your feelings about her, know this: Hope was always going to be a person defined by dichotomy. Her voice has been invaluable in many ways; she has drawn attention to some essential issues within the game and challenged the established order. She sparked a debate about female athletes and sporting behavior. In 2018, she contributed a powerful op-ed to the *Guardian*, pointing out the overwhelming whiteness of the USWNT and raising the issues of diversity and investment. In her words, "silence never changed the world."

In some ways, Hope's relationship with US Soccer echoes the mark left by her father.

"It's a complicated thing," she wrote in her memoir, knowing that he had caused her pain, "yet I still hold love for him in my heart."

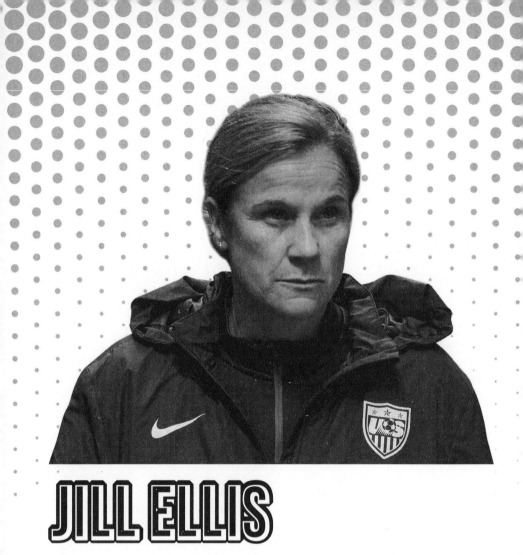

JILL ELLIS

JILL ELLIS
COACH

In the early 1990s, Graham Taylor, manager of the England men's soccer team, described his role as an "impossible job." Such was the level of pressure, scrutiny, and coverage in the UK tabloid press—not exactly known for their sensitivity or patience—Taylor felt that failure was inevitable.

The same must go for the job of USWNT coach, a role imbued with such high levels of expectation that only continuing to win everything in perpetuity will suffice. Jill Ellis, who took over from Pia Sundhage in the spring of 2014, has led the team to resounding success at the 2015 World Cup and stumbling defeat at the 2016 Olympics. The former, the team's first World Cup trophy in sixteen years, led to glowing accolades, while the latter, the first time the US team hadn't made it to the gold medal match or advanced to the semifinals of a major tournament, brought Jill's methods into sharp focus.

Although the USA lost in a penalty shoot-out to Sweden in the 2016 Olympics, the consensus was that the real defeat had come in open play, in Jill's lack of a clear game plan and an overreliance on long balls. But that failed to account for other factors: Sweden parked the bus, meaning they put every player behind the ball to defend. USA had twenty-six shots to Sweden's three and had close to 70 percent of the possession. Still, the pundits laid blame: Jill's team had been too frantic in attack, not "measured" enough. Additionally, she had taken a risk in bringing on Megan Rapinoe, who wasn't yet match fit after a long layoff, only to sub her out in extra time.

When Hope Solo called the Sweden team "cowards" after the game for their defensive tactics, Jill oversaw the punishment that was meted out: a six-month suspension followed by the termination of Solo's contract. Her official statement declared, "It's not simply a decision made about comments, it was based on the sum total of actions that have unfortunately shone a negative light on our program."

But the negative light continued to shine, even after Hope's departure. In 2017, a year many decried as dire for the USWNT, Jill came under yet more scrutiny. She was doing what any savvy coach would do following a big tournament defeat: tinkering, trying things out, experimenting with a three-four-three formation that fell flat and led to defeat in the She Believes Cup.

Most top-level coaches suffer under high expectations and intense scrutiny, and if results aren't immediate, the crowds will turn on you. But the USWNT coach is expected to maintain the team's overwhelming dominance at all times. In defeat, Jill faced a surge of disproportionate criticism, petitions calling for her to be fired, disgruntlement among supporters, and rumors of a mutiny from veteran players. It was reported that some senior members of the team allegedly approached former USSF president Sunil Gulati at the 2017 Tournament of Nations in Seattle to tell him that if the doubts they had weren't addressed, they wanted a new coach. Some of those issues reputedly stemmed from Jill's communication style, or lack thereof. At her best, the UK-born coach is known for being a calm, steadying presence; at worst, she is perceived as stern and aloof. In the past, she has admitted she is "quite content to sit in the corner and chat with people who walk by." But she added, "Coaching forced me to come out of my shell."

It was a harsh response to a coach who, only a couple of years previously, had led the USWNT to victory in the World Cup. But Jill came into the job with an awareness of what lay ahead. "I understand the expectations," she said at her first news conference as USA coach. She knew that there would be no pleasing some people, heeding her father's advice that 50 percent would be with her and 50 percent against. "That's life," she said. "You have to deal with a lot of different things that are not going to be perfect."

In a world with so few female coaches, one wonders whether Jill would be subject to the same level of scrutiny if she were male. She certainly wasn't subject to the same level of remuneration.

After the 2015 World Cup win, it came to light that Jill still earned less than many USSF officials, including the chief medical officer, staff attorney, and the director of events. Indeed, sexism has reared its head on many occasions during her tenure, and she has consistently stood up to it. During the 2015 victory tour, Jill refused to let her team play on a substandard field in Hawaii, a surface that would never have been deemed appropriate for the men's team. She has been vocal in encouraging FIFA to treat the women's game as a game in its own right. At the 2018 men's World Cup, she said she expected the tournament's new video assistant referee to be in place for the women's World Cup in 2019: "I think it would be a little bit insulting if we weren't afforded the same opportunity."

USSF has stood behind Jill, and the results have paid off: the USWNT were unbeaten in 2018, even though the competition in women's soccer is fiercer than ever. In November, Jill presided over the team's historic five hundredth win, taking the side into 2019 in formidable form.

She has observed, learned, tinkered, and rebuilt to startling effect, structuring her system around key players and giving young talent plenty of game time. As she continues to shore up her roster, she keeps her focus on the field. When asked if she ever checked Twitter or read match reports, she said, "Hell, no. The game is the best indicator for me."

CARLI LLOYD

CARLI LLOYD

MIDFIELDER

It should be a crisp, bright morning in July, but the sky over Vancouver is yellow grey. Wildfires are raging on the outskirts of the city, and the air is thick with the acrid tang of smoke. Carli Lloyd hasn't slept well. All night she's been waking up from vivid dreams, wondering if it's morning yet.

From her window on the twenty-fourth floor of this sleek, skyscraping hotel, she should be able to see for miles over the whole city, to the mountains and the bay. Not today. Today there is only haze.

All her bags are already packed, everything neat and in order. Nothing left to do but go for her morning jog, burn off some of the pent-up energy she's feeling. She pulls on her sneakers and her headphones, heads out of the lobby, and takes off running through the smoggy city. As she jogs, she passes fans out walking to breakfast in their USA shirts, draped in flags. They cheer her on and yell, "Good luck!" as she skips past them.

She's so ready. She wants the game to start right now. But there are still hours to go before she will take to the field for the 2015 World Cup final. It won't be her first; that was four years ago, and she can still taste the defeat. A hard-fought game against Japan, extra time, penalty kicks, the crucial moment when she took hers and blasted it over the bar. She wants nothing more than to show how strong she is now—to beat Japan this time around and bring the trophy home.

It's a Tuesday morning in July, three years after the World Cup final of 2015, and the USWNT is on the East Coast of the United States for the Tournament of Nations. The squad has a day off from training, and Carli is sitting in her hotel room, diligently conducting her phone interviews. She is desperate to play in a few days' time, but it looks as though she may not figure in Jill Ellis's plans. At thirty-five, some may feel that Carli's peak playing years are behind her, but she doesn't see it that way.

"Right now, I'm probably playing the smartest football that I've played with my decision making on the field, my runs," she says. "I feel I'm fitter than I've ever been; I feel I'm more explosive than I've ever been. But then I have other people who continuously don't wanna believe in me, who continuously doubt my age, who continuously doubt if I can even contribute to this team."

She pauses. "It usually isn't a good idea to bet against me."

That has been evident throughout her career. As a player, Carli is the epitome of hard work, a one-woman master class in dedication. When, at fourteen, she didn't make the final soccer team for the regional Olympic Development Program, she went back to the training field and focused on her game. When Coach Chris Petrucelli cut her from the Under 21s, she played against the team in a friendly and proved herself on the field. When she thought about ending up on the fringes of the national team, never quite breaking in, she sought help with her training regimen. And when the trainer she linked up with, James Galanis, told her she wasn't anywhere near fit enough, Carli got to work.

Galanis became Carli's coach, free of charge. It was a gesture of faith that gave her the impetus to show up in the rain, heat, or snow and put in the hours, the runs, and the reps.

"James saw the talent that I had and knew that there was definitely something special in me," she says. "He took me on and told me that he would turn me into the best player in the world if I listened and dedicated my whole life to soccer."

The duo worked as much on her mentality as they did on her physical fitness and skills. Self-doubt and self-criticism were Carli's demons; she was in the habit of losing faith in herself, worrying that her slightest mistakes would manifest as huge failures. Six months into working with Galanis, she had begun challenging those thought processes and improving her fitness levels. And then she was selected to join the national team for camp.

It was an incredible feeling to be picked, especially having been told once by Petrucelli that she was unlikely to become a national team player. But when Carli joined the group of veteran players, household names she had grown up admiring, she found the atmosphere intimidating, describing it in her book *When Nobody Was Watching* as a "girls club" where new members were "not exactly welcome."

Carli hunkered down and focused on her own game, becoming a regular fixture on the USA roster. But it was not an easy time. New coach Greg Ryan wanted Carli to focus on her defensive play, which felt unnatural to an attacking midfielder. At the same time, tensions were mounting at home, cracks appearing in her relationships with her immediate family. Carli's parents felt that they had put in the hours, made all the sacrifices to give her this career, and had earned the right to give their input, to analyze her decision making on the field, and to keep close tabs on her training regime. But Carli found it stifling, and she pushed back; the family bonds started to disintegrate as the 2007 World Cup began. Later, she made the decision to open up about it in her memoir.

"It was a difficult thing to talk about my family situation," she says. "Obviously, when you are a private person like myself, it's not something that I just want to babble on about. But it was part of my journey."

Such discord at home can cause a person to become cautious and guarded. While Carli developed firm friendships with a few other players, including Hope Solo, and maintained her close professional relationship with Galanis and her romance with her high school boyfriend, Brian Hollins, she may have been slow to open up to others. Some teammates felt they wanted more from her, and after the drama of the 2007 World Cup, Carli was told her position on the team was in jeopardy.

She sought assurances from Ryan that it wasn't the case, and then Ryan was replaced by Pia Sundhage. The new coach put her faith in Carli by shoring up her defense and giving her the freedom to go forward. Sundhage's strategy paid off as the USA progressed through the 2008 Olympics and Carli scored the decisive goal in the final game against Brazil, clinching gold for her team.

It was the best of times on the field and the worst of them at home. A parade in Carli's hometown welcomed her back from the Beijing Olympics, complete with a marching band. The main thoroughfare was lined with little kids in soccer shirts, all waiting to catch a glimpse of their local hero. Her family turned out for the celebrations, but within a few months, she was no longer on speaking terms with them.

The following season was a tricky one for Carli. She wasn't at her best on her club team, the Chicago Red Stars. The afterglow of the Olympics had faded, and Sundhage notified her that her contract with the USWNT wasn't going to be renewed on account of her poor form. Sundhage gave Carli three months to show she had improved and earn her contract back. Once more, the world was doubting Carli Lloyd, and once more she fought back.

Training, fitness, work ethic—these were the things over which she had control. And as she continued to apply herself, jogging every morning, taking part in long training sessions with Galanis at the fields on Ark Road in New Jersey, the results showed. She reached new levels of fitness, had her USWNT contract renewed, and earned her one hundredth cap.

Then came the 2011 World Cup. It wasn't the easiest tournament for the USA; they lost a game in the group stage for the first time and only just edged past Brazil on penalties in the quarterfinals. Carli knew she wasn't playing well in the semifinal against France, and Sundhage subbed her out. She watched from the bench as her team clinched a 3–1 victory. In the final against Japan, she was back in the side and put in a solid performance—until she missed her kick in the penalty shoot-out.

Heading into the 2012 Olympics, Carli needed to regain her confidence and composure quickly. The USWNT made it to the final again, and so did Japan. Determined to put the memory of the missed spot kick behind her, she was at her best in front of a packed Wembley Stadium in London. It was always going to be a one-goal game between these two sides, but Carli gave the USA breathing room, scoring twice to put them 2–0 up with a little over half an hour left to play. Japan pulled a goal back, but USA clung on to win gold.

After the games were over, everyone was talking about Carli Lloyd. She was named US Soccer Athlete of the Year. She signed an endorsement deal with Nike. She made the FIFA World Player of the Year shortlist. She was on course to becoming the world's greatest, just as she had intended.

⚽

What happens next is the stuff of legend.

The wildfires are still burning outside Vancouver, but BC Stadium is full, all fifty-three thousand seats taken on this smoggy July evening. Across the world, over 750 million viewers are tuned in to watch the 2015 World Cup final. The smell of smoke hangs in the air as the game kicks off, so it feels fitting to see Carli out there, scorching up the field like a lit spark. Every disappointment, every setback, the words of every doubter and hater, every workout, every visualization, every motivational message, they all burst out of her the moment the whistle blows.

It takes her just three minutes to score, to make the stadium erupt into cheers. Two minutes later, she gets another, this time beating two defenders and knocking it past Japan goalkeeper Ayumi Kaihori. The juggernaut will not stop. In the fourteenth minute, Lauren Holiday makes it three. It's breathtaking, this performance. And it's the World Cup final.

Then comes the screamer, the one everyone will remember above all the others. Carli takes a chance, sees Kaihori off her line, and decides it's worth a shot. She has been practicing these long kicks with Galanis out on empty playing fields for over a decade. The ball has fifty-four yards to travel from Carli's boot to the back of the net; it sails over Kaihori, kisses the post, and lands in the goal. It's audacious; it's masterful. It's the first hat trick in a women's World Cup final and the fastest in any World Cup final. It cements Carli's place at the pinnacle of world soccer.

The USA wins 5–2. Carli holds her dream, the World Cup, in her hands.

⚽

After the final, Carli won the FIFA Player of the Year award twice in a row. She signed endorsement deals with Visa, Whole Foods, and Pepsi. There were ticker-tape parades, this time in New York City, and a visit to Barack Obama's White House. Then came more landmark moments: 250 international caps, one hundred international goals.

It's easy to be complacent when you're on top, but Carli is not the kind of person to let it go to her head. "I didn't get here because of my looks," she says pointedly. "I didn't get here because I was kissing ass with the coach or the press officer or anything. I got here on sheer hard work, day in and day out. There's been loads of coaches and people who wanted to push me out time and time again. But if you let your performance speak for itself, they can't ignore you."

The outcast, the underdog, this is how Carli identifies. She didn't travel a conventional route to become a soccer star, and at times she didn't fit in, either as a player or personality.

"I'm not here to be friends with everyone," she explains. "I'm not here to just be a participant of a World Cup or Olympics. I'm here to separate myself from every single person in the world of soccer."

When you set the bar so high, it only raises expectations. "If I'm not scoring hat tricks now, people are like, 'Well, why is she on the national team anymore?' But what they fail to recognize is that I'm working on things in between these cycles, on my game, on the tactical side, on the technical side. There are these in-between years where I'm constantly developing in order for there to be a big bang come World Cup, come Olympics. That's usually when the big, big moments happen."

Carli still works closely with Galanis, whom she describes as the best coach she has ever had. When she married her long-term partner, Brian Hollins, in 2016, it was Galanis's two sons who walked her down the aisle.

It's hard to see why anyone would count her out of contention for the 2019 World Cup, given how hard she works and how talented she is. If it's the challenges that makes us stronger and the way we choose to overcome them, then Carli is a shining example of that. She wants to pass along the message, "It doesn't matter what you look like; it doesn't matter where you're from; it doesn't matter if you're nice to this person or that person. You can get there by sheer hard work day in and day out."

"And I'm still not done," she says. "I'm still having to prove myself to people."

Perhaps that's for the best.

NADIA NADIM
FORWARD

Herat, Afghanistan. A multiethnic city of minarets and mausoleums, arid summers and freezing winters, a city damaged by the Soviet-Afghan War of the 1980s but one that remained resilient and cosmopolitan in its aftermath.

Nadia Nadim enjoyed her childhood here and felt safe and protected by her parents. Her father, Rabani, loved sports and would take Nadia and her four sisters to play soccer in the local fields. She enjoyed being out there, running free, hearing the thunk of their feet kicking against leather, learning to control and pass the ball around with her family.

Then, everything changed. Around the time Nadia turned eight, Herat fell to the Taliban, a political group notorious for misogyny and violence against women. Under Taliban control, women were persecuted. They weren't allowed to work; to be educated beyond the age of eight; to speak loudly in public; to wear high-heeled shoes; or to appear on radio, on television, or at any public gathering. Girls were forced into underage marriages, and any violation of the laws resulted in public flogging or execution. It was a terrible place to be female.

Nadia was no longer allowed to go to school and certainly not to play the sport she was growing to love. One day Rabani—a general in the Afghan National Army—was summoned to a meeting with Taliban leaders. It was the last time Nadia saw her father. He never returned home. Six months later, Nadia's mother, Hadima, discovered that Rabani had been taken out to the desert and executed. Hadima's options were terrifyingly limited: stay put and raise five daughters alone under gender apartheid, without income or personal freedom, or take her girls and flee in the middle of the night, pay somebody to traffic them to safer climes, and hope for the best. She chose the latter.

Hadima escaped with her daughters to Pakistan, where they boarded a plane with fake Pakistani passports, all of them afraid and trying not to seem it. Soon they were huddled together in the dark in the back of a truck with a smuggler at the wheel, terrified they might not make it out alive. Nadia closed her eyes as the truck jostled and swerved, willing it all to work out, for them to be safely delivered to London where they could track down distant relatives. For thirty hours, nobody spoke or made a noise. They just held each other and hoped.

In the early hours of the morning, the truck stopped. The driver opened the door and ordered Hadima and her girls out onto a dirt road. Carrying two bags between the six of them, they walked for almost an hour through the quiet, dawn-lit countryside. They weren't sure where they were, but Nadia was fairly certain it wasn't London. Finally, they came across a man walking his dog.

Hadima asked in haltering English, "Where are we?"

"Randers," he replied.

The family looked quizzical, so the man added, "Denmark."

⚽

It took nearly twenty years, but in the winter of 2017, Nadia made England her home. She could barely sleep the night before she signed her deal for Manchester City, she was so excited.

But Nadia's soccer career is just one of her many achievements. She speaks nine languages: Danish, English, German, Persian, Urdu, Hindi, Arabic, and French. She is in medical school studying to become a reconstructive surgeon, and she was named Danish Sports Personality of the Year in

2017. Her story stands in stark contrast to the damaging political rhetoric that dehumanizes refugees and downplays their capabilities.

While Nadia and her family found their bearings in Denmark, they were housed in a refugee center in Visse. It was there, in the adjacent playing fields, that she began kicking a soccer ball around again with her little sister Diana and a group of boys who had escaped other troubled homelands: Iraq, Bosnia, Armenia. They spoke only one common language: soccer.

Nadia's passions were reignited; she was desperate to keep playing. Her mother was worried that their asylum application would fail and they would be sent back to Afghanistan, but in the meantime, she took great pleasure in seeing how much her daughter loved soccer—and how good she was. Despite the family's lack of resources, Hadima bought Nadia a pair of secondhand cleats. It was her way of saying, "Pursue what you love; enjoy your freedom." Nadia was so in love with the cleats that she was rarely without them. Sometimes she even slept with them on her feet so that they'd fit better.

Her playing career began in earnest shortly after, first with local side B52 Aalborg and then Team Viborg and IK Skovbakken, before moving to Fortuna Hjørring in 2012. She came over to the United States in 2015, playing on loan for Sky Blue until she signed a long-term deal with the club. In 2017, she led Denmark to their first European Championship final, scoring in the quarterfinal, the semifinal, and the final, where they lost 4–2 to the Netherlands.

On arriving in Manchester later that year to play for City, she was over-awed by the size of the club. But the club was equally impressed by Nadia, describing her as "much more than a footballer." In her first season, she got to fulfill her ambition of playing in the Champions' League when City made it all the way to the semifinal.

Nadia knows how differently her life might have turned out; she has even said that her indefatigable sense of independence would have been such a curse in Afghanistan that she probably wouldn't have survived. It's why she exudes enthusiasm, exuberance, and a vitality that comes from having escaped violent oppression. It's there in the way she plays, in the way she wears her trademark colorful headbands, the ones she makes herself out of spare fabric—or underwear—and it's there in her infectious grin.

A fan of the Drake lyric "started from the bottom now we here," Nadia uses it as a hashtag on Instagram posts as a means of referencing her journey. Somehow, you get the feeling that "here" is still only the beginning of her story.

NILOUFAR
ARDALAN

NILOUFAR ARDALAN
FORWARD

When Iran won the Asian Football Confederation (AFC) Women's Futsal Championship in 2015, its team captain and star player, Niloufar Ardalan, was watching on TV at home in Tehran. As her team lifted the cup in the air and cheered, Niloufar's seven-year-old son, Radan, looked up at her and asked, "Mom, why aren't you with them?" She smiled, holding back tears. "Mom," he said again, "you should be lifting the cup right now."

Niloufar, whose proficiency in front of goal had earned her the nickname "Lady Goal," hadn't been held back by illness or injury but by her husband. Married women in Iran still require permission from their husbands to travel abroad independently. Niloufar's husband, sports journalist Mahdi Toutounchi, had denied her.

Women's futsal, an indoor five-a-side game, is hugely popular in Iran, and its team is one of the best. When they qualified for the inaugural AFC Cup in Malaysia, everyone expected Niloufar to be there. She was widely regarded as the best female player in Iran, was the daughter of one of the country's best-known male goalkeepers, and had played every game in the qualifying rounds. But Niloufar's husband forced her to stay home, insisting that she needed to be present for the first day of her son's new semester at school.

Teammate Feretesh Karimi put it plainly in an interview with ESPN: "He didn't want her to go because he knew it was her dream."

News of Niloufar's plight had been shared on social media using the hashtag #WeAreAllNiloufarArdalan. Her teammates played with Niloufar's name scrawled across their shirts. And when they won, they dedicated the victory to her. "We had an overwhelming sad feeling because she wasn't there," said Karimi.

Niloufar felt the same mixed emotions. "I was happy for them that the game went well but deep down I was going through hell."

There was a bright spot on the horizon: the women's Futsal World Cup was taking place that year in Guatemala. "I didn't think [my husband] would deny me permission again," Niloufar said. But he did.

She knew she had to fight back. After all, she had railed against Iran's laws before. In 2005, she was among a small group of women who lobbied the Iranian football association to be permitted to attend a soccer match, since women in Iran have been banned from attending male sports events for over thirty years. During the game, a qualifier for the 2006 World Cup between Iran and North Korea, the group of women was seated near the Korean supporters and surrounded by security officers.

"Many young women in Iran are in love with football but they are frustrated that they cannot come to watch," Niloufar said.

Despite their small victory, the ban remained in place. Ten years later, with her husband standing in the way of her footballing dreams, Niloufar took her fight to the Iranian government once again.

"I wish authorities would pass a law for sportswomen so we can defend our rights in these circumstances," she told Iran's NASIM news agency.

It was a courageous move, seeking to change the law, not only for herself but for all Iranian women.

"I'm not going abroad for fun," she said. "My goal is to bring home glory for my national flag and my country. I'm a woman and a mother and I won't forego my rights for being either one."

Niloufar had support from news outlets and campaigners. Several high-profile Iranian men took to social media, holding signs that said, "I return the right to travel to my wife."

Just seventy-two hours before the Futsal World Cup was due to kick off, Iranian president Hassan Rouhani granted her a single exit visa to travel and play. The move was seen cynically by some as a hollow political attempt at public relations, yet it was still a victory for women's rights.

Although Iran lost in the group stages of the Futsal World Cup, Niloufar was there in Guatemala and able to compete.

In 2017, an amendment to the travel ban was accepted by the Iranian Parliament. While permission broadly remains with husbands, women who work as athletes, academics, diplomats, and in certain other high-profile careers are seemingly exempt from the ban. It is a small step toward female emancipation, and it all began with Niloufar and her teammates, who used soccer as a vehicle for political and social change.

BECKY SAUERBRUNN

BECKY SAUERBRUNN
DEFENDER

Wannabe soccer stars of the world, take heart from Becky Sauerbrunn. Either that, or take umbrage at the way the world forces women to constantly question themselves.

Becky is widely regarded as one of the best defenders in the world. She's the beloved captain of the USA, the top-ranked women's soccer team in the world, and a World Cup winner to boot, and yet she still struggles with self-confidence.

She refers to that struggle as an "ongoing process." "I think it's really easy to say, 'I'm going to be confident today,' but it's very hard for that to actually happen."

As a defender, the success of the team rides on your performance and individual errors can be lethal. It's not an easy space to live in and requires a great deal of mental strength. Becky's playing style has always relied more on a problem-solving mentality, her reaction speed, and deft footwork than brute force. She focuses on positional awareness, assessing where the opposing attacker is heading and using her skill to intercept. It's a sophisticated strategy, one that doesn't develop overnight and can only be learned through a willingness to make mistakes.

As a younger player, this left Becky enduring crippling episodes of self-doubt. "It was affecting the way I was playing and the way I was off the field. I was overanalyzing how I was playing. I needed to stop the overanalysis and have my time taken up with something more empowering."

An English Literature major, Becky began reading more, devouring books as often as possible. When she was called to camp with the USWNT, she would bring several novels—sci-fi being her favorite genre—and finish one every few days. "Reading is such an escape, it's so nice to just get away," she said. "Plus, I want to continue learning. Soccer will only last for so long and I'd still like my brain to function, so it's good to keep exercising it."

Reading gave her something else to think about while she worked to assert herself in the team. Despite a great performance coming into the 2011 USA side in the World Cup semifinal after Rachel van Hollebeke (formerly Buehler) received a ban for a red card in the quarterfinal, Becky still wasn't first choice of center-back. A regular on the subs bench, she replaced the injured van Hollebeke for the last ten minutes of the 2012 Olympic final, helping the USA hold on to their narrow 2–1 lead to claim gold. Teams require consistency and fortitude from their back line and are often loath to

make changes in defense. Joining such a high-stakes game late on and keeping her composure showed what a centering presence Becky could be.

"Here's a player that had to step in under the most unbelievably pressure-packed moment, and the poise there, it resonated with me," Jill Ellis said during the 2015 World Cup, when Becky had firmly established herself in the heart of defense, an invaluable player on the team's path to glory. "It was like, 'Wow, she's got some grit and some resolve.' Just her confidence to step into that moment, for me it was a big indicator of what she had inside of her."

Even if she doesn't always feel confident, Becky surely conveys it in the way she plays and leads her team. Now she wears the captain's armband for both club and country. She's a player her teammates describe as a leader, mentor, and role model. The captaincy, she says, carries weight and responsibility, and she doesn't take the role lightly. Her aim is to support all the players around her, to welcome newer players into the fold, and, ideally, to lead them to another World Cup victory in 2019 so that they can experience it for themselves.

ASISAT OSHOALA
FORWARD

From the bustling streets of Lagos to Liverpool, London, and Shanghai, soccer has taken Asisat Oshoala on a peculiar path.

Born and raised in Ikorodu, on the banks of the Lagos Lagoon, she began her club career with FC Robo in the overcrowded, industrial suburb of Mushin. Before long she was playing for the Nigeria youth team, the Falconets, and in 2014, she led them all the way to the U-20 World Cup final, scoring seven goals along the way. The Falconets lost in the final, but Asisat's star was rising. Great things were to come.

Later that year, she transitioned to the senior team, the Super Falcons, helping them win the African Cup of Nations. By then, Asisat was on the radar of some of the biggest teams in Europe. She was still only twenty when she signed for Liverpool Ladies, with manager Matt Beard saying she was "one of the best young players in the world." She won the inaugural BBC Women's Footballer of the Year award. Then it all went quiet.

Asisat missed two months of the season due to injury while Liverpool languished at the bottom of the Women's Super League. She switched to Arsenal, but things didn't go well there either. She scored twice in eleven appearances and was reportedly upset at the wage disparity among the players in the newly professionalized league. Some of the more established names were on relatively lucrative contracts, while young players like Asisat were earning far less. When Chinese Super League team Dalian Quanjian offered her a contract, she took it, even though it seemed an obscure destination for someone who had made such an early impact in her career.

Meanwhile, strange happenings were afoot with the Nigeria women's soccer team, long hailed as the best in Africa, having lost only five games to African opposition in twenty years. The Football Federation fell into financial difficulty, and head coach Florence Omagbemi went without pay for most of 2016 while the players marched on Parliament over their unpaid win bonuses. Despite being champions of Africa, they didn't play any games at all for a whole year, and Omagbemi was fired, despite being on a shortlist for FIFA World Coach of the Year.

But even while the Nigerian women's team was inactive and Asisat couldn't play international soccer, she was voted African Women's Player of the Year for the third time in 2017.

She stood on the podium in a sparkly white dress, clutching her award, as tears welled in her eyes. "They said my career was finished when I left Arsenal for China," she said. "But here I am tonight. This award is for every young African girl: don't let them tell you that you can't do it."

Nigeria is a difficult place to be female. The extremist group Boko Haram is notorious for kidnapping girls on masse, and the nonprofit group Human Rights Watch believes that the Nigerian government is not doing enough to protect them. Violence against women and LGBTQ+ people is rife—any public display of affection between same sex couples is punishable by ten years in prison. Girls tend to lack access to education, and nothing can be taken for granted.

After her Player of the Year win, Asisat appealed to Nigerian parents to encourage their daughters' independence and agency.

"In most cases, the girl is always taken out of school for the boy to further his education because women's education means nothing to some parents," she said in an interview with a Nigerian newspaper. "While the boys move about, making friends with their peers, the girl is confined to the house in order to be seen as a 'good child' by suitors. It's a big problem in Africa. In Europe, it's no problem at all. Here [in Nigeria] we need to tell them that girls also have the capacity to do well in sports and still read and pass their exams very well."

In 2018, Asisat and Nigeria were back on the international scene, and she netted twice as the Super Falcons beat Gambia 7–0 in June. As far as club soccer goes, she is enjoying life in China and her status as the Super League's top scorer. Thanks to the relatively high salaries in the league, she was able to buy her parents a new home in Lagos.

For now, Asisat seems content to stay put, but there's no telling where soccer will take her next.

AZIZE AY

Azize Ay (center) meeting the Fenerbahce coaches in 2017.

AZIZE AY

FORWARD

When Azize Ay made her debut in 2017, she stood out.

A young women's team, Diyarbakirspor, who were in the third tier of the Turkish women's league, were 2–0 up against a local team with twenty minutes left to play when Coach Melek Hanim brought Azize on as a substitute. Cheers erupted from the smattering of supporters gathered on the sidelines. At forty-eight years old, Azize was at least three decades older than most of her teammates, and her enthusiasm was unparalleled.

Azize had been waiting her entire life for such a moment and had just about given up hope that it would ever happen. Yet there she was, out on the soccer field, wearing the number twenty-one shirt, racing down the wing with the ball at her feet.

⚽

Azize was born and raised in the small, rural village of Karacali in a modest home surrounded by lush fields, bordered by a creek and an old stone bridge. Her father died when she was just three months old, and she grew up knowing very little about him, only that he played and loved soccer.

When she was six, she began playing herself, finding in it a connection to the father she had never known. By that time, her mother was remarried—to her uncle—and had two sons. The household was very strict and traditional, much like the village, and when Azize was seen playing soccer with the neighborhood boys, she was castigated by the locals; it was unfeminine, against the natural order of things. As she grew older and more independent, she would sneak away when she could, ride her horse way out into the fields, and kick a ball around with the local farm laborers, away from judgmental eyes.

Word of her soccer skills spread. When she was seventeen, the same age as many of the Diyarbakir players, two nearby teams, Ankara Sitespor and Adana Dostlukspor, invited her to join them. She went back home and began packing her suitcase, but her uncle forbade her from moving away to join a soccer club.

He told her, "We would rather kill you."

"Fine," Azize replied. "Then bury me under a corner flag."

After that, Azize continued to play in secret. She turned down several marriage proposals, preferring to keep her energies focused on the one thing she was desperate to achieve: her dream of playing for a soccer team.

Years passed, then decades. Azize moved to the city of Diyarbakir and began working as a cook. When she turned forty, she met a man and agreed to marry him.

"When I first met my husband, he told me that he too was a Fenerbahçe fan," she told Turkish news agency Andalou. "But, after we got married, I understood that he had lied and was actually a Galatasaray fan. I was very upset."

Fortunately, her husband was happy to endorse her allegiances. At their wedding, Azize insisted they forgo the traditional Halay music for the Fenerbahçe anthem. She tried to have her wedding dress made in the team colors of yellow and navy, but the dressmakers refused. So she settled for Fenerbahçe-colored flowers instead.

"In my life, [soccer] has always been very important," she said. "And Diyarbakir realized my dream."

Azize shares a special bond with her teammates, who see her as both a mother figure and a mascot. "I love them very much, I respect them, we play in harmony. They even tell me, 'Do not run, we'll bring you the ball so you do not get tired.' I have never had children but now I have 11 daughters."

She is proof that it pays to hold on to your dreams. "I got to take to the field for the first time in my life," she said after making her debut. "I [was] very happy and excited. I have never given up and I won't. I feel like I'm 17."

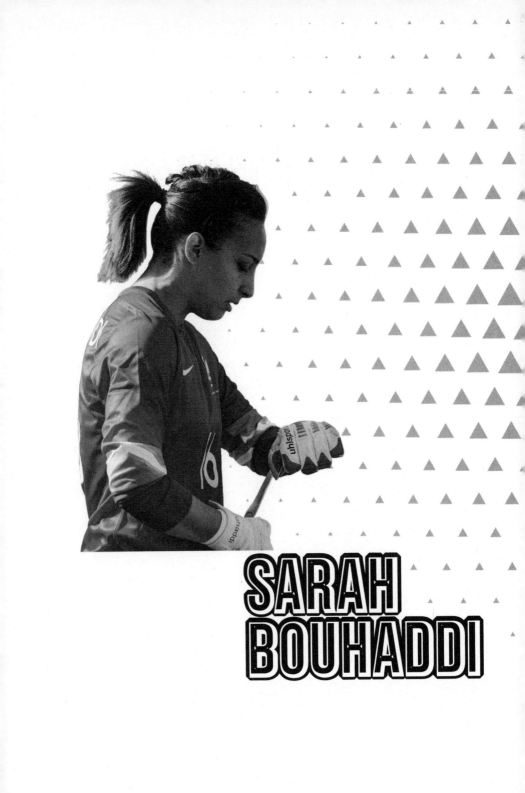

SARAH
BOUHADDI

SARAH BOUHADDI
GOALKEEPER

When goalkeepers try to show off some fancy footwork, it tends to strike fear into the hearts of their defenders. Gaffes usually ensue as opposing forwards lurk in wait, ready to pounce on stray balls or dispossess those shot stoppers who think they can pass the ball around as well as the outfield players. But Sarah Bouhaddi can.

The France goalkeeper loves having the ball at her feet, a throwback to her preprofessional playing days as a midfielder. It's what makes her both an exciting and nerve-inducing keeper to watch: you never know what she might do next.

Sarah has a great first touch and is confident playing off her line, dribbling out of defense if she feels the need. Her teammates can count on her distribution being as effective as her shot stopping, and they can also count on her to take a penalty should the moment arise.

The Champions League Final in 2017 was at a deadlock. The all-French affair between Olympic Lyonnaise and Paris Saint Germain remained goalless through extra time, and as the penalty shoot-out began, neither was any closer to breaking the deadlock. Kick after kick, everything remained tied until each side had scored six and exhausted their lists of primary penalty takers. Going into the eighth round of kicks, it was the keepers' turn.

Sarah and PSG goalie Katarzyna Kiedrzynek were up against each other. Kiedrzynek took her kick and missed, scuffing the ball wide. Then it was Sarah's turn. A lean figure in neon yellow, she placed the ball on the spot, took her run-up, and blasted it past Kiedrzynek to win the Champions League for Lyon, their third major trophy that season.

Elated, Sarah ran to her teammates to celebrate, sliding across the turf on her knees as they rushed to her, and immediately disappeared in a bundle of white-clad bodies.

"Sarah is great with her feet," Lyon coach Gerard Precheur said after the game. "I think she's the best goalkeeper in the world anyway, but she's outstanding with her feet. I asked her to take a penalty in a league match too, because I thought she could score."

Sarah grew up in Cannes with parents of Algerian descent and began playing soccer when she was eight, discovering her goalkeeping talents at fourteen when her team needed a stopper and she stepped in. A graduate of the prestigious French national soccer school at Clairfontaine, Sarah was

only sixteen when she was picked to play for France's Under 19s in the 2003 European Championship finals. In their three qualifying games, she kept two clean sheets and maintained her unbeatable streak as France progressed and won the tournament.

She was called up for the senior team soon after, starting for France in Euro 2005. But the following year, a moment of recklessness tarnished her growing reputation. In the 2006 Algarve Cup, Sarah was in goal as France took on Sweden. Hanna Ljungberg, a veteran on the Swedish side, rose to meet a lofted ball in the France penalty box, but Sarah leaped to intercept it and smashed into Ljungberg in midair. The Swede was rushed to hospital with a severe concussion.

While it looked to many like dangerous play, Ljungberg was more forgiving, saying later that Sarah "probably just timed it wrong."

There was more drama when Sarah was left out of France's squad for the 2011 World Cup, seemingly inexplicably. Later, rumors came to light that she and French captain Sandrine Soubeyrand didn't get along. When Soubeyrand retired, Sarah returned to the international fold once more.

She has amassed over 120 caps for the French side, assisted in five Champions League victories for Lyon, and was voted the world's best women's goalkeeper in 2017.

There is plenty more to come from Sarah; in 2019, she will relish playing a World Cup in her homeland. With or without the ball, you will want to keep your eyes on her.

SILVIA NEID

SILVIA NEID

COACH

There was almost nothing left for Silvia Neid to win. Almost.

In her twelve-year tenure as head coach for Germany, she had taken home nearly everything: the World Cup, the European Championship, and the FIFA World Women's Coach of the Year award three times over. But when she announced that she would be retiring after the 2016 Rio Games, she had yet to get her hands on Olympic gold.

As a player, Silvia had been integral to the birth and rise of women's soccer in Germany. She made her debut at eighteen in Germany's first international game and made headway from there, winning the Bundesliga with SV Bergisch Gladbach. In 1989, seven years after her first international appearance, Germany won the European Cup, a moment that she described as "pivotal" in bringing women's soccer to the fore.

As soon as she stopped playing, Silvia moved into coaching, taking charge of the German Under 19s and guiding them to win a European Championship. Before long, she was involved in the senior setup, assisting Tina Theune-Meyer before succeeding her as coach.

Silvia became one of the most recognizable female coaches in the world; her cool manner as she observed from the technical area made her seem imperturbable. Nadine Angerer, who came to be Germany's first-choice goalkeeper under Silvia, described her as the "kind of coach who can really improve players." Angerer elaborated: "She sees weaknesses and she has solutions to make every single player better."

In Germany, Silvia also became an object of desire. Before the 2011 World Cup, *Playboy* invited her to pose nude for their magazine. She declined, not wanting to devalue her achievements by doing something she felt would keep people from taking women's soccer seriously.

Instead, Silvia wanted her success to help demonstrate how important it is to nurture female coaches. "[Germany] has always tried to encourage female players to train as coaches," she told a reporter from UEFA. "And it's paid off. Since 1996, the DFB [German Football Association] has only employed women as head coach of the women's team."

⚽

Germany progressed through the women's soccer tournament at the 2016 Olympics, as many thought they would with Silvia at the helm, setting up a showdown with Sweden in the final. Pia Sundhage's Sweden had been criticized for their defensive play during the tournament; it was going to be tough for the German side to break them down and send Silvia off to retirement with a gold medal around her neck.

Everyone expected Sweden to win, since they had been so organized and clinical under Sundhage's direction. But for the final game, Sundhage gambled and changed their system. It worked in Germany's favor. After a tight first half, the scoring was level at 1–1. Early in the second half, Dzsenifer Marozsan stepped up with the decisive strike for Germany, and Silvia's side held on to claim victory.

At the final whistle, Silvia's notoriously cool demeanor finally vanished. She dashed onto the field, arms outstretched, and dived onto a pile of her players. It was the perfect end to an illustrious coaching career.

Still, it was difficult for her to conceive of stepping away from the German national team. "When I think about it, it's a strange feeling," she said. "Thirty-four years! Thirty-four years as player, assistant and head coach. It's wonderful that I've been able to experience it all and I am proud of that, but now I am setting up a scouting department for women's football at the DFB.

You need to be able to realize when it's the right time to stop, and I want a new challenge."

In the end, the new challenge was a continuation of the old one. Silvia now heads up the scouting operations for German soccer's women and girls. She still maintains a pivotal role in shaping the framework of German women's soccer.

"It's important to be looking out for new trends and developments in women's football," she said. "That's my responsibility. Our aim is to be a few years ahead of the game and the players need to be trained accordingly."

With Silvia's continuing influence, Germany will be a dynamic force on the international soccer scene for generations to come.

HAJRA KHAN

HAJRA KHAN
FORWARD

Hajra Khan pulls her long, dark hair tighter in its ponytail, adjusts her uniform, and stretches her calves out one last time.

She is standing on the field in one of the best stadiums in Karachi, the capital city of Pakistan, about to play the state quarterfinals, and there are only ten people in attendance. Maybe twelve. And this is Lyari, the part of Karachi they call "mini Brazil" for its love of all things soccer related.

In Lyari, soccer is everything. Here, where three-wheeled auto rickshaws speed past stray street animals and delicious smells waft from food carts over trash-strewn gutters, every TV in the area beams out live soccer from around the world. The bustling streets are filled with soccer fans in replica shirts. It can be dangerous here in this overcrowded enclave, which is governed by drug cartels and known for a brutal, decades-long gang war—except when there's a game on. But even here, women's soccer still lags behind.

Hajra is trying to change that. She has been through a lot to get here to Lyari on this muggy afternoon. She has made a name for herself as a soccer star, been named vice-captain of the national team, and yet she still doesn't know how she will be received on any given day. So, when the referee, who is supposed to be checking her cleats and uniform, comes to a stop in front of her, she is quiet.

"My wife had a daughter last week," he says.

She smiles warily and congratulates him.

"We named her Hajra," he adds. "Because we hope one day she'll grow up to be like you."

⚽

A serious, studious, introverted girl who found her outlet in sports, Hajra was born and raised in Karachi. While Karachi is a progressive city, Pakistan is an Islamic republic and largely conservative. When she was eleven, Hajra's parents risked the wrath of their families to send her to India so that she could compete in a half marathon. Political relations between Pakistan and India are hostile and historically complex, and Hajra's extended family disapproved.

"They were like, 'How are you gonna send her to India? That's not how it works here. She's Muslim, and she should stay at home.'"

But Hajra's parents allowed her to go. They could see how much enjoyment and confidence she took from playing sports. Then, a year or two later when a local soccer team put a notice in the local newspaper offering tryouts, it was Hajra's mother who brought it to her.

"I just looked at her," Hajra says. "The only soccer I had ever played was out in the street. Because I used to play basketball, the kids in the neighborhood would put me in goal, against a goalpost that we chalked out on the wall.

"But my mom said, 'You're strong; you're fit; you run a lot. You have the stamina. Why don't you give it a shot?' And I did. She took me to the tryouts, and I got picked by a club team, which is a level higher than the provincial team."

Hajra was called into the senior side, although she was just fourteen, and began playing as a forward. That year, she was the top scorer in the national championship. The following year, she scored even more goals and was called up to the Pakistan national team.

But there was fallout. "My parents were comfortable letting me play in shorts," she explains. "But my extended family again, they were like, 'She's a disgrace to this family; she's a disgrace to the country. What have you done to her?'" They didn't speak to Hajra's parents for years.

⚽

To some, she's a disgrace, but to others, she's an icon, the young woman in the dark-green soccer uniform of Pakistan with the big smile, all confidence on the ball. The kind of woman girls look up to and people name their daughters after.

By the time she was made captain of the Pakistan team, Hajra was having difficulties in her personal life. In October 2016, her friend and fellow Pakistan strike partner Shahlyla Baloch was killed in a car accident late one Wednesday night. It was a loss, both personal and professional, that Hajra is still coming to terms with.

Then, just a day after Baloch's death, Hajra's father called to tell her that his industrial equipment business had gone bankrupt. "He was like, 'We've been cheated, and we don't have any more money,'" she recalls. "I'm the oldest of six siblings; we're five sisters, and the youngest is a boy. So, I felt that direct responsibility of being the oldest and trying to make things okay."

A year later, there was no more international soccer. FIFA suspended the Pakistan Football Federation for third-party interference, meaning there would be no more competitions for the foreseeable future. "Soccer has been my sanctuary," she says. "And I couldn't find anywhere to go."

It was the final straw for her mental health. Without soccer as an outlet, Hajra found herself in a downward spiral, diagnosed with depression and high-functioning anxiety. She knew things were bad when she started using drugs, nullifying her physical health and numbing her feelings. She sought help from a therapist who prescribed medication and encouraged her to regain her focus. Hajra made a

concerted effort to kick a soccer ball around whenever she could, often playing alone, making sure she kept her skills sharp.

Now she has an additional mission: to shed light on mental health issues
in sport. "When an athlete gets physically injured, there's tons of people
trying to fix them," she says. "But when an athlete's going through mental
health problems, the treatment is absolutely not the same at all. As an athlete, you're supposed to be strong, and you're supposed to be this macho
person who everybody looks up to. But nobody really knows what's going on
inside."

Hajra wanted to be open, to let people know that successful athletes
suffer with their mental health as much as anyone. Athleticism doesn't negate
emotional fragility.

This is what courage looks like: to play soccer when only a few people
are watching, to play even though others tell you it's wrong, to reach the top
of your game and share your personal struggles publicly so that others feel
more able to deal with their own. This is why Hajra is destined to make a
difference.

ALEX MORGAN

ALEX MORGAN
FORWARD

It's early, so early the sky is only just getting light outside, and Alex Morgan is standing on a soccer field in full uniform and makeup. There's a camera trained on her, and lights. There's a boom operator holding a stick mic over her head, a wardrobe assistant, a grip, and a hair-and-makeup person hovering nearby who keeps reapplying gloss to her lips and sweeping stray strands of hair out of her face. Turns out it takes a long time and a lot of people to make a soccer movie.

The first assistant director calls out, "Last touches!" and for a moment, she thinks he's talking about the ball at her feet. But it's another one of those things people yell on set, a cue for her hair and makeup to be checked one more time before the director calls, "Action!"

She's a little nervous, because she's never done this before. But she's Alex Morgan, so she's prepared. When she agreed to be in this movie, she hired an acting coach, even though she's portraying a fictionalized version of herself. In *Alex & Me*, she's a poster on a young girl's bedroom wall come to life. And isn't this part of what it means to be the current face of American soccer? That simply being on a poster is no longer enough.

⚽

But first, the soccer.

The USA, the best women's soccer team in the world, are on the verge of crashing out of qualifying for the 2011 World Cup. Since they lost to Mexico in the CONCACAF (Confederation of North, Central America, and Caribbean Association Football) Gold Cup—one of the most shocking results in the history of women's soccer—it looks as though the team might not make it to the World Cup. How could this be happening? Not to win the World Cup is one thing—it's already been more than ten years since that last happened—but not to qualify at all? Unthinkable.

On a rainy night in November, the USA is up against Italy in the first leg of a crucial qualifying playoff for the 2011 tournament. The stadium in Padua, the oldest city in northern Italy, is only a quarter full, but the few thousand or so Italian fans are setting off fireworks from the stands, filling the night with sparks and smoke. It's a foreboding atmosphere; the USA team looks unsettled and is unable to find their way through the Italian defense.

Alex is twenty-one years old, the youngest player on the roster, not yet signed to a professional team. She has impressed at youth level, scoring the winning goal in the U-20 Women's World Cup final in 2008, but she's only just beginning to prove herself at the senior level. She's watching the game unfold from the sidelines as she warms up. Every now and then, she glances over at the bench, willing Pia Sundhage to put her in.

Finally, in the eighty-sixth minute, she gets her chance. Sundhage calls her over and looks her straight in the eye. "Just go to the goal," she says. Alex nods and runs out there. The minutes tick by. Still no goal. Then, in the fourth minute of injury time, Carli Lloyd lofts a long ball to Abby Wambach, who heads it down, and Alex runs onto it. She takes it into the box, and before you can blink, she fires it home.

It's a big goal, one of the most crucial, and it helps send the USA to the World Cup. For Alex, it marks her as a future star.

⚽

Going into the 2011 World Cup, Alex knew that she'd be on the subs bench and that when she came into a game, she'd have to make every second count.

Sundhage brought her on in the second half of the semifinal against France, and she scored to make it 3–1. She was a second-half substitute once again in the final against Japan, and once again she made an instant impact and scored, then provided the assist for USA's second goal. It wasn't enough to win the World Cup in the end, as the USA was edged out on penalties, but Alex had burst onto the scene and made her name. She was adept at reading the play, knowing where the ball was going to land, and striking it goalward. She looked every inch the world-class forward, an unstoppable force in front of goal.

Overnight, Alex accumulated a whole generation of young fans who wanted to find out everything they could about her. Who was this young, pretty forward who wore a pink hairband, the one her teammates nicknamed "Baby Horse" for the way she sped toward goal? What was her favorite kind of food? Mexican. Favorite workout other than soccer? Yoga. Favorite app? Instagram.

Alex's club team, Western New York Flash, drew record attendances in the first games after the tournament. Everyone was clamoring to see her in action. The endorsement deals started rolling in: Chapstick, Chobani, McDonald's, Nike. She became the *New York Times* best-selling author of the middle grade series *The Kicks*, which was later made into a series on Amazon Prime.

"That was the one time that I was like, 'Wow, a lot of things are getting thrown at me and I just don't know when to say yes or no,'" she admitted. "I had to learn just by going through it because I didn't have the experience."

For many players, such intense interest at such a young age could spell disaster on the field, but not for Alex. For starters, she signed with Dan Levy, the agent who looks after Mia Hamm. "We were very, very careful about who we wanted to work with," he says. "The most important thing for any player is that they put their sport first. If they're not playing at the highest level possible for themselves, then the rest of it doesn't work."

Alex's focus remained on the field. In 2012, she was officially a starter, and she proved her worth immediately in the 2012 Olympics, scoring twice in the USA's opening game against France. Just like she had in Italy, she popped up to score another crucial goal, a winner in the dying minutes of extra time in the semifinal against Canada, powering the USA to the game where they'd win gold. Meanwhile, she racked up one of the best year-long tallies of goals and assists in USWNT history.

The Alex Morgan brand continued to thrive, even when Alex the player was sidelined with an ankle injury for seven months in 2013. But the brand wasn't where she wanted to put all her energies. "I don't want to focus on the things I do off the field because there wouldn't be a reason for that unless I performed on the field," she said. "I want to show people that the product that I put on the field is good, is great."

Alex Morgan, center

A knee injury kept her from starting the 2015 World Cup. True to form, when she took to the field against Nigeria, she immediately renewed her strike partnership with Abby Wambach, bringing an extra dose of speed and movement to the American attack. As the team progressed, headlines around the world called her a "golden girl" with "the world at her feet."

Three days later, she was on the field at BC Stadium waving to the crowd as a World Cup winner. The cameras showed her draped in a US flag after the final whistle, crying tears of joy. The cameras love her, and it would be remiss not to acknowledge that this is what makes her so marketable. In a culture where women are celebrated for their looks first and foremost, Alex fits the mold of sporting superstar. She looks like a movie star, so it makes sense that she eventually became one. Her life is eminently Instagrammable, and she has over five million followers. But she knows that the world tends to treat women reductively, making beauty their most essential component. She has been quick to point out that "you can have beauty *and* brains *and* athletic ability."

Knowing she had the world's attention after the 2015 World Cup, Alex used her platform to further the fight for equal pay. She appeared with her teammates on NBC's *Today* show and said, "Every single day we sacrifice just as much as the men. We work just as much. We endure just as much physically and emotionally. . . . We're really asking, and demanding now, that our federation and our employer really step up and appreciate us as well."

USSF agreed to give the women's players a better deal, although not an equal one as yet. The players have accepted it, for now. Meanwhile, Alex continues to find new ways to improve her game. In 2016, she made a surprise move to Lyon in France, making the difficult choice to leave her husband, her dog, her family, and her home behind, all in the pursuit of sporting excellence.

"I hope that this change will help push my game to another level," she said when she signed the deal. "Importantly, I will be immersed in a soccer culture that I believe is precisely what I need at this point in my career."

Alex won the Champions League with Lyon that season and returned to the United States an even more accomplished player, albeit an injured one with a strained hamstring. Once she had battled back to fitness again, she took her goalscoring to another level, netting seventeen goals in an eighteen-game run, in which the USA didn't lose once. She looks set to become the seventh woman in US history to reach one hundred goals and one of the youngest to get there. Alex is entertaining and dangerous, drawing fouls, scoring goals, and linking up beautifully with Megan Rapinoe. All of which points to an even more exciting future in the years to come.

If there is pressure that comes with being Alex Morgan the movie star and brand ambassador, Alex Morgan the player isn't fazed by it. As her dad once said, "She has a competitive spirit that is almost scary."

KELLY LINDSEY

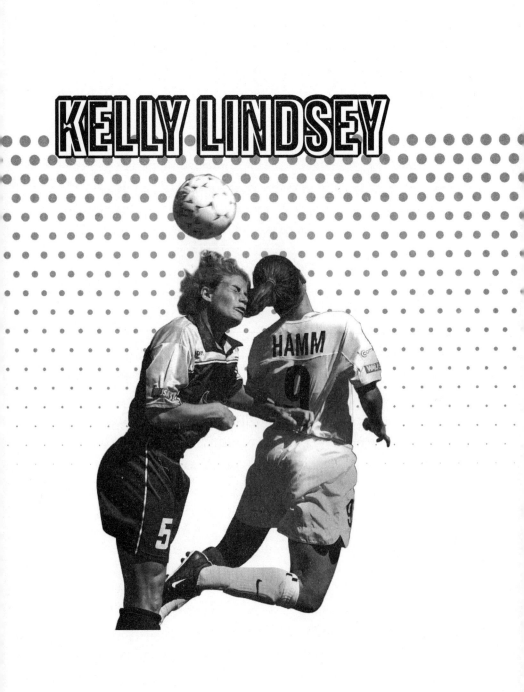

KELLY LINDSEY
COACH

Kelly Lindsey pulls up in the parking lot of a California grocery store. She's on a mission to get coffee for her staff on the way to the morning's coaching session. She grabs her wallet from the center console and unbuckles her seat belt. As the strap slides away from her chest, she pauses for a moment and looks down at what she's wearing. The training jacket is a rich, forest green, and on it, thick, block letters spell out "AFGHANISTAN."

Shoot, she thinks, *can I wear this in here?*

Afghanistan holds a potency in American discourse that makes emblazoning it across one's body seem like a subversive act, even when strolling around a store. To many Americans, Afghanistan is an enemy, a hotbed of terrorism. It is a country that has been reduced to caustic cable news soundbites. Most Americans would feel nervous out in public with the word "Afghanistan" written across their chest.

To someone less pensive and empathetic, this brief, jarring moment would quickly be forgotten. But to Kelly, it's a revelation. From it, she takes the understanding, "on a very small level," of what her players go through every day.

"Whoever you talk to, when the word 'Afghanistan' is thrown out, all people think about is terrorism, evil, horror," she says. "And I think that's the exact reason they're playing, because they say that's not the truth of their country. They say that they live in a very beautiful country with very wonderful people. Everyone views [Afghanistan] based off this one group [the Taliban] who are so negative and evil."

The Afghanistan women's team formed in 2007 at the grassroots, with a group of schoolgirls from Kabul. Support from overseas grew, and within three years, they'd signed a deal with Danish kit brand Hummel, who created their uniforms and an integrated hijab for them to wear while playing. Kelly joined as head coach in 2016, with Haley Carter as her assistant and former player Khalida Popal the program director.

Kelly has said before that her players' commitment to soccer is a matter of "life or death." As women, they are constantly under threat—if not from Taliban militants, then from members of their communities or even their own families, for making the choice to play soccer. In one instance, the brother of former player and program director Popal was stabbed near his home and nearly killed by men who were angry that he "allowed" his sister to play soccer.

Kelly recalls somebody asking her why they continue to play. "My jaw dropped," she says. "I thought, well, do you think that they have a million options to go do whatever they want? This is one of the few things they get to do to try to make their country a better place."

The team is beginning to see the positive effects of their efforts in their homeland. Kelly says she thinks their social media feeds are reflecting a steady groundswell of change. "We've gone from about ninety percent hostile and negative to about fifty-fifty. But the fifty percent that's positive, we can stand on that."

There are times, she says, when soccer feels very small, and there are times when it feels huge. "We've been through the days where everyone on social media was dogging the girls and telling them how they're not Afghan, they're not real women, they're a disgrace to their country. They still get that, but now we're starting to get some more of the positive responses. Men especially are stepping up, from inside Afghanistan, and saying, 'We're proud of you; we're proud of what you do. I hope my daughter can be like you someday. I hope my daughter can play for our country.'"

Kelly's journey to becoming coach of the Afghanistan national women's team wasn't a smooth one; the most worthwhile journeys never are. She grew up in Omaha, Nebraska, without much access to organized soccer. When she was still in middle school, she was so desperate to play that her father, who knew nothing about the sport, stepped up and became her coach. Later, she acquired a mentor: Tracey Bates Leone, a USWNT midfielder and assistant coach at nearby Creighton University. Bates Leone was someone to look up to and emulate, and she guided Kelly through her early playing days.

A highly promising defender, Kelly played college soccer for Notre Dame, helping them to a runner-up spot in the NCAA Division 1 Championship. After graduation, she joined the San Jose CyberRays and was soon called up to the USA team, where she made her debut in an 8–1 win over the Czech Republic. With her strength and skill shoring up the defense, the CyberRays won the WUSA in 2001. She was so impressive that *Soccer America* named her Rookie of the Year.

But Kelly was beset by injuries; her knees were persistently bad. She was in and out of contention over the next two seasons, battling back over and over again to be able to play. By the end of the 2003 season, she was forced to face the terrible truth: her playing career was over. Kelly announced her retirement from the game when she was only twenty-three years old. It's still hard for her to talk about that crushing blow, the agony of having to walk away from her dreams. Even now, the wounds remain fresh.

"I think I'm still dealing with it," she says. "It's one thing to choose to retire when you've done what you can, and it's another to have to just physically hang up the boots and move on to something else in your life. It's not easy. I think it lingers with you for years. But I also think the sport teaches you a lot about how to deal with that stuff in life."

Kelly has chosen to learn. She is constantly listening, observing, thinking, putting herself in other people's shoes. Perhaps that's a result of living through heartbreak; it has deepened her understanding and empathy for other people's hardships. Certainly, it has prepared her in some way for this coaching role.

"I believe everything happens for a reason," she says. "I know that all the challenges I went through as a player were building toward something that would have greater meaning."

Kelly was told constantly throughout her playing career that she'd never play again, that she might never even walk again if she had surgery on her knees. But she felt she had to keep trying until there were no other options.

"I get it when these girls are told every single day in lots of different ways from lots of different people, 'Your dream is stupid. You're not allowed to do that.' And I get their courage to say, 'It doesn't actually matter how far I get; I just want to keep doing it to see where it ends up.'"

Rarely do you find coaches who see themselves not as the central figure around whom the team is structured but as a custodian, working with others to help change the political landscape.

"I came in trying to own my ignorance and know that I didn't know everything," she says. "I've worked really hard to try to ask the right questions and not always be the leader, but to let them teach me. Let them be the leaders of their country."

She is adamant that she won't be the one leading them to big tournaments or trophy wins, whenever that might be. "This country needs an Afghan woman to lead. That is when they will succeed."

⚽

In November 2018, Kelly's prediction came true, though under seemingly the worst possible circumstances. The Afghanistan Football Federation (AFF) said it had opted to move in a "different direction" without Kelly, her staff, and most of the team's established players. Team captain Shabnam Mobarez stated that she had declined to sign a contract that purportedly denied the players payment for playing, as well as the opportunity to seek external sponsorship. Beneath the contractual dispute were more nefarious allegations. It soon came to light that the players had reported being subjected to horrific mental, physical, and sexual abuse by male AFF officials both inside and outside the country, including at the federation headquarters. The allegations caused Hummel to cut ties with the AFF, who put out a statement "vigorously reject[ing] the false accusations." FIFA says it is investigating.

In the light of her experiences with Afghanistan, Kelly's thoughts have turned to her own country. In the fight for equality and inclusion swirling around her head, she can't fathom why things aren't further along in the United States.

"There is no excuse in a country like this. US Soccer is not leading the way. Our women should be paid equal to the men, no questions asked. If other countries can do it, there is no excuse. I cannot think of a single argument US Soccer can put forward and buy into it."

Kelly has seen what it is for her players to live in a country where they are forbidden from public life, treated as second-class citizens, and confined to the home. It has only fueled her frustration and anger at wage inequality in America.

"The US women's team has won everything; the men have won nothing. And the fact that we're not leading the movement for women's equality and pay in a sport that we dominate shows why girls feel [less important] in our country. And it's our own fault. And it's the leaders of our soccer's fault, because they could change it in a heartbeat and they're choosing not to. They're choosing to tell girls they're not equal. Our leading soccer organization is choosing to tell girls in our country, 'You are not enough.' If it doesn't start here, where does it start?"

For now, it starts with women like Kelly, those fearless, passionate advocates who sow the seeds of change.

ENIOLA ALUKO

ENIOLA ALUKO
FORWARD

The Palace of Westminster lies on the north bank of the River Thames in London. Grand and archaic, its regal halls have been the center of political life in Britain for centuries. In October 2017, England soccer player Eniola Aluko was called to one of the buildings here, the most intimidating arena in the country, to testify in front of a parliamentary inquiry.

If the enormity of the occasion made her feel nervous, she didn't show it, appearing calm and poised in front of panel of politicians. But aside from being a star player, Eni is also a qualified solicitor who holds a first-class law degree from Brunel, a degree she completed while playing international soccer at the highest level.

Born in Lagos, Nigeria, Eni arrived in the United Kingdom with her parents when she was six months old. The family moved into a high-rise housing project in the industrial city of Birmingham. She grew up playing soccer with her brother and the boys from the neighborhood in local parks until she "realized [she] was better than most of them." She is used to holding her own among tough crowds.

Eni, whose literary hero is Atticus Finch of *To Kill a Mockingbird*, was giving evidence at the inquiry because she believes in justice and equality and in challenging racism, no matter the cost. She was there because she wanted the Football Association to take action against England coach Mark

Sampson for allegedly racially abusing her. In her written testimony, Eni recounted the incidents. "[Fellow England player] Drew [Spence] informed me that Mark Sampson addressed her in a midfielders' meeting to ask her directly: 'How many times have you been arrested? 4 times isn't it?'"

As she wrote in her statement, "I informed Drew that this was not the first time such an offensive comment had been made by Sampson that I believed was related to race/ethnicity. . . . Sampson said in 2014 that my family should 'make sure they don't come over with Ebola' prior to an England game v Germany at Wembley."

When Eni first spoke out about Sampson's remarks in 2016, she lost her place in the England team, even though she had been capped over a hundred times over the course of her career and had scored fifteen goals in sixteen starts during Sampson's two-year tenure. Sampson, meanwhile, stated that his conscience was clear. "I've been cleared of any wrongdoing," he said after the first of three inquiries into the allegations.

Eni refused to back down or be silenced. Only an hour before parliamentary hearing, she was told that a third inquiry had finally ruled in her favor, but the caveat was that Sampson would keep his job as England coach since his comments were deemed to be "ill-judged" rather than racist. With this knowledge, she took the FA to task on their handling of her complaint and its protracted aftermath.

Eni stood in front of the panel of MPs and told them about a meeting with FA chief executive Martin Glenn in which he implied that she wouldn't receive the second half of a compensation of an $100,000 compensation package unless she wrote a favorable statement saying the FA was not institutionally racist. There were audible gasps in the room as she delivered this damming indictment of the UK's soccer chief.

"I felt [it] was bordering on blackmail," Eni continued. "I categorically refused to write any statement because I'd already suggested that it wasn't up to me to come up with that determination. I've never said that publicly. My comments have always been based on what I felt were racist [remarks] made to myself and to Drew Spence. So, for Martin Glenn to effectively suggest that I should say the FA are not institutionally racist in order to get a payment that they had already contractually agreed to, I think is again a suggestion that the case has been handled appallingly."

Glenn later disputed the claim but came in for serious criticism, though he kept his job. After over four hours of grueling testimony, Eni emerged from the halls of political justice vindicated, having received "a full and unreserved apology" from the FA and the admiration of many. She later received the remainder of her compensation settlement too. But not everyone was supportive.

Several of Eni's England teammates had made it clear they stood behind their coach. A few weeks before the hearing, those players made a public show of support for Sampson during the team's 6–0 win over Russia. When Nikita Parris scored the opening goal after eleven minutes, she and several others rushed to celebrate with Sampson on the touchline while Eni watched

in horror. Parris said afterward that the celebrations showed the England team was "united," but other players strongly disagreed. "I'm actually lost for words and feel physically sickened by all of this," said midfielder Lianne Sanderson. "They successfully manipulated the players into a *them* against *us*."

Playing for England meant everything to Eni. As a seventeen-year-old, she was so proud to be attending her first England training camp that she wore a skirt-and-blazer set, while the rest of the squad arrived in tracksuits. She scored her first goal for England in 2005 against the Czech Republic and played at the

European Championships that year while finishing high school. She even sat a history exam on the morning of England's group game against Denmark. She featured in the team at the World Cup in 2007 and was critical of the FA for their lack of investment in the women's team after they crashed out of the tournament. She was the top scorer in qualifying for the 2015 World Cup with thirteen goals, although she didn't feature as prominently at the finals.

Eni played club soccer in the United States for Saint Louis Athletica, Atlanta Beat, and Sky Blue FC and in England for Birmingham City, Charlton Athletic, and Chelsea.

She has also become a well-known TV pundit and newspaper columnist. During the men's World Cup in 2018, Eni found herself in the center of another controversy. After she delivered perceptive analysis of a game between Serbia and Costa Rica, former Manchester United forward Patrice Evra applauded her. Evra was accused of being patronizing for his palpable surprise that a woman could be so knowledgeable about men's soccer.

Sampson was eventually fired from his job as England manager for alleged conduct in his previous post at Bristol Academy, described as "overstepping the professional boundaries between player and coach." According to the FA, Sampson's dismissal was unrelated to the racist comments he was found to have made—though Eni described that as "highly questionable." Eni has yet to return to the England team, but she is enjoying her soccer again, playing in Italy for Juventus. Whatever happens next, she clearly has a bright future ahead and is strong enough to meet any challenge head-on.

As she once said, "Sport gives you real-life lessons that make you bulletproof."

MEGAN RAPINOE

MEGAN RAPINOE
FORWARD

Beneath the floodlights, the first, familiar strains of "The Star-Spangled Banner" chimed out across the still evening air. Almost everyone was standing, from the bleachers to the field. Down by the dugout, a line of substitutes in blue bibs held their hands to their hearts and sang. Alex Morgan. Alyssa Naeher. And then there was Megan Rapinoe, down on one knee.

Through the crowd, you could just about see her: the crop of short white-blonde hair, the dark, long-sleeved tracksuit, the solemn expression on her face.

It was September 2016, a few weeks before Donald Trump would be elected president and a year before "taking a knee" would escalate into a wild political firestorm, igniting social media and sparking vehemence and vitriol and a debate over the First Amendment. Pinoe was the only pro soccer player and the first white athlete in any sport to show solidarity with Colin Kaepernick, then an NFL quarterback for the San Francisco 49ers, who knelt during the national anthem to protest racial injustice in the United States.

Pinoe remained on the sidelines while the USWNT demolished Thailand 9–0 in the game, Heather O'Reilly's last for the team, but condemnation for her protest came soon after the final whistle blew. US Soccer released a strongly worded statement rebuking her, even though she had cemented her position as one of their marquee players: "As part of the privilege to represent your country, we have an expectation that our players and coaches will stand and honor our flag while the National Anthem is played."

But Pinoe continued her protest. She knelt again a few days later when the USA took on the Netherlands in another international friendly. When Coach Jill Ellis brought her on in the sixty-fourth minute, the crowd greeted her with a mix of cheers and boos, a sign of the divisiveness engulfing the country on the issues of protest and patriotism.

Pinoe said afterward she had spoken to people who were inspired by it and others who were outraged. "I welcome both of those conversations," she said. "I think they're both incredibly important." ESPN commentator Kate Fagan noted that she had bravely "opened the discussion to a new demographic."

US Soccer president Sunil Gulati made it clear where the federation stood. "There is a right to freedom of speech," he said. "She also has obligations to putting on a national team uniform, and we think those are pretty strong when you're representing the US national team and wearing the crest."

Before the NFL banned its players from protesting during the anthem, US Soccer set a precedent of reprimand. Within a few months, the board had voted unanimously to insist players stand or face serious consequences, although it was unclear exactly what those consequences would be.

The soccer writer George Quraishi criticized the move in a strongly worded op-ed for the *Washington Post*, saying that "it verbalized a message that the soccer establishment has been sending to black Americans for decades: This sport is not for you."

Pinoe accepted USSF's decision and released her own statement, making it clear that her protest was never intended to be a mark of disrespect: "It is an honor to represent the USA and all that we stand for—to be able to pull on the red, white and blue to play a game that I love. I will respect the new bylaw the leadership at USSF has put forward. That said, I believe we should always value the use of our voice and platform to fight for equality of every kind."

In a piece for the *Players' Tribune*, Pinoe explained she felt she had to "do something. Anything. We all do."

She went on to describe herself as "the same Megan Rapinoe you have known for years now . . . the same woman who has worn the Stars and Stripes across her chest, proud and beaming . . . one of the women you have called an American hero, and not just once. . . . I haven't experienced over-policing, racial profiling, police brutality or the sight of a family member's body lying dead in the street," she said. "But I cannot stand idly by while there are people in this country who have had to deal with that kind of heartache."

Although the anthem protests have been derided by those who feel that there is no place for politics in sporting competitions, as the stories in this book show, everything is impacted by politics. Sporting competitions are vital spaces for those wishing to engage in peaceful protest on the world stage. And Rapinoe is here for it.

"It's really obvious that we have very serious inequality in this country across many different spectrums," she told the *Guardian*. "Yes, we can talk about the form of protest, or the way it's done, or this or that. But it's still not really the conversation that I think we desperately need to have more of in this country."

Aside from protesting racial injustice, Pinoe has advocated for equality across the board, delving into the concept of intersectionality. "As I got more into gay rights, I got more into equal pay and you just see that it's all connected," she said. "You can't really speak out on one thing and not another. . . . We need . . . a larger conversation in this country about equality in general and respect."

⚽

It's 2019, and Pinoe is in arguably the best form of her career. Assist after assist, she is both a goalscorer and a playmaker in the USWNT, setting up eight goals in six appearances and displaying inimitable set-piece skills. She plays long balls that slice through opposition defenses, inch-perfect crosses and corners. Her game is so poised and precise that she makes it all look easy, the way only the greatest athletes can. Her strike partnership with Alex Morgan has solidified into something deep and symbiotic, and Jill Ellis has built the team around them.

Pinoe is often unselfish in her play, a trait that fits her sense of philanthropy and social justice. Here's one goal that sums her up: at the 2011 World Cup, it was she who teed up Abby Wambach to score a late equalizer against Brazil with an inch-perfect, finger kiss of a cross. It was a pivotal goal in the history of the USA team, one that propelled the women to the final and the apex of world soccer once more.

Pinoe arguably should have been among the finalists for the FIFA Player of the Year award in both 2017 and 2018. In 2017, FIFA opted to elevate an amateur player—Deyna Castellanos—to the shortlist, somewhat inexplicably. Perhaps it was Castellanos's performance at the U-17 World Cup, or perhaps it was her one million Instagram followers that turned FIFA heads; either way, the nomination annoyed many of the world's best players, Pinoe included. Without wishing any disrespect to Castellanos, Pinoe spoke out against the world game's governing body.

"It signals to us and it signals to the rest of the world that FIFA doesn't really care," she said. "If some random male player, who was not even a full professional, was nominated, I'm sure they would step in for that, so it's disappointing that the same hasn't been done for us."

Pinoe continues to speak her mind and break down barriers, although she brings a great deal of levity to her environment too. An energetic, boisterous, and quick-witted presence in the locker room, she is serious when she needs to be and a wisecracker when the mood takes her.

This year, she and her partner, WNBA star Sue Bird, became the first same-sex couple to appear on the cover of *ESPN the Magazine*'s body issue. Pinoe describes herself as a "cannon ball" who uses Sue as a sounding board before reacting to posts on social media. Megan and Sue are able to support each other's respective careers, sharing their experiences of common themes in elite sports. Their schedules match up well, and they often work out at the same time each day, sharing fitness tips and injury advice.

Pinoe came out publicly in 2012 in an interview with *Out* magazine because she felt it was necessary. "Sports in general are still homophobic," she said. "People need to see that there are people like me playing soccer for the good ol' U.S. of A."

If empathy evolves from heartbreak, then Pinoe has plenty of cause to feel for others. In the course of her career, she has suffered several major injuries, most notably a torn ACL at the end of 2015. In her personal life, she knows what it is to see a close family member lose their way: her older brother Brian has been in and struggling with drug addiction. He was incarcerated during the 2015 World Cup, watching with his fellow inmates at the Vista Detention Center as his little sister won the trophy.

She described the situation as a heartbreak unlike any she'd ever been through. "Going through that basically from the age of 10 was really hard. For a long time, you blame yourself, you think, 'What can I do?' and you're mad at him, but his addiction is not really about you. He's not doing the things that he's doing in order to hurt us—that's just a byproduct. It took me a long time to wrap my head around that."

Perhaps USA coach Ellis described her best as an ambassador on "so many levels, for women, for gay women, for people. She's just been a performer in big games. . . . She's an incredibly smart woman who can crack a room up and bring some levity. She's very special on the field, which is a given, but she's a player that recognizes there's also a life outside the game. All these players have the ability to support different things, but I think Megan has confidence in expressing herself and supporting causes that she feels strongly about. It's part of what makes her unique and special."

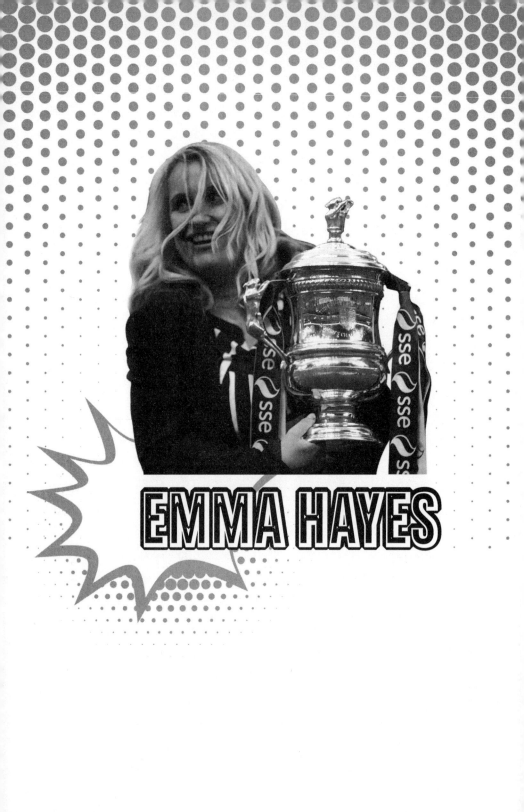

EMMA HAYES

EMMA HAYES
COACH

She has led her team to major cup finals before and led them home again clutching silverware.

For years, she has been a familiar sight on the sidelines at Stamford Bridge, this fair-haired figure in royal blue with the Chelsea crest emblazoned on her coat. What draws the attention, finally, of curious journalists who rarely spend their prose on women's soccer isn't her coaching record. Nor is it her winning methodology, tactics, or technique. It's the bulge of her stomach.

She is out there in the technical area, as she always has been, animated and focused, but now she is pregnant with twins. And the British newspapers can't get enough of it.

Pregnancy is the most arresting display of femaleness there is. How, those reporters wonder, can it be combined with something as traditionally male as soccer coaching? Motherhood has long been seen as incompatible with sport—and pregnancy, its precursor, as a fragile state of being best endured with nine months of rest. So, it figures that in the prematch press conference before Chelsea's FA Cup final game against Arsenal in 2018, Emma Hayes is met with a mixture of awe and bemusement from the waiting press. When one journalist attempts to compliment her on being a "role model," she balks.

"You wouldn't call [Manchester City Women coach] Nick Cushing a role model," she replies. "You'll call me one because I'm female."

Emma is a straight talker. It's one of the many reasons she commands respect from her players.

"While, of course, I want to influence other females in the game," she adds, "more importantly, I want to be renowned for being good tactically, being an outstanding coach who delivers well on the grass, who gets the best out of my players, and who ultimately competes for titles year in, year out."

She is clear that archaic attitudes toward motherhood need to change, that players and coaches should be celebrated for their achievements, not for an "otherness" that comprises womanhood.

"It does make it hard when there's not a lot of us doing it," she admits. "But we have to remove the gender-specific conversation about it."

"I just see myself as a coach."

⚽

There was a time, in her early twenties, when Emma considered a career in politics. She had graduated from the University of Liverpool with a bachelors' degree in European Studies and was honing in on the possible paths ahead. But the lure of soccer continued to beckon; she couldn't shake the feeling that it was her calling.

Emma grew up in north London and fell in love with soccer early on. Watching World Cups throughout the 1980s and 1990s, she developed a passion for Brazilian and Argentine soccer, what she describes as a "fluid, pacey" style of play.

Forced to end her playing career at the age of seventeen when she suffered cartilage damage to her leg, Emma found she had an affinity for coaching. She had always been an easy, open communicator with an innate understanding of the game. Coaching came naturally.

"Of course, [my] playing experience helps me to understand the kinesiology of the game—what it feels like to do certain things," she told the Coaches' Voice. "But ultimately, being able to influence people to carry out instructions on a football pitch is about your ability to connect with them. I always had a natural ability to do that."

She began coaching at the age of twenty. At twenty-five, she was living in the United States and working for the Long Island Lady Riders. One afternoon, the team's general manager, who also played for the side, turned to the team bench and offered Emma the job of head coach.

"You're twelve years older than me," Emma replied. "I'd have to coach you."

The team manager asked if she thought she could handle that.

Emma thought for a moment, then gave a direct and self-assured response: "Only if you can cope with being dropped."

The player/manager told Emma that it didn't worry her, and she hired her as coach.

Despite being younger than most of her players, Emma took the Lady Riders to the playoffs in her first season in charge. She coached them to play the "fluid, pacey" style of soccer she had grown up admiring, which she felt gave her players the most creative freedom. Meanwhile, Emma thought that the player who was also her boss had been underperforming.

Presented with the prospect of dropping her employer, Emma turned to her team. She asked each of them to anonymously fill out a form and score the others on their training performances. Then she asked them to pick their own starting lineups for the big game.

Most of the group left the player in question on the bench. When it came to picking the side for the next game, Emma opted to not to include the woman who had given her the job. "I showed her what the team thought of her, which came as quite a shock. But what it did was remove a degree of argument between her and I. And she accepted the decision."

The Lady Riders made the conference final, won the championship, and Emma was voted national coach of the year. But her tenure as team coach came to an end.

"It was a great lesson because I took a risk, knowing that I could have played it safe," she said. "I took a decision to pick winning over everything else."

⚽

Playing and working for Emma means taking responsibility. As a coach, she implements a "no excuses" culture, encouraging all team members—players and coaching staff alike, herself included—to analyze each game and think about what they can improve upon the next time.

But her approach is also especially sensitive and empathetic. When she led Chelsea to the FA Cup final in 2015, she thought deeply in the run-up to the game about how to make sure her players felt loved and appreciated. She wanted to give them "something special . . . to acknowledge how significant it was, just like you would on your wedding day or if you have a child."

A keen gardener, Emma grew pink roses, spending weeks tending and pruning them. When the players boarded the team bus to take them to the game, they discovered one on each seat, along with a poem. Instead of traveling to the game in the usual manner, headphones on or bantering at the back, the players enjoyed a quiet, tender moment with the gifts their coach had left them. Chelsea won the cup that day.

As Emma says, "To be a top coach, you have to be more than the *X*s and *O*s on the grass. You have to be able to influence their minds and their hearts."

⚽

Fast-forward to the spring of 2018.

Chelsea were playing away at Arsenal when Emma felt unwell. She was in her third trimester of pregnancy and quickly called for the doctor, who confirmed that her blood sugar levels were extremely low. Although she brought them back up again by sipping on tomato soup, something didn't feel right. She met with her consultant at the hospital the following day and was informed that one of her twins had passed away in the womb.

Emma had known from the beginning of the pregnancy that the loss of one baby was a possibility, and her doctors had prepared her for it as best they could. Even so, the impact was devastating. Yet she decided not to inform her team, instead opting to maintain her solid and focused presence in the crucial last weeks of the season. Emma led Chelsea to victory in the league and was there on the field celebrating with her players when they won the FA Cup. Not long afterward, she gave birth to both a healthy son, Harry, and Albie, the little boy she'd lost.

"I didn't start dealing with it until I'd given birth," she told the *Times*. "I'd gone from seeing my born child in one moment, then whisked off into intensive care and, within 30 minutes, saw my dead child. It was a moment I don't think I'll ever forget."

Soccer gave her a way through the grief and the elation, a chance to focus on her obligations. As she lay in hospital, recovering from the birth, she was working hard to sign new players before the transfer window closed. Emma believes that motherhood has brought an extra component to her professional life.

"I feel more energized now," she said. "My coaching has gone up a notch. I'm just driving standards at a whole new level, not letting anything go."

She is also acutely aware of how precarious life can be and grateful for what she has. When Harry was a few weeks old, Emma brought him along to France for the first of Chelsea's preseason games. Just before the trip, she posted a picture to her Twitter account. In it, she is kneeling on the field at Stamford Bridge, grinning at the camera. To her left is the FA cup, to her right the Women's Super League trophy, and in the middle, holding her hands, is baby Harry.

Her caption? "The treble."

NILLA FISCHER

NILLA FISCHER
DEFENDER

Sometimes the simplest acts take the most courage.

When Wolfsburg defender Nilla Fischer pulled on her captain's armband for a Bundesliga game against Bayern Munich, her pride took on a new resonance. With the support of her club, although not the German football federation at the time, she had insisted the armband be rainbow colored.

The Sweden defender, who came out in 2013, wanted to show her allegiance to the LGBTQ+ community and support others who are subjected to shame and stigmatized for their sexual orientation. The response she got from fans and social media was overwhelmingly positive, and the DFB lent their support. But there were shocking comments too. Like any woman or LGBTQ+ person in the public eye, especially one who engages in activism, Nilla was targeted with vitriol and death threats. One Facebook comment, she recounted to the Swedish magazine *Offside*, called her a "pervert" and suggested she "should die."

But Nilla isn't easily cowed. She is pragmatic about the misogyny and bigotry that simmers to the surface online, describing it as a "hard climate." She is determined to be strong for all the other people out there who encounter the same kinds of prejudice.

"I have to suck it up," she told the *Guardian*. "There are always going to be idiots but I still want to put things out on social media and there are a lot more good comments than bad ones."

In the course of her career, Nilla has accrued over 150 international caps, two Swedish league titles, two German league titles, three German Cups, and a Champions League. She has changed position too. In an unusual move, Sweden coach Pia Sundhage switched Nilla, by then the team captain, to the center of defense in 2013, after she had played for more than a decade in midfield. She settled into her new role immediately and scored three goals in the European Championships that year before transferring to club team Wolfsburg when the tournament was over.

What makes her a great center-back is her fearlessness. At thirty-three, Nilla is one of the world's best defenders and one of the game's leading advocates for equal pay and LGBTQ+ rights. She believes it's a battle we must all undertake. "We have to fight all the time to improve everything around us—economic factors, training times, everything."

LISA COLE

LISA COLE
COACH

I t's late February in Goroka, and Lisa Cole is standing at the edge of a soccer field.

Around her, the lush Highlands and ice-capped peaks of Papua New
Guinea (PNG) jut into the clouds. Out there in the dense canopy of forest
are some of the last remaining hunter-gatherer tribes on earth.

On the soccer field, a squad of thirty-seven girls is vying to impress her.
They hail from all around PNG; there's Christo from Kimbe, Jaqueline from
Alotau, Nicolette from Bougainville, regions as disparate as squares on a
patchwork quilt. Lisa's task is to craft a soccer team out of these girls, to convince them to play for a flag that has little meaning for any of them.

The nation of PNG is in its early forties, younger—by a whisker—than
its new women's Under 20s soccer coach. The concept of national pride is
still foreign. This is a country foisted upon a people who put tribal loyalty
before all else, an outsider's notion of nationhood that hasn't quite set yet. In
a few months' time, these girls will play for their country in the U-20 Wom-
en's World Cup. They will be the first team representing Papua New Guinea
to qualify for any major tournament ever, even if it is by the default of being
hosts.

Lisa couldn't have known the nuances of the task when a friend for-
warded her the job description or when she sent an e-mail just before the
closing date to express her interest. But she knows what it is to be in the
wilderness, figuratively at least.

A protégée of Tony DiCicco—the beloved coach of the USA women's team of the 1990s—Lisa took over his role as coach of the Boston Breakers when he retired. All was going well as she guided them through their first year in the NWSL. The Breakers were in the playoff hunt with four games left when the team owner fired her because of a minor philosophical disagreement over youth development and how to grow the team's youth program.

Nobody asked questions, not the fans or the local reporters, not like they would if a male coach had been let go while on a winning streak. It was just assumed that she had done something wrong, that perhaps she was one of those *difficult* women. She even considered reaching out to some of the reporters she knew to explain what had happened. "What they should have done is had me continue as head coach and just taken me out of the role of technical director for the club," she says, given that her coaching abilities weren't in question. As a result of the firing, she was out of the professional game for years.

Now she's here in the mists of PNG, in charge of a group of young women who will barely speak to one another. Lisa's first task is to get them to raise their heads, then to maybe make eye contact with her. They are meek and subdued. This is a society where gender violence and sexual assault are endemic. Some put the figure above 80 percent, leaving only a fraction of young women who haven't been assaulted, if that. Every player on the squad has almost certainly been through it. It has even happened since the girls arrived in Goroka for the training camp.

One morning, one of the players suffered an asthma attack during practice and went to a local hospital with one of the team assistants. While there, a doctor took the young woman into a cubicle by herself, under the premise of treating her, and sexually assaulted her.

"She wouldn't tell us initially," Lisa recalls. "We just saw her go into this really dark shell of a place. Finally, she said something."

Even though expectations for the PNG women's Under 20s team are extremely low, since they've never even played a game before, Lisa's task here is so much bigger than winning a match or even a championship—it's helping these young women to use their bodies, to reclaim them for their own. It's uniting a group of diverse players who lack confidence and skill. It's making sure that they try their best at the 2016 women's U-20 World Cup, even when they inevitably lose.

The task of the tournament itself is to "inspire the young women," or so David Chung says. He's the president of the Oceana Football Confederation (OFC) and a senior vice president of FIFA, and he's the reason Papua New Guinea is hosting this tournament, despite not having a transport system or an array of stadiums or a network of roads. Chung is adamant that the point of this U-20 World Cup is to leave a positive legacy and inspire the next generation of Papua New Guineans.

⚽

November is approaching. The tournament will soon kick off, and Lisa thinks she has whittled down the group into a team.

Goroka was tough, but less so for Lisa. She knows she had it easier as an expat living in a hotel, despite water shortages and daily power outages. They had internet, at least. She got her girls into the local school by making a deal with the headmaster. She gave them breaks to go home, even though leaving Goroka was at times almost impossible. On one occasion, a tribal argument left a debt unsettled, and violence ensued along the only road.

"The highlanders were pulling the coastal people out of vans, and they were beating them," Lisa explains. "My players were stuck for four days until this tribal war was settled, till the chiefs got together and shared a meal and somebody paid."

Lisa thinks her players might all be on the same page now, but getting here has been a process. The girls were mean to one another. They stole each other's things. Often, Lisa felt they were just telling her what they thought she wanted to hear.

"I would be looking at them and asking, 'Isn't this so-and-so's shirt?' And they're like, 'No.' I'm like, 'I'm looking at you wearing the shirt,' and they're like, 'No.' And I go, 'Okay, turn around,' and I pull the tag out, and, like, it is so-and-so's shirt. Then they'd say, 'Oh, I didn't know, Coach,' and apologize, cry, apologize."

She feels frustrated by them, sure, but mostly she feels protective. They've had to let many players go, including Mary, who, at sixteen, already has a three-year-old son. Some of the players left willingly; others were pulled out of contention by parents who didn't want their daughters to be embarrassed by losing heavily in the tournament. The ones who remain, well, she just wants them to give everything they've got.

"Let's just represent our country from the start of the game to the end of the game," she tells them. "We're going to fight. We don't care what the score is. In every minute, we're going to make the country proud. They're going to watch us, and they're going to think, 'I'm proud of their effort,' because we're not going to give up. We're not going to quit."

It may be audacious, but she wants them to score a goal. Just one goal. She has her team practice their celebrations, to get them into the mind-set of scoring more than anything. They think she's crazy, but they go along with it, trying out different styles of celebration, wheeling away from the goal, hugging, dancing.

Off the field, there are all kinds of issues trying to get the tournament off the ground. Before the opening game in Port Moresby, one of lighting banks at the Sir John Guise Stadium almost falls and smashes to the ground. Without it, there would have been no way to host games at night, since one corner of the field would have remained in total darkness.

Somehow, with a great deal of effort, it all comes together. Lisa brings in some of her most trusted people for the tournament, including Anthony DiCicco, son of her mentor, Tony, a stalwart of women's soccer whose first job as a teenager in the 1990s was as the USWNT's first team intern.

The young women of Papua New Guinea take to the field against Brazil in the World Cup opener. The Port Moresby stadium is filled with locals, cheering on their team. The lights are working. But it doesn't go well. Brazil scores after six minutes, then again five minutes later, then five minutes after that, and so on.

Lisa sends some of her subs down the touchline to warm up, and one of her players, a seventeen-year-old, walks back to the dugout in tears.

"The men in the stands were booing and heckling her and calling her nasty names and stuff because we were losing. *Of course* we're losing; we're playing Brazil. In our first-ever international game, we're playing Brazil, and we actually did pretty well for a while. We just aren't at that level."

The game ends 9–0. At the press conference after the game, Lisa lets rip. She tells the Papua New Guinean fans by way of the press, "Don't come. If you're not going to cheer, then don't come. If you're going to heckle, then don't come. We'll play in an empty stadium. Only come if you're going to support our women and recognize the sacrifices they've made."

Afterward, one of the aides tells her, "Do you realize what you said? You could probably get hung for that." She agrees. "Yeah, probably." But, still. It needed saying.

Next up: Sweden. PNG plays with a little more confidence, stringing together several passing moves while, this time, the entire crowd cheers them on. Ramona, a PNG midfielder, tries a shot from distance, but it sails just over the crossbar. It's not enough to save PNG from elimination when Sweden wins 6–0, although it's an improvement on the nine-to-nothing score line against Brazil. Most importantly for Lisa, it's a good showing overall.

All that remains for the young PNG women is to show up for the final group game, against a strong North Korea side, and play their hearts out. Seven minutes into the game, North Korea takes the lead through a defensive error. *Come on*, Lisa gestures from the bench. *Keep your heads up. Focus.*

Ten minutes pass, and all of a sudden PNG is on the break. Nicolette, the young woman from Bougainville Island, bursts forward and chips the ball over the onrushing goalkeeper. Screams of excitement reverberate through the stadium as the ball sails up and over the keeper, landing in the back of the net.

An explosion of sound. The crowd goes absolutely wild. Nicolette and her teammates completely forget the celebrations they practiced back in Goroka. She races back toward them in utter, unbridled ecstasy, arms outstretched, and they leap onto her, hugging and screaming. The entire PNG bench leaps to their feet, and Anthony DiCicco is jumping for joy because here it is, here is

World Cup '99 still making an impact nearly two decades later, on the other side of the world. Here is the USA coach's son and his mentee sharing a moment of pure joy and hope and strength with the maligned women of a small archipelago in the South Pacific through the universal language of soccer.

The only person not really celebrating is Lisa. Everyone's rushing her. The players mob her, but she stands there, like, "Yeah. They deserve it."

And they do.

North Korea wins 7–1 in the end, but it doesn't matter. PNG got their goal. All around the stadium, all around the capital city, little girls and boys are watching these young women show their fight, their power. A tiny seed of change has been sown.

⚽

What happened next is emblematic of women's soccer: some losses, some gains. The plan was for Lisa to remain in charge for four more years, to perhaps shepherd PNG to a senior World Cup and bring another group of young women up through the Under 20s. She thought she was to implement the legacy Chung had heralded, but as soon as the tournament was over, she felt him grow cold on the idea. "It was about him, you know what I mean? And not about growing the game ultimately." The FIFA vice president dismissed Lisa, ending her work with the young women's team. "Basically, once the World Cup was over, he was like, 'Okay, get out of the country.'"

Less than eighteen months later, Chung suddenly quit soccer, citing "personal reasons." Beneath it were "potential irregularities" revealed during an external audit into a multimillion-dollar construction project he was overseeing as OFC president. Chung denied any wrongdoing, and FIFA stopped short of accusing him of anything but accepted his abrupt resignation. The legacy building he had vaunted in PNG skidded to a halt.

Some of Lisa's players have been able to use the U-20 World Cup as a springboard to a better life. Nicolette, the goalscorer, is going to school in Madang. Yvonne, the captain, returned to Goroka to resit the school year and will likely go to college. Lisa's assistant, Rachel, got her OFC B coaching license and found her voice.

"She was timid," Lisa says. "She didn't talk, didn't have an opinion. Now everyone says, 'We have to tell her to shut up.' We had to tell her to be quiet because she's like, 'And you should do this.' She had the answers, and she was clear."

"There are some really good stories," Lisa says. But there are sad ones, too, with some of the young women returning home, lacking agency, already domesticized and raising children. "It's a little bit all over the place."

But the memory of that tournament and what they took from it will always remain. "When we were driving in the bus down to the stadium and swarms of people were coming and cheering on the team, it changed them in some way. They used to walk with their heads down, and when men groped them, they'd allow it. That was their reality before. Their reality today is not that."

Lisa is back in the United States, working as a coach for the Washington Spirit Academy and as a scout for the senior team. She possesses a level of experience and insight that most coaches don't have.

"It gave me a totally different perspective," she says. "Also, just such an appreciation for the game and the power of the game for bringing change."

THE FUTURE IS FEMALE
2020s

Moving into the next decade, this much is clear: women's soccer is growing exponentially and becoming increasingly competitive.

Dan Levy, who has been a key figure on the commercial side of the women's game since the 1990s, says the signs are all there. "If you look at the investment in the US alone, at what Fox has paid for the women's World Cup rights, it's much, much greater than what's been done in the past. That makes a huge difference. And now there's all sorts of ancillary coverage about the players so people are feeling more connected to the journey that is the World Cup."

International sides like Spain and England are improving as the game becomes more global and investment increases at club level. "You look at what's happening at the major clubs in Europe: Manchester City, Chelsea, Barcelona," says Levy. "They're starting to spend money on their women's program in ways that they never did before. They're looking at [starting] a Women's Club World Cup too. It's all trending in the right way."

Players like Barcelona's Patricia Guijarro and Man City's Georgia Stanway look like the kind of future stars who could lead their respective international teams to success in major tournaments. With a European Championship win under their belts and the outstanding Lieke Martens in midfield, the Netherlands also look like a team to be reckoned with in the coming years.

In the United States, the NWSL is still going strong and gaining ground, but more investment is needed to bring the facilities and conditions up to the highest standards. A 2018 exposé on Deadspin suggested that conditions at Sky Blue FC, the longest-running women's team in the United States and lone survivor from the days of the WPS, were "unsafe, unsanitary [and] unprofessional." They quoted the team's former assistant coach David Hodgson describing some of the players' living quarters as a house "you would not let your dogs sleep in" with windows boarded up with cardboard and plastic bags. This despite the fact that New Jersey governor Phil Murphy is the club's majority shareholder.

Sky Blue players have suggested the problem lies with the NWSL leadership, which has been without a commissioner since March 2017. Meanwhile, Hope Solo has criticized the leadership at the top of US Soccer, for allowing poor conditions to exist for the women. Solo believes the $100 million or so in surplus funds that the federation has accrued by virtue of its charitable status must be reinvested at a grassroots level in order to ensure the game's continued growth and an increase in diversity. Otherwise, the USWNT will not retain its dominance in future generations.

Indeed, the Under 19s side performed poorly at the 2018 World Cup, with some pundits suggesting the college system in the United States will be left behind by the player development schemes at major European clubs. Even younger than that, the participation of six- to twelve-year-olds dropped by nearly 14 percent in the USA in three years leading up to 2018. The youth system is widely regarded as bad for the game; it is a pay-to-play system where the parents of young participants pay $1,500 a year on average for them to play for a local team. Exclusionary and prescriptive, it can fail to cultivate creativity and flair.

That said, the current crop of young players in the USWNT isn't short on either of those attributes. If they can channel them into victory at the 2019 World Cup, it will help continue the dialogue about the youth system and ensure the progression of women's soccer in the United States for years to come. The pressure to remain the most successful team of all time is immense—as it is on all female athletes to keep developing the infrastructure of their own sports.

Inclusivity and diversity are key. As long as those who fund and administrate the game continue to support women from all walks of life in their efforts to play at the highest level, women's soccer will continue to be an unstoppable force, ever increasing its popularity and audience share, all over the world.

ROSE LAVELLE

ROSE LAVELLE

MIDFIELDER

"Rose Lavelle is a cheat code."

That's what the official Twitter account of the USWNT tweeted out after Lavelle's second game for the team. The accompanying clip showed the quick, rangy midfielder leaving Russia players for dust in the 2017 She Believes Cup, executing fancy footwork with the aplomb of an experienced international.

But then, Rose is experienced. She has played for the USA team at every level since the Under 18s, one of those rare talents who seem destined for greatness from the moment they have a ball at their feet.

She is, according to Jill Ellis, a unique and dynamic prospect. "Rose is a very different player," Ellis said when asked which players stood out for her. "I just think her creativity and her sense of reading the game and how she can bring out the best in her teammates is going to be an important strength for us. She's showed enough to me that she's going to be an important piece of this puzzle."

After a lengthy spell on the sidelines with a hamstring injury, Rose picked up where she left off in the 2018 Tournament of Nations. A sweetly struck half volley against Brazil reminded everyone just what she's capable of.

For the fans, it's exciting to see such prodigious ability from a player still in her early twenties. Nicknamed "Sweet Baby Rose" by her teammates, she once played a game with a list of homework assignments scrawled across her hand. Rose is funny too. She posts clips of dance breaks with teammates and

dresses her beloved bulldog, Wilma, in bikinis and rain boots. Wilma is so well known that she even has her own social media following, and Rose is such a renowned dog lover that the USWNT started the hashtag #Rosewithdogs.

Rose is emblematic of the new wave of USWNT players, as social media savvy as she is cerebral, as lighthearted as she is competitive, and as industrious as she is tricksy. All of which points to a promising future.

MALLORY PUGH

MALLORY PUGH
FORWARD

As the USWNT came back out from the halftime break in the final game of the She Believes Cup in 2018, a fan reached down from the stands to wave frantically at Mallory Pugh. The nineteen-year-old forward didn't miss a beat; she simply glanced up and blew a kiss with two fingers. It was the kind of move of which GIFs are made and circulated—such style, such swagger.

Mal has an abundance of both. When she has the ball at her feet, the crowd seems to hush, waiting with bated breath to see what she will do with it. She has blistering pace, sublime ball skills, and the kind of composure in front of goal that makes keepers quiver—and she's not averse to slotting it through their legs.

Mal is one of the most exciting of Ellis's new crop of young players. She's the youngest player to debut on the national team in nearly fifteen years and the youngest player ever to score a goal for the USA in an Olympic game, with her strike against Colombia in 2016. She was poised to play college soccer for UCLA but decided to turn professional instead, signing for the Washington Spirit in 2017. "The second she came in, we knew big things were going to come from her," said USWNT teammate Julie Ertz.

Born in Highlands Ranch, Colorado, to sporty parents Karen and Horace Pugh—Karen ran long distance; Horace played football—Mal was hooked on soccer by the time she was four years old. According to her father, she would sit in her bedroom, glued to her Hello Kitty TV as it broadcast soccer games on the Spanish-language channel Telemundo. She grew up watching her sister, Briana, who is five years her senior, play soccer in a local league and credits Briana with helping develop her ball skills as a youngster. "My sister was, of course, my role model," she told Soccer America. "The fact that she played really made me want to stick with it, keep playing and be the best player I could."

At nineteen, Mal had already secured an endorsement deal with Gatorade and been interviewed for *Teen Vogue*, with more high-profile projects to come, including rumors of a book. Her burgeoning celebrity at such a nascent stage of her career is both indicative of her obvious talent and of how much more attention the women's game attracts now as compared to those pre–World Cup winning years of the 1990s, before Mal was born.

In 2016, *Sports Illustrated Kids* ran an interview with Mal, calling her "the future of women's soccer." Her social media feeds are awhirl with praise and prom-date requests. If all this hype adds a large dose of pressure, it doesn't appear to faze her. She remains close with her high school friends, texting

with them every day, and goofs around in interviews, showing off a passion for singing by jokingly crooning through a range of different musical genres.

When she spoke to *Teen Vogue*, Mal talked about the pressures of being in the public eye, particularly how female athletes were expected to look and behave differently to their male counterparts. "Obviously, there is [a] difference," she said. "There is the pressure, but I think that staying true to yourself and your beliefs is a great way to express those things that people are expecting and I think that being authentic and real about all that stuff is the most important thing you can do."

She is now a regular starter in the USWNT alongside the heroes she looked up to when she was growing up, players like Carli Lloyd and Tobin Heath. And she has sound advice for all the young girls who are watching and hoping to emulate her.

"When I was growing up, it was about always working as hard as you can and while you're doing that, just have fun with it. You see a lot of girls in high school and they're not having fun anymore and I think that stops them from playing sports. So, I think [my advice is to] just have fun and not really take it too seriously."

LIEKE MARTENS

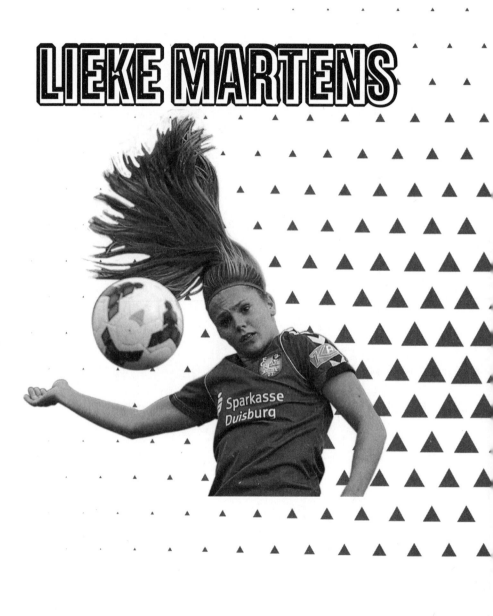

LIEKE MARTENS
MIDFIELDER

She's pressed up against the touchline with the ball at her feet and a German player snapping at her heels. Then another dashes over and crowds her out. For a split second, there's nowhere for this spry winger to go. Lieke Martens, a figure in Netherlands orange, boxed in by Bavarian black and white. A right-footer on the left wing, playing inside-out soccer.

Then, all of a sudden, she pulls out the turn, the one invented by and named for Netherlands legend Johan Cruyff. A deft little back heel, a swift change of direction, and Lieke skips away, leaving the two German players to clatter into each other like cartoon villains.

It's the kind of flair you long to see on the soccer field, rare and poetic. The Cruyff Turn. The most patriotic move she could pull out at a European Championship tournament hosted by her home nation. It's a message to the Dutch crowd: *You need a new legend? Here I am.*

⚽

Kick, thud, kick, thud.

Lieke kicks the ball against the wall of her home. She's seven years old, and this is all she wants to do. *Kick, thud.* In her mind, she's Ronaldinho, the Brazil and Barcelona legend with the incredible ball skills and the infectious grin. She wants to be like the Brazil players in the famous Joga Bonito Nike commercial for the 1998 men's World Cup, dinking and flicking the ball around an airport, wowing onlookers with their tricks.

Kick, thud. Kick, thud. She continues for hours, until her parents call her in for dinner.

In eight years' time, all this practice will pay off. She will leave her little village for the first time and join the Netherlands Under 19s team in Amsterdam. Still only fifteen, she will feel lonely and homesick, but she will stick it out. Because she has known from the very beginning that she was born to do this.

⚽

The Netherlands defeat Germany, thanks in large part to Lieke, and go on to win the 2017 European Championships on home soil. During the compe-

tition, Lieke goes from being a well-known and much-admired player within the world of women's soccer, to being well known and much admired outside of it as well. She gains a Nike contract and amasses a substantial Instagram following.

At twenty-five, she plays club soccer for Barcelona, the team she grew up adoring, the team her idol, Ronaldinho, played for. Eleven years after he was named FIFA World Player of the Year, Lieke collects the same accolade. Now, she is laser focused on the prospect of competing in World Cup 2019. One of the faces of UEFA's "Play Anywhere" campaign, Lieke is keen to show a new generation of girls that if they want to emulate her one day, all they really need are a ball and a wall.

"When I was young, I had no idea there were women players or what I could achieve. Now we are role models."

SAM KERR

SAM KERR
FORWARD

When the final whistle blew on a balmy November night in Melbourne, Australia's brightest soccer talent made her way over to the crowd. Sam Kerr had just scored twice as Australia beat China 3–0, making it nine goals in her previous five appearances.

She held out her hand to greet a group of awestruck young boys who were leaning over the barricades, grinning up at her. Somebody snapped a picture and shared it widely on social media. *Now little boys finally have someone to look up to—how great is this!*

Australia is known for its machismo, a culture firmly steeped in traditional gender roles, and yet here was an image that challenged that: a group of boys looking up to a female athlete. Yet more evidence that Sam is changing the landscape, one goal at a time.

Before soccer, the Kerr family's sporting lives revolved around Australian Rules (Aussie Rules), a hugely popular antipodean sport similar to rugby. Her father had played professionally, and Sam grew up playing on a boys' team until she came home one day with a black eye and he insisted she try soccer instead. She reluctantly agreed and quickly found that the skill set she had developed made her a standout soccer player.

By her early twenties, Sam had made a name for herself as one of the best women's soccer players in the world, smashing records and winning awards. She was the first player to score fifty goals in the NWSL. She won the ESPY for best international women's soccer player in 2018, and she has been nominated for FIFA Player of the Year twice. In addition, she was named Asian Women's Footballer of the Year, ABC Australia Sports Personality of the Year, and the NWSL's Most Valuable Player in 2017.

And that was all before she turned twenty-five. A player with pace, power, strength, creativity, and agility, Sam is a natural goalscorer who launches into a backflip every time she scores a goal. Her enthusiasm for the sport is infectious. She's humble and approachable, yet she's savvy, too, aware that she has a platform that can help effect change and promote diversity, being of Anglo-Indian heritage. In many ways, Sam is the complete package.

In 2018, she was named Young Australian of the Year. As she made her speech, she fought back tears. She said, "This award isn't just for me, it's an endorsement of the achievements of the Australian women's football team and, more broadly, Australian women's football and women's sport in general."

When the accolades come thick and fast, they can have an unmooring effect, creating off-field distractions and heaping pressure on young players. But Sam has the benefit of experience. Her older brother Daniel was a famous Aussie Rules player for the West Coast Eagles who became

Sam Kerr, left

tabloid-news fodder for bad behavior off the field. When Sam was beginning her international soccer career, traveling the world while still only a teenager, she heard about her brother's troubles from afar. There were allegations of drug use and brawling, an assault charge, and a five-night stay in maximum-security prison. She couldn't bear seeing Daniel behave in such a way and didn't speak with him for two years until he recovered, got sober, and turned his life around.

"When times were good for the West Coast Eagles, they were like movie stars," she told the *Sydney Morning Herald*. "They couldn't go out. He gave up too much of his personal life to be a professional athlete and it got to a stage where he just didn't care what people thought: he just wanted to do what he wanted. He'd be the first to admit he really stuffed up."

Sam feels she has learned from his experiences, "one hundred per cent."

In July 2017, soccer magazine *FourFourTwo* described Sam as being potentially the "best player on earth." Even with such an unassailable title, she has displayed a levelheadedness that belies her years.

"Footballers know that things like this come and go. Obviously, it's nice, right now, because sometimes you don't get the recognition, or you're not playing well. I would never sit down and say, 'Yeah, I agree with being the best in the world,' but it's obviously nice that people say that."

CARSON PICKETT

CARSON PICKETT

DEFENDER

"Imperfection is Beauty."

Those are the words inked in looping cursive script on Carson Pickett's wrist, a permanent motto for us all.

Carson is fast becoming one of the NWSL's most highly rated defenders. The Orlando Pride left-back was also born without a left forearm and hand, but she doesn't let that define her. Her playing style, poise, and passing ability are what's been getting her attention as she uses her wiles to shepherd the ball out of danger.

Simply put, "she is a very good footballer," as Pride coach Tom Sermanni told the *Guardian*.

In soccer, balance and agility are key. As a defender, Carson needs to go shoulder to shoulder with opposing players and use her body to protect the ball and herself. Achieving all that at the highest level without the use of one arm is highly impressive.

Long before she became a pro soccer player, Carson knew what it was to be watched and evaluated. The attention she got bothered her. "When I was younger I was like, *why are they staring at me?* But I always knew the answer," she said. As she grew up, she decided she would no longer worry about what people thought. Instead, she would use her perceived physical disadvantage to set a positive example.

Carson is very careful about the language others use to describe her, as well as how she defines herself. "Disability is a harsh word. It's a hold-you-back word." She prefers "unique." As in, "we're all unique in our own ways. Just because I'm missing an arm doesn't mean it's different than somebody else's uniqueness."

It was Carson's father who sparked her love for soccer. He played at college and began encouraging her to play from a young age, later coming on board as a coach for her school teams. The obsession took hold from there.

"I wasn't ever allowed to say 'no' or 'I can't.' 'Can't' was like the worst word in my vocabulary." As she grew her game, she had to become a more cerebral player to overcome the challenges. "I have to position myself before the ball even comes. I don't want to get in an arm-wrestling contest because that's just not my strength."

Carson's dedication to her game is clear. When the NWSL season ends, she travels to Australia to play for Brisbane Roar in the W-League, a schedule that allows for year-round soccer. But even more important to her than soccer is the desire to become a positive influence, someone for youngsters to look up to and feel inspired by.

"If I can give back to kids that need it most, who need that extra boost of confidence, I think that's winning in life. I don't think anything in soccer will ever come close to feeling as good as knowing that I gave back to people who needed it most."

ACKNOWLEDGMENTS

Thank you to the outstanding team at Nation Books—Clive Priddle, Katy O'Donnell, and especially Remy Cawley, who worked tirelessly on the text and artwork, improving everything with patience and enthusiasm.

This book exists thanks to the generosity of many incredible women: firstly Andrea Shallcross, to whom I can never express enough gratitude; Alessandra Bastagli, who championed the idea and guided it through its early stages; Lisa Gallagher, the agent I always hoped for—wise, warm, and erudite; Ali Lawrence, whose encouragement and feedback in the early days were invaluable; Ashley Gartland, who gave me the courage to call myself a writer; and Victoria Barrett, who thought the *Observer* sports desk needed more women way back when and who thought I should be one of them.

Thank you to the remarkable soccer stars who gave their time to this book, told their stories so beautifully, and put up with my questions and occasional outpourings of emotion. To Briana Scurry, who did this when it was still just a concept; Abby Wambach; Brandi Chastain; Joy Fawcett; Julie Foudy; Kristine Lilly; Carli Lloyd; Michelle Akers; Sun Wen; Tiffeny Milbrett; Christine Sinclair; Fara Williams; Hajra Khan; Kelly Lindsey; and Lisa Cole. Thanks also to Anthony DiCicco (an ally if ever there was one) and Dan Levy.

I am so grateful to those who helped facilitate: Aaron Heifetz, Elizabeth Sanchez, Susan Lipton, John Archibald, Brian Levine, Jake Mallen, Marcus Campbell, Haley Carter, and Catherine Marsh.

Championing and supporting other women is often done in the dark, without recognition, so for the much-needed encouragement, love, and help, thanks to Casey Hayes, Ruby Parra, Domonique Franklin, Dani Vergara, Jacqui Stix, Kay M., Alicia Johnson, and my fellow survivor, Miranda Nagalingam.

My thanks to Jonathan Santlofer, whose patience and generosity helped improve my writing and then some. And the same goes to the wholehearted, eclectic CFA-ers.

To my Sands family, who welcomed me in, thanks for the love and support. Much appreciation to all at RMC for both kindness and diligence. Gratitude for Moozie and Syd, who we lost this past year and who are sorely missed.

For those endless hours watching our beloved Leicester City lose heavily and occasionally tie, thanks always to my brother, Luke. Those were some of the best times of my life because it meant hanging out together. Who needs a Premier League title? (Although that was pretty sweet.) Thanks and love to Rachel, Bea, and Sasha too.

To my Jonpa, in whose footsteps I followed to become a writer and journalist. Thank you for the unwavering support and thoughtful suggestions and for showing me that parenting is a choice, not an obligation.

To my mum, the original soccerwoman—still playing coed every week!—whose indomitable spirit imbues every courageous thing I've ever done. Thank you for the steadfast belief and unconditional love and for reading everything I've ever put forward with an open heart and a judicious eye.

To my incredible kids, who make me catch my breath at how lucky I am. Griffin, thank you for all your "help" with this book, especially bouncing on the yoga ball—that was so helpful—and for being immensely sensitive, sweet, and wise. Thank you, Devon, who was in my tummy while I began writing this and within arm's reach while I finished, and whose future is in every word.

To Stark, a partner in the truest sense and the best pep talker there ever was: thank you for seeing how much I still loved this sport, even when I was broken by it, and for insisting I could still write about it. I am so grateful to you for making this possible, for putting your work on hold, for parenting so beautifully, and for your love, laughter, strength and positivity. Eternal thanks to last-minute London trips, QPR v. Watford, and Rob McCartney, wherever he is.

Lastly, to anyone who has ever been told they can't do the thing they love: don't listen.

Do it anyway.

IMAGE CREDITS

A League of Their Own: 2000s

Fighting for Equality: 2010s

The Future Is Female: 2020s

BIBLIOGRAPHY

AAMDSIF. "Stories of Hope: The Family of Garrett Hamm." YouTube. January 7, 2010. https://www.youtube.com/watch?v=n6ACHq5OxkU.

Abdul, Geneva. "Pakistan Captain Hajra Khan: 'It's Changing. Slowly, but It's Changing.'" *Guardian*. May 18, 2018. https://www.theguardian.com /football/2018/may/18/pakistan-hajra-khan-its-changing-geneva-abdul.

Akers, Michelle, and Gregg Lewis. *The Game and The Glory*. Grand Rapids, MI: Zonderkidz, 2000.

Ames, Nick. "Sweden's Nilla Fischer: 'There Will Always Be Idiots—But You Can't Give Up.'" *Guardian*. July 16, 2017. https://www.theguardian.com /football/2017/jul/16/nilla-fischer-sweden-idiots-not-give-up.

Associated Press. "Lyon Wins Champions League on Goalie's Kick." *New York Times*. June 2, 2017. https://www.nytimes.com/2017/06/01/sports/soccer/lyon -paris-st-germain-champions-league-final-sarah-bouhaddi.html.

———. "Neid Goes out with Gold as Germany Defeats Sweden 2–1." *USA Today*. August 20, 2016. https://www.usatoday.com/story/sports/olympics /2016/08/19/neid-goes-out-with-gold-as-germany-defeats-sweden-2-1 /89018674/.

Australian of the Year Awards. "Samantha Kerr's Speech." YouTube. February 22, 2018. https://www.youtube.com/watch?v=mjTZW9QojcU.

Ayala, Erica L., and R. J. Allen. "The NWSL's Sky Blue FC Is Falling Apart, On the Field and Off." Deadspin. August 10, 2018. https://deadspin.com/the -nwsls-sky-blue-fc-is-falling-apart-on-the-field-an-1828043155.

Barnard. "Abby Wambach: Barnard Commencement 2018." YouTube. May 18, 2018. www.youtube.com/watch?v=wJe40l2waxs.

BBC News. "Papua New Guinea Country Profile." January 14, 2018. https://www .bbc.com/news/world-asia-pacific-15436981.

BBC News (World). "Azize Ay's Family Said 'We Will Kill You' If You Play Football,' She Replied, 'Fine—but Bury Me Under the Corner Flag.' Twitter. March 10, 2017. https://twitter.com/bbcworld/status/840125414034948097 ?lang=en.

BBC Sport. "Kelly Lindsey: Afghanistan Women's Coach Says It Is 'Life or Death' for Players." BBC News. February 23, 2018. https://www.bbc.com/sport /football/43167059.

Berndt, Michael E., Jr. "Becoming Alex Morgan." ESPN Films. September 13, 2015.

Best, Katelyn. "Megan Rapinoe's New Focus: Make Soccer Inclusive for LGBTQ Kids." Outsports. June 7, 2018. https://www.outsports.com/2018/6/7 /17435834/megan-rapinoe-soccer-lgbtq-kids-project.

Borden, Sam. "Pia Sundhage of Sweden Is a Coach at Home on the Move." *New York Times*. June 9, 2015. https://www.nytimes.com/2015/06/10/sports/soccer /for-pia-sundhage-swedens-itinerant-coach-its-old-home-week.html.

Bradley, Sharon. "Matildas Star Samantha Kerr's Advice to Young Girls Playing Soccer." *Sydney Morning Herald*. November 24, 2017. https://www.smh.com .au/lifestyle/matildas-star-samantha-kerrs-advice-to-young-girls-playing-soccer -20171114-gzknrq.html.

Brennan, Patrick. "The Dick, Kerr Ladies' FC." Donmouth. Accessed October 19, 2017. http://donmouth.co.uk/womens_football/dick_kerr.html.

———. "Nettie Honeyball." Donmouth. Accessed October 23, 2017. http://www .donmouth.co.uk/womens_football/nettie_honeyball.html.

Burke, Jason. "Gambia Goalkeeper Who Died in Mediterranean Wanted to Play in Europe." *Guardian*. November 3, 2016. https://www.theguardian.com /world/2016/nov/03/gambian-goalkeeper-who-died-in-mediterranean-wanted -to-play-for-major-club.

Cabrera, Daniela. "The Best Quotes from Inspirational Badass Mia Hamm." Bustle. April 25, 2018. https://www.bustle.com/articles/91313-8-inspirational-mia -hamm-quotes-that-can-get-you-through-anything.

Carlisle, Jeff. "Becky Sauerbrunn at Heart of U.S. Defense in Run to World Cup Final." ESPN. July 3, 2015. http://www.espn.com/espnw/news-commentary /2015worldcup/article/13195659/becky-sauerbrunn-heart-us-defense-run -world-cup-final.

Cathal, Kelly. "FIFA Does Canadian Women's Soccer a Favour by Suspending Christine Sinclair: Kelly." Thestar.com. October 15, 2012. https://www.thestar .com/sports/soccer/2012/10/15/fifa_does_canadian_womens_soccer_a_favour _by_suspending_christine_sinclair_kelly.html.

————. "The Greatest Game of Women's Soccer Ever Played." *Globe and Mail.* June 19, 2017. https://www.theglobeandmail.com/sports/soccer/an-oral-history-soccer/article24914992/.

Central Intelligence Agency. "The World Factbook: PAPUA NEW GUINEA." September 26, 2018. https://www.cia.gov/library/publications/the-world-factbook/geos/pp.html.

Chastain, Brandi, and Gloria Averbuch. *It's Not about the Bra: How to Play Hard, Play Fair, and Put the Fun Back into Competitive Sports.* New York: HarperResource, 2004.

The Coaches' Voice. "Emma Hayes: My Calling." February 21, 2018. https://www.coachesvoice.com/my-calling/.

————. "Emma Hayes on the No-Excuse Culture That Forms Part of Her Coaching Philosophy." YouTube. February 27, 2018. https://www.youtube.com/watch?v=Vow9ZCqQ1lk.

Cohen, Andrew. "The Women's United Soccer Association Breaks Mold." Athletic Business. October 2000. https://www.athleticbusiness.com/the-womens-united-soccer-association-breaks-mold.html.

Conheeney, Kelly. "Over and Over Again." July 17, 2018. https://ckelly919.wixsite.com/website-1/single-post/2018/07/09/Over-and-Over-again.

Cooky, Cheryl, Michael A. Messner, and Michaela Musto. "'It's Dude Time!' A Quarter Century of Excluding Women's Sports in Televised News and Highlight Shows." *Communication & Sport* 3, no. 3 (June 2015): 261–287.

Cretaz, Britni De La. "This 19-Year-Old Soccer Star Just Became Gatorade's Youngest Female Athlete." *Teen Vogue.* February 20, 2018. https://www.teenvogue.com/story/mallory-pugh-gatorade-youngest-athlete.

Culver, Jordan. "Orlando Pride Star Alex Morgan Makes Movie Debut in 'Alex & Me.'" Pro Soccer USA. June 12, 2018. https://www.prosoccerusa.com/nwsl/orlando-pride/orlando-pride-star-alex-morgan-makes-movie-debut-in-alex-me/.

Daily Sabah. "Age Just a Number as Female Footballer, 49, Takes Field." February 27, 2017. https://www.dailysabah.com/football/2017/02/28/age-just-a-number-as-female-footballer-49-takes-field.

Das, Andrew. "In Fight for Equality, U.S. Women's Soccer Team Leads the Way." *New York Times.* March 5, 2018. https://www.nytimes.com/2018/03/04/sports/soccer/us-womens-soccer-equality.html.

————. "U.S. Soccer Suspends Hope Solo and Terminates Her Contract." *New York Times.* August 25, 2016. https://www.nytimes.com/2016/08/25/sports/hope-solo-suspended-for-six-months-by-us-soccer.html.

Davis, David. "How the Most Iconic Photo in Women's Soccer Was Almost Never Taken." Deadspin. June 8, 2015. https://deadspin.com/how-the-most -iconic-photo-in-womens-soccer-was-almost-n-1708269396.

Davis, Noah. "From Last Chance to the American Messi: The Rise of Rose Lavelle." Bleacher Report. October 3, 2017. https://bleacherreport.com/articles /2721506-from-last-chance-to-the-american-messi-the-rise-of-rose-lavelle.

Dewey, Caitlin. "DIY." *Players' Tribune*. January 16, 2018. https://www.theplayers tribune.com/en-us/articles/moya-dodd-common-goal.

———. "Her Biggest Save." *Washington Post*. November 2, 2013. Accessed October 3, 2018. http://www.washingtonpost.com/sf/national/2013/11/02/her -biggest-save/.

———. "Women's Struggle in the Beautiful Game." *Aspetar Sports Medicine Journal*. June 2018. http://www.aspetar.com/journal/viewarticle.aspx?id=401.

Drape, Joe. "Youth Soccer Participation Has Fallen Significantly in America." *New York Times*. July 14, 2018. https://www.nytimes.com/2018/07/14/sports/world -cup/soccer-youth-decline.html.

Dunn, Carrie. "Sylvia Gore Obituary." *Guardian*. September 15, 2016. https:// www.theguardian.com/football/2016/sep/15/sylvia-gore-obituary.

Dure, Beau. "Suspended WPS Season Brings Uncertainty." ESPN. January 30, 2012. http://www.espn.com/espnw/news-commentary/article/7520830 /suspended-wps-season-brings-uncertainty.

ESPN. "The Body Issue 2018." June 29, 2018. http://www.espn.com/espn/ feature/story/_/id/23851669/espn-body-issue-2018/?sf192505289=1#! bird-rapinoe.

ESPN Media Zone. "Julie Foudy." August 13, 2018. https://espnmediazone.com/us /bios/foudy_julie/.

Farley, Richard. "Why Jill Ellis and the USWNT Can't Afford Another She Believes Cup Catastrophe." *FourFourTwo*. February 27, 2018. https://www.fourfourtwo .com/us/features/why-jill-ellis-uswnt-shebelieves-cup-preview-world-cup.

FIFA.com. "FIFA U-20 Women's World Cup France 2018—News—Scott's Inspiring Journey to PNG—FIFA.com." December 8, 2016. https://img.fifa.com /u20womensworldcup/news/scott-s-inspiring-journey-to-png-2859047.

———. "A Fond Farewell to Birgit Prinz." March 28, 2012. http://www.fifa.com /fifaworldcup/news/y=2012/m=3/news=fond-farewell-birgit-prinz-1607891 .html.

———. "Sissi, a Brazilian Trailblazer." August 12, 2016. http://www.fifa.com /womens-football/news/y=2016/m=8/news=sissi-a-brazilian-trailblazer -2821914.html.

FIFATV. "Greatest Women's World Cup Goal? Rise in 1999." YouTube. May 11, 2015. https://www.youtube.com/watch?v=RrVZahMI_sw.

———. "Homare Sawa: A Trophy Full of Laughter and Pain." YouTube. June 7, 2015. https://www.youtube.com/watch?v=SPh0S747JF8.

———. "Match 17: Korea DPR v Papua New Guinea." YouTube. November 20, 2016. https://www.youtube.com/watch?v=i-kxgfrZSVk.

———. "Nadine Angerer: The Pressure was On Marta." YouTube. June 5, 2015. https://www.youtube.com/watch?v=Th85shgSwQI.

———. "Sun Wen: 1991 Debut Was Unforgettable." YouTube. June 4, 2015. https://www.youtube.com/watch?v=uAVi3Qg1O5I.

Foudy, Julie. *Choose to Matter: Being Courageously and Fabulously You*. Los Angeles: ESPN W, 2017.

FourFourTwo. "Reading's Fara Williams Scores Incredible Goal from Kick-Off Against Arsenal." November 7, 2017. https://www.fourfourtwo.com/features /readings-fara-williams-scores-incredible-goal-kick-against-arsenal.

French, Scott. "Why Tiffeny Milbrett Is One of U.S. Soccer's All-Time Greats." *FourFourTwo*. May 4, 2017. https://www.fourfourtwo.com/us/features/why -tiffeny-milbrett-us-soccer-uswnt-all-time-greats.

Goff, Steven. "WPS Shutdown Might Mark the End of U.S. Women's Pro Soccer Efforts." *Washington Post*. January 30, 2012. https://www.washington post.com/blogs/soccer-insider/post/wps-shutdown-might-mark-the-end-of -us-womens-pro-soccer-efforts/2012/01/30/gIQAGBHKdQ_blog.html?utm _term=.842da918dd15.

Goldberg, Jamie. "After Storied Career, Nadine Angerer Guiding Next Generation as Portland Thorns Goalkeeper Coach." OregonLive.com. March 7, 2018. https://www.oregonlive.com/portland-thorns/2018/03/portland_thorns_goal keeper_coa.html.

———. "Alex Morgan Prepared for Spotlight at Women's World Cup, Both on and off the Pitch." OregonLive.com. May 9, 2015. https://www.oregonlive.com /sports/index.ssf/2015/05/alex_morgan_prepared_for_spotl.html.

Goldman, Bruce. "Researchers Identify Biomarkers Associated with Chronic Fatigue Syndrome Severity." EHR National Symposium. July 31, 2017. https:// med.stanford.edu/news/all-news/2017/07/researchers-id-biomarkers-associated -with-chronic-fatigue-syndrome.html.

Gordon, James Bridget. "US Soccer Is Getting Ready to Crack Down on Megan Rapinoe's Kneeling Protests." Pastemagazine.com. November 14, 2016. https:// www.pastemagazine.com/articles/2016/11/us-soccer-is-getting-ready-to-crack -down-on-megan.html.

Gowon, Akpodonor. "My Voice Is for the Nigerian Girl-Child, Says Asisat Osho-ala." *Guardian Nigeria.* January 13, 2018. https://guardian.ng/sport/my-voice -is-for-the-nigerian-girl-child-says-asisat-oshoala/.

Hall, Matthew. "Hope Solo Interview: 'I Was Told to Shut My Mouth and Play Soccer.'" *Guardian.* February 7, 2018. https://www.theguardian.com/football/2018 /feb/07/hope-solo-interview-i-was-told-to-shut-my-mouth-and-play-soccer.

———. "'I Use What God Gave Me': Carson Pickett on Life as a One-Handed Professional Footballer." *Guardian.* June 1, 2018. https://www.theguardian .com/football/2018/jun/01/carson-pickett-orlando-pride-womens-national -soccer-league.

Hamm, Mia, and Aaron Heifetz. *Go for the Goal: A Champions Guide to Winning in Soccer and Life.* New York: Quill, 2002.

Harwell, Drew. "Why Hardly Anyone Sponsored the Most-Watched Soccer Match in U.S. History." *Washington Post.* July 6, 2015. https://www.washingtonpost .com/news/wonk/wp/2015/07/06/the-sad-gender-economics-of-the-womens -world-cup/?utm_term=.2d25eae5a542.

Hays, Graham. "Mallory Pugh Powers U.S. Women's National Soccer Team to 5–1 Win in 2018 Opener." ESPN. January 21, 2018. http://www.espn.com /espnw/sports/article/22173575/mallory-pugh-powers-us-women-national -soccer-team-5-1-win-2018-opener.

Hays, Kate, Owen Thomas, Ian Maynard, and Mark Bawden. "The Role of Confi-dence in World-Class Sport Performance." *Journal of Sports Sciences* 27, no. 11 (2009): 1185–1199.

Hill, Jemele. "Rapinoe on Body Issue Cover: 'Visibility Is Important.'" ESPN. June 25, 2018. http://www.espn.com/wnba/story/_/page/espnwbodybirdrapinoe /wnba-sue-bird-uswnt-megan-rapinoe-debate-better-athlete-body-issue-2018.

Hjelm, Jonny, and Eva Olofsson. "A Breakthrough: Women's Football in Sweden." *Soccer & Society* 4, no. 2–3 (2003): 182–204.

Hoff, Eli. "Mia Hamm on LAFC Ownership, Inaugural Season, More." Angels on Parade. July 22, 2018. https://www.angelsonparade.com/2018/7/22/17600816 /lafcs-mia-hamm-on-mls-ownership-inaugrual-season-more.

Hollersen, Wiebke. "The Beautiful Game: Germany Feels Strain of World Cup Ex-pectations." Spiegel Online. July 5, 2011. http://www.spiegel.de/international /germany/the-beautiful-game-germany-feels-strain-of-world-cup-expectations -a-772399.html.

Jackson, Melanie. "Four Years Later: Abby Wambach's 2011 Header Heard 'Round the World." ESPN. June 15, 2015. http://www.espn.com/espnw/news-commentary

/2015worldcup/article/13075090/abby-wambach-2011-header-heard-round
-world.

Jacobs, Barbara. *The Dick, Kerr's Ladies*. London: Robinson, 2004.

Japan Times. "Sawa Ending Illustrious Career with No Regrets." December 17, 2015. https://www.japantimes.co.jp/sports/2015/12/17/soccer/sawa-ending
-illustrious-career-no-regrets/.

Johnk, Zach. "National Anthem Protests by Black Athletes Have a Long History." *New York Times*. September 25, 2017. https://www.nytimes.com/2017/09/25
/sports/national-anthem-protests-black-athletes.html.

Jung, Chris. "Germany's Silvia Neid Looks to Sign Off with Gold." UEFA.com. August 19, 2016. https://www.uefa.com/womensworldcup/news/newsid
=2396727.html.

"Keeping Score Episode 1." Vimeo. November 26, 2018. https://vimeo.com
/183582880.

Kelner, Martha. "Eniola Aluko: The Footballing Whistleblower Whose Hero Is Atticus Finch." *Guardian*. October 21, 2017. https://www.theguardian
.com/football/2017/oct/21/footballer-whose-hero-is-atticus-finch-from
-to-kill-a-mockingbird.

———. "FA Needs Urgent Change at the Top after Damning Day at Eni Aluko Hearing." *Guardian*. October 18, 2017. https://www.theguardian
.com/football/blog/2017/oct/18/fa-needs-urgent-change-at-the-top-after
-damning-day-at-eni-aluko-hearing.

Kessel, Anna. "Hope Powell's Ruthless Brilliance Will Not Be Missed by England Players." *Guardian*. August 22, 2013. https://www.theguardian.com/football
/blog/2013/aug/22/hope-powell-england-players.

Kulish, Nicholas. "Women's World Cup 2011: New Doubts Surround Birgit Prinz." *New York Times*. July 4, 2011. https://www.nytimes.com/2011/07/05/sports
/soccer/womens-world-cup-2011-new-doubts-surround-birgit-prinz.html.

Laverty, Rich. "Nilla Fischer in Conversation: The 150-Cap Sweden Star's Journey to the Top." These Football Times. July 31, 2018. https://thesefootball
times.co/2018/01/26/nilla-fisher-in-conversation-the-150-cap-sweden
-stars-journey-to-the-top/.

Lee, James F. *The Lady Footballers: Struggling to Play in Victorian Britain*. London: Routledge, 2011.

Leigh, Mary H., and Thérèse M. Bonin. "The Pioneering Role of Madame Alice Milliat and the FSFI in Establishing International Trade and Field Competition for Women." *Journal of Sport History* 4, no. 1 (1977): 72–83.

Leighton, Tony. "Farewell to Kelly Smith, England and Arsenal's 'Once in a Life-time' Forward." *Guardian.* January 12, 2017. https://www.theguardian.com /football/2017/jan/12/farewell-kelly-smith-england-arsenal-retired.

Leyden, Erin. "Nine for IX: The '99ers." ESPN Films. August 20, 2013.

Lilly, Kristine. "Always Believe!" KristineLilly13.com. Accessed October 3, 2018. http://kristinelilly13.com/kristine/.

Lindsey, Kelly. "American Coach of Afghanistan Women's Soccer Team Has One Goal: Hope." Interview by Amy Bracken. PRI's *The World.* February 21, 2018.

Lloyd, Carli, and Wayne R. Coffey. *When Nobody Was Watching: My Hard-Fought Journey to the Top of the Soccer World.* Boston: Mariner Books, Houghton Mifflin Harcourt, 2017.

Longman, Jere. "Norway's Rivalry with U.S. Is Intense." *New York Times.* June 13, 1999. https://www.nytimes.com/1999/06/13/sports/women-s-world-cup -norway-s-rivalry-with-us-is-intense.html.

———. "Women's Soccer League Folds on World Cup's Eve." *New York Times.* September 16, 2003. https://www.nytimes.com/2003/09/16/sports/soccer -women-s-soccer-league-folds-on-world-cup-s-eve.html.

Los Angeles Times. "WUSA's Inaugural Game Is a Big Winner at the Gate." April 15, 2001. http://articles.latimes.com/2001/apr/15/sports/sp-51398.

Loudin, Amanda. "The Crusader Protecting Child Athletes from Sex Abuse." Outside Online. April 5, 2018. https://www.outsideonline.com/2277976 /fighting-sexual-abuse-behalf-young-athletes.

MacDonald, Frank. "When the U.S. Women's National Team Was Made in Washington." Society for American Soccer History. July 6, 2015. http:// www.ussoccerhistory.org/when-the-u-s-womens-national-team-was-made-in -washington/.

Mahr, Krista. "The Swift Kicker Behind Japan's Women's Soccer Rise." *Time.* July 19, 2012. http://olympics.time.com/2012/07/19/womens-football-nadeshiko -japan-homare-sawa/.

Marta. "Letter to My Younger Self." *Players' Tribune.* August 24, 2017. https://www .theplayerstribune.com/en-us/articles/marta-brazil-letter-to-my-younger-self.

Martens, Lieke. "Be Like Ronaldinho." *Players' Tribune.* March 8, 2018. https:// www.theplayerstribune.com/en-us/articles/lieke-martens-be-like-ronaldinho.

Martinelli, Michelle R. "U.S. Soccer Is Forcing Players to 'Stand Respectfully' for National Anthem." *USA Today.* March 4, 2017. https://ftw.usatoday .com/2017/03/national-anthem-protest-us-soccer-megan-rapinoe-colin -kaepernick-racial-injustice-lgbtq.

McCauley, Kim. "What on Earth Is U.S. Soccer Doing with Jaelene Hinkle?" SBNation.com. July 25, 2018. https://www.sbnation.com/soccer/2018/7 /25/17609060/jaelene-hinkle-uswnt-roster-tournament-of-nations-roster -homophobic-700-club-interview.

McRae, Donald. "Fara Williams: 'I Had Football. A Lot of Homeless Girls Have Nothing.'" *Guardian*. November 17, 2014. https://www.theguardian.com /football/2014/nov/17/fara-williams-football-homeless.

Met Office. "August 1920." Monthly Weather Report of the Meteorological Office. Accessed February 11, 2018. https://www.metoffice.gov.uk/binaries/content /assets/mohippo/pdf/g/9/aug1920.pdf.

Meuren, Daniel. "Im Gespräch: Birgit Prinz: 'Ich Wollte Nie Die Welt Retten.'" *Frankfurter Allgemeine*. March 26, 2012. http://www.faz.net/aktuell/sport /fussball/im-gespraech-birgit-prinz-ich-wollte-nie-die-welt-retten-11698795 .html.

Miller, Gretchen, Jonathan Scheyer, and Emily Sherrard. "Women's United Soccer Association—Soccer Politics." Duke University. 2015. https://sites.duke.edu /wcwp/research-projects/womens-soccer-in-the-u-s/womens-soccer-after-1999 /womens-united-soccer-assocation/.

Missio, Sonja Cori. "Moya Dodd: 'Football Was for Men for So Long. I'd like to Deliver a Better Game.'" *Guardian*. August 12, 2014. https://www.theguardian. com/football/2014/aug/12/moya-dodd-football-women-fifa.

Moore, Glenn. "Alex Morgan Has the World at Her Feet." *Independent*. June 25, 2015. https://www.independent.co.uk/sport/football/international/womens -world-cup-2015-alex-morgan-has-the-world-at-her-feet-10346675.html.

———. "How Nadia Nadim Escaped the Taliban to Become a True Football Trailblazer." *Independent*. August 6, 2017. https://www.independent.co.uk /sport/football/international/womens-euros-2017-european-championship -spain-vs-denmark-nadia-nadim-taliban-a7866206.html.

Morgan, Alex. *Breakaway: Beyond the Goal*. New York: Simon & Schuster BFYR, 2017.

Murdock, Sebastian, and Michael McLaughlin. "Athletes Who Inspired off the Field in 2016." *Huffington Post*. December 22, 2016. https://www.huffington post.com/entry/athletes-who-took-a-stand-in-2016_us_58557f29e4b08deb b7897eee.

Murray, Caitlin. "Women's World Cup: Bigger, Better—But Still Treated as the Poor Relation." *Guardian*. July 4, 2015. https://www.theguardian.com /football/2015/jul/04/womens-world-cup-fifa-tournament-mens.

Myers, Rebecca. "Emma Hayes: 'Losing a Child Makes You More Vulnerable but More Grateful.'" *Sunday Times*. August 5, 2018. https://www.thetimes.co.uk /article/06763938-97fe-11e8-9fa4-edef73b234ec.

National Research Council. *Learning, Remembering, Believing: Enhancing Human Performance*. Washington, DC: National Academies Press, 1994.

National Soccer Coaches Association of America. "NSCAA Member Lisa Cole Taking on New Challenges." February 16, 2016. http://ww2.nscaa.com/news /2016/02/lisa-cole-as-png-u20-coach.

Newsham, Gail J. *In a League of Their Own: The Dick, Kerr Ladies 1917–1965*. S.l.: Paragon Publishing, 2018.

NWSL Soccer. "Lifetime Player Spotlight: Carson Pickett, Orlando Pride." You-Tube. July 8, 2018. https://www.youtube.com/watch?v=X9gkaCxg5LY.

Oatway, Caroline. "Nadia Nadim | An Incredible Journey." Manchester City FC. September 28, 2017. https://www.mancity.com/news/mcwfc/mcwfc news /2017/september/nadia nadim man city women long read.

Omaha.com. "Kelly Lindsey—No. 70—Nebraska's Greatest Athletes." 2005. https://dataomaha.com/neb100/player/70.

Oxenham, Gwendolyn. "Pinoe's Biggest Fan." US Soccer. June 16, 2017. https://www .ussoccer.com/stories/2015/06/14/15/21/150614-wnt-rapinoe-brother-feat.

———. *Under the Lights and in the Dark: Inside the World of Women's Soccer*. London: Icon Books, 2017.

Parker, Dani. "Alex & Me: A Film Inspired by a Daughter's Love of the Beautiful Game and Her Idol." Girls Soccer Network. July 7, 2018. https://girlssoccer network.com/lifestyle/alex-morgan-me-film-girls-soccer/.

Pantorno, Joe. "USA vs. Thailand Women's Soccer: Score and Twitter Reaction for 2016 Friendly." Bleacher Report. September 27, 2017. https://bleacherreport .com/articles/2663979-usa-vs-thailand-womens-soccer-score-and-twitter -reaction-for-2016-friendly.

Pentz, Matt. "Megan Rapinoe: 'God Forbid You Be a Gay Woman and a Person of Color in the US.'" *Guardian*. March 25, 2017. https://www.theguardian.com /football/2017/mar/25/megan-rapinoe-gay-woman-person-color-us.

———. "Why U.S. Women's Soccer Pioneer Sharon McMurtry Matters to This Generation of Players." *Seattle Times*. August 30, 2016. https://www.seattle times.com/sports/reign/why-us-womens-soccer-pioneer-sharon-mcmurtry -matters-to-this-generation-of-players/.

Peterson, Anne M. "Rapinoe Says She Will Respect US Soccer Policy for An-thems." AP News. March 7, 2017. https://www.apnews.com/e7de95b78

c9b42e5bc344b501b23f80e/Rapinoe-says-she-will-respect-US-Soccer
-policy-for-anthems.

Pirnia, Tara. "How an Iranian Soccer Star Fought to Play for Her National Team."
ESPN Films. 2016. http://www.espn.com/espnw/video/17124272/how-iranian
-soccer-star-fought-play-national-team.

Powell, Hope, and Marvin Close. *Hope: My Life in Football*. London: Bloomsbury,
2016.

Q13 Fox. "Sue Bird and Megan Rapinoe: WA Most Wanted." YouTube. July 2,
2018. https://www.youtube.com/watch?v=zT4uCSkdFh8.

Quraishi, George. "U.S. Soccer Is Trying to Dodge Politics by Banning Anthem Protests. It Can't." *Washington Post*. March 9, 2017. https://www.washingtonpost
.com/posteverything/wp/2017/03/09/banning-anthem-protests-means-u-s
-soccer-is-siding-against-black-lives-matter/?utm_term=.ae17c20b6cd6.

Rapinoe, Megan. "Why I Am Kneeling." *Players' Tribune*. October 6, 2016.
https://www.theplayerstribune.com/en-us/articles/megan-rapinoe-why-i-am
-kneeling.

Rape, Avery. "Carla Overbeck Still Inspires." ESPN. August 27, 2013. http://www
.espn.com/blog/espnw/post/_/id/6919/carla-overbeck-still-inspires-at-unc?
utm_source=twitterfeed&utm_medium=twitter.

Roberts, Gareth. "My Knowsley: Sylvia Gore." Knowsley News. Winter 2005.
http://www.knowsley.gov.uk/pdf/issue4_winter05.pdf.

Rohn, Tim, and Tariq Panja. "FIFA Vice President Quits After Audit Raises Questions." *New York Times*. April 6, 2018. https://www.nytimes.com/2018/04/06
/sports/soccer/fifas-vice-president-david-chung-resigns.html.

Rogers, Martin. "Sweden Coach Pia Sundhage Rips U.S. Players." *USA Today*.
June 9, 2015. https://www.usatoday.com/story/sports/soccer/2015/06/09/pia
-sundhage-rips-uswnt/28773877/.

Rumsby, Ben. "Mark Sampson Found Guilty of Racially Abusing Eni Aluko and
Drew Spence." *Telegraph*. October 18, 2017. https://www.telegraph.co.uk
/football/2017/10/18/mark-sampson-found-guilty-racially-abusing-eni-aluko
-drew-spence/.

Rutherford, Kristina. "The Evolution of Christine Sinclair." Sportsnet.ca. 2015.
https://www.sportsnet.ca/soccer/big-read-the-evolution-of-christine-sinclair/.

Saul, Heather. "Niloufar Ardalan: Women Launch Hashtag in Solidarity with Iranian." *Independent*. September 18, 2015. https://www.independent.co.uk/news
/people/niloufar-ardalan-women-launch-hashtag-in-solidarity-with-iranian
-footballer-stopped-by-husband-from-10508093.html.

Scott, Mark. "Bougainville: Island of Scars." *New Zealand Geographic*, Issue 46, April–June 2000. Accessed October 3, 2018. https://www.nzgeo.com/stories /bougainville-island-of-scars/.

Shah, Syed Ali, and Imtiaz Ali. "Pakistan Football Team Striker Shahlyla Baloch Dies in Karachi Car Crash." DAWN.com. October 13, 2016. https://www .dawn.com/news/1289729.

Shafqat Khan, Maha. "Hajra Khan: The World at Her Feet." *Nation*. April 27, 2018. https://nation.com.pk/28-Apr-2018/hajra-khan-the-world-at-her-feet.

Shipley, Amy. "Milbrett: U.S. Women's Unsung Star." *Washington Post*. June 18, 1999. http://www.washingtonpost.com/wpsrv/sports/soccer/longterm/world cup99/teams/articles/milbrett18.htm.

Sieff, Kevin. "She Was Gambia's Star Goalkeeper. But She Died as Yet Another Drowned Migrant in the Mediterranean." *Washington Post*. November 4, 2016. https://www.washingtonpost.com/news/worldviews/wp/2016/11/04/a -gambian-soccer-star-becomes-the-tragic-face-of-this-years-migrant-deaths-in -the-mediterranean/?utm_term=.bc85ccb60245.

Simkin, John. "History of Women's Football." Spartacus Educational. March 2015. https://spartacus-educational.com/Fwomen.htm.

———. "Nettie Honeyball." Spartacus Educational. August 2014. http:// spartacus-educational.com/Fhoneyball.htm.

Smith, Gary. "Everyone Knows Mia Hamm, No One Knows Mia Hamm." SI.com. September 22, 2003. https://www.si.com/vault/2003/09/22/350152 /mia-hamm-us-womens-national-team-greatest.

Smith, Kelly, and Lance Hardy. *Footballer: My Story*. London: Corgi Books, 2013.

Solo, Hope. "Something Is Broken When the USA Women Are Dominated by White Girls Next Door." *Guardian*. September 4, 2018. https://www.theguardian .com/football/2018/sep/04/usa-womens-soccer-team-white-hope-solo.

Solo, Hope, and Ann Killion. *Solo: A Memoir of Hope*. New York: Harper, 2013.

Straus, Brian. "Women's Pro Soccer League Forced to Fold." *Washington Post*. September 16, 2003. https://www.washingtonpost.com/archive/politics/2003/09 /16/womens-pro-soccer-league-forced-to-fold/d3e974bd-62a9-4e41-ad11 -ab524c2961e3/?utm_term=.ad72f41040cd.

Svrluga, Barry. "U.S. Women Win Soccer Gold Medal." *Washington Post*. August 27, 2004. http://www.washingtonpost.com/wp-dyn/articles/A36021-2004Aug26 .html.

Tait, Robert. "Iranian Women Kick Out Against Football Ban." *Guardian*. June 5, 2005. https://www.theguardian.com/world/2005/jun/06/iran.roberttait.

Taylor, Louise. "England's Fara Williams: 'We're Feeling the Pain but If You Want to Win It Needs to Hurt.'" *Guardian*. July 13, 2017. https://www.theguardian.com/football/2017/jul/13/england-fara-williams-euro-2017-mark-sampson.

———. "Leading Coaches Question FA Line over Phil Neville's England Appointment." *Guardian*. January 26, 2018. https://www.theguardian.com/football/2018/jan/26/phil-neville-fa-england-women-vera-pauw-carolina-morace.

Theisen, Lauren. "Megan Rapinoe Calls FIFA 'Old, Male, And Stale' After Awards Controversy." Deadspin. October 23, 2017. https://deadspin.com/megan-rapinoe-calls-fifa-old-male-and-stale-after-a-1819781188.

———. "Megan Rapinoe Is Still Pulling All the Right Strings." Deadspin. July 30, 2018. https://deadspin.com/megan-rapinoe-is-still-pulling-all-the-right-strings-1827970577.

Time. "Women's World Cup: See the Top 8 Moments in Its History." June 9, 2015. http://time.com/3907383/womens-world-cup-extraordinary-moments/.

Unicef. "Alex Morgan's Global Mission." November 20, 2016. https://unicefkidpower.org/champions/global-mission-alex-morgan/.

UEFA.com. "'Women's Football Hasn't Had Its Heyday Yet'—Silvia Neid." October 3, 2018. https://www.uefa.com/insideuefa/football-development/technical/coach-education/news/newsid=2453887.html.

US Soccer. "The Journey: Becky Sauerbrunn." YouTube. November 8, 2017. https://www.youtube.com/watch?v=5eQaF5NBVQA.

———. "Midfielder Rose Lavelle Joins U.S. WNT Training Camp Prior to China Friendlies." June 3, 2018. https://www.ussoccer.com/stories/2018/06/03/18/48/20180603-news-wntvchn-lavelle-joins-camp.

———. "10 Things About Mallory Pugh." YouTube. August 26, 2013. https://www.youtube.com/watch?v=zKA0abpcOQU.

———. "U.S. WNT Flashback—20th Anniversary of First-Ever Match." August 18, 2005. https://www.ussoccer.com/stories/2014/03/17/13/13/u-s-wnt-flashback-20th-anniversary-of-first-ever-match-sharon-mcmurtry.

———. "U.S. WNT Responds to Women's United Soccer Association Suspending Operations." September 16, 2003. https://www.ussoccer.com/stories/2014/03/17/13/55/u-s-wnt-responds-to-womens-united-soccer-association-suspending-operations.

Wahl, Grant. "USWNT Players Voiced Deep Concerns about Ellis in 2017." SI.com. July 26, 2018. https://www.si.com/soccer/2018/07/26/insider-uswnt-players-concerned-jill-ellis-firing-jaelene-hinkle-call.

Walker, Sam. *The Captain Class: The Hidden Force Behind the World's Greatest Teams.* New York: Penguin Random House, 2017.

Wallerson, Ryan. "Why Women's Soccer Was Banned in Brazil—Until 1979." OZY. October 25, 2016. https://www.ozy.com/the-huddle/why-womens-soccer -was-banned-in-brazil-until-1979/72241.

Wambach, Abby. *Forward: A Memoir.* New York: Dey St., 2017.

Washington Spirit. "Lisa Cole Joins Washington Spirit as Academy Coach, Pro Team Scout." May 23, 2018. http://washingtonspirit.com/pro/lisa-cole-joins -washington-spirit-as-academy-coach-pro-team-scout/.

Welch, Ashley. "Number of U.S. Women Taking Maternity Leave Unchanged for Two Decades." CBS News. January 19, 2017. https://www.cbsnews.com/news /number-of-u-s-women-taking-maternity-leave-unchanged-for-two-decades/.

Wheeless, Tanya. "Remove 'Women' from 'Women's World Cup.'" *Time.* June 18, 2015. http://time.com/3926940/sports-soccer-female-player/.

Whitbourne, Susan Kraus. "Why Don't We Trust Angry Women?" *Psychology Today.* November 3, 2015. https://www.psychologytoday.com/us/blog/fulfillment -any-age/201511/why-dont-we-trust-angry-women.

Woitalla, Mike. "Mallory Pugh: The Teen Star's Amazing Rise and How It All Started." Soccer America. April 28, 2016. https://www.socceramerica.com /publications/article/68353/mallory-pugh-the-teen-stars-amazing-rise-and-how .html.

The World's Sport. "History Follow Up: Ljungberg and Bouhaddi." July 19, 2011. https://theworldssport.wordpress.com/2011/07/19/history-follow-up -ljungberg-and-bouhaddi/.

Worthen, Whitney. "Female Coaches on the Rise in the NWSL." Girls Soccer Network. February 8, 2018. https://girlssoccernetwork.com/profiles/female -coaches-rise-nwsl/.

Wrack, Suzanne. "Fifa Examining Claims of Sexual and Physical Abuse on Afghanistan Women's Team." *Guardian.* November 30, 2018. https://www .theguardian.com/football/2018/nov/30/fifa-examining-claims-sexual-physical -abuse-afghanistan-womens-team.

———. "Hope Powell: 'I'm a Builder, so This Is Great for Me—It Is What I like to Do.'" *Guardian.* October 10, 2017. https://www.theguardian.com/football /blog/2017/oct/10/hope-powell-brighton-england-mark-sampson-mo-marley.

———. "Lieke Martens: 'Ronaldinho Was My Idol. Long Hair, Great Dribbles . . . I Loved Him.'" *Guardian.* April 24, 2018. https://www.theguardian .com/football/blog/2018/apr/24/lieke-martens-barcelona-ronaldinho.

Yannis, Alex. "Kelly Smith's 90 Minutes of Fame Yet to Come." *New York Times.* November 2, 1999. https://www.nytimes.com/1999/11/02/sports/soccer-kelly -smith-s-90-minutes-of-fame-yet-to-come.html.

Zeigler, Mark. "US Soccer and the Continued Failure of Its Pay-to-Play Model." *San Diego Tribune.* August 14, 2018. http://www.sandiegouniontribune.com /sports/sd-sp-us-soccer-pay-to-play-u20s-20180814-story.html.

Gemma Clarke is a British writer and sports journalist based in the United States. She has written for the *Guardian*, the *Observer*, the *Times* (UK), the *Daily Telegraph*, and the *London Evening Standard*. She wrote minute-by-minute reports on the FIFA Men's World Cup for the *Guardian* online, reported on the Women's European Championships and the Men's blind World Cup, and covered the London Marathon, Boat Race, and Wimbledon Lawn Tennis Championships. She was the first female publications editor for a Premier League soccer club and worked as a production assistant at Sky Sports News. She lives in New York with her husband and two children.